PHILOSOPHICAL ESSAYS

The Library of Liberal Arts
OSKAR PIEST, FOUNDER

PHILOSOPHICAL ESSAYS

Discourse on Method; Meditations;
Rules for the Direction of the Mind

RENÉ DESCARTES

Translated, with an Introduction and Notes, by
LAURENCE J. LAFLEUR
Professor of Philosophy, The University of Akron

J. B. Taylor

. . . .

The Library of Liberal Arts
published by
THE BOBBS-MERRILL COMPANY, INC.
A Subsidiary of Howard W. Sams & Co., Inc.
Publishers • Indianapolis • New York • Kansas City

René Descartes: 1596-1650

. . . .

CONTENTS
. . . .

PHILOSOPHICAL ESSAYS

DISCOURSE ON THE METHOD OF RIGHTLY CONDUCTING THE REASON AND SEEKING TRUTH IN THE FIELD OF SCIENCE

INTRODUCTION

In proposing to present the philosophy of Descartes as he himself expounded it, and without extensive piecing together of originally independent material, it becomes important to decide which parts of the great volume of material Descartes left should be selected. Because our special interest is philosophy, and the continuing importance of Descartes is dependent upon his philosophical ideas, his many articles on specialized subjects, on mathematics, music, physics, physiology, and similar topics, need not be considered. Nor need we consider the Objections and Replies, consisting of letters written to Descartes in criticism of the views expressed in his writings together with Descartes' answers to these, for though this large body of material contains much of philosophical importance, it does not form a coherent whole, and therefore is not especially useful for a first survey. Finally, we have hundreds of letters touching upon all sorts of personal matters as well as upon many points in philosophy, theology, and the various other subjects which interested Descartes. Still more so than the Objections and Replies, this material is formless and unsuitable for the first study of the philosopher.

Eliminating all of these, as well as the fragmentary beginnings of contemplated essays, we are left with four works primarily concerned with philosophy: *Rules for the Direction of the Mind, Discourse on Method, Meditations Concerning First Philosophy,* and *Principles of Philosophy*. To understand the relationship of these it is perhaps well to go back to the paper, *Olympia,* in which Descartes describes a series of three dreams he had on November 10, 1619. Though this paper was lost, a detailed description of the dreams was given by Baillet in his *Vie de Monsieur Des Cartes*. These dreams, or Descartes' interpretation of them, seemed to the philosopher, he explains to us, "to lay the foundations of a new

method of understanding and a new and marvelous science." [1]
What this method in science may have been is not entirely
clear. One is inclined to assume that it is the same as that
which he later planned to expound in *Rules for the Direction
of the Mind,* and to discuss in the still later *Discourse on
Method,* but this is only conjecture. It could have been, as
Charles Adam writes, universal mathematics, algebraic reform, the expression of quantities by lines or lines by algebraic notation, or a variety of other things.[2] All of these might
well suit Descartes' description, since each of them did, in
fact as well as in expectation, transform mathematics and science. But even if one of these more limited achievements was
the burden of Descartes' insight of 1619, it must have become
generalized in the ensuing years into the principles of investigation which formed the starting point of Descartes' work.

We do not know whether these principles concerning the
pursuit of truth were well formed in November 1619, or
whether they developed only gradually in the ensuing years;
but it is clear that they could and did lead Descartes into two
sorts of activity: one, the development of the principles of research themselves for his own benefit and for the benefit of
mankind, and the other, the investigation of particular problems in many fields, in which he was spectacularly successful.
For most of the remaining years of Descartes' life, his interests
fluctuated among the many areas involved in these two
activities.

Rules

We do not know, either, exactly when the decision to write
the first exposition of the principles of investigation, the
Rules, was made, when the task was begun, or when abandoned; but it seems most likely that the writing occurred

[1] Quoted in Baillet, *La vie de Monsieur Des Cartes* (Paris, 1691), I, 50-51;
see also Adam and Tannery, eds., *Œuvres de Descartes* (Paris, 1897-1913),
X, 179.

[2] Adam and Tannery, XII, 50 ff.

during 1625-1628, and probably late in that period. Somewhat less than half of the planned work was accomplished before Descartes turned to "a little treatise on metaphysics" and other investigations. His work on the *Rules,* thus abandoned, was never resumed, and the book in its incomplete form was first published posthumously. Descartes did, indeed, return to his principles of investigation, but only to write a completely new and markedly different work entitled *Discourse on Method.*[3] This latter work, published in 1637, achieved fame for itself and for Descartes and, somewhat unfortunately, obscured the merits of *Rules,* especially in English-speaking countries.

Let us examine, then, the different concepts involved in the *Rules* and in the *Discourse on Method.* The former is an earnest attempt by Descartes to expound the rules of his method so that an attentive reader, willing to devote considerable time and effort to the consideration and practice of these rules, might hope by following them to discover new truths. The *Discourse,* on the other hand, appears to be intended to whet the reader's curiosity and to advertise the author's importance rather than to explicate the method in such a way that the reader could make use of it. It contains only a brief description of the method; the remainder of the *Discourse* and the three appended essays, *Optics, Meteorology,* and *Geometry,* are devoted to proving the usefulness of the method.

The fact that the enlightening *Rules* was abandoned while the *Discourse* with its pretentious claim was completed and published raises the interesting question of whether or not this was deliberate on Descartes' part. For it would be quite in accordance with the traditions of the time to tantalize the public with a suggestion of a great discovery rather than to disclose it. The idea was to use the special information one had discovered for one's personal advantage, or to enhance one's reputation by indicating enough of an original knowledge to prove it existed without actually revealing it com-

---

[3] Complete title in French: *Discours de la méthode—pour bien conduire la raison, et chercher la verité dans les sciences.*

pletely. One might, for example, after discovering a practical method for finding the prime factors of any number, give the prime factors of all numbers between 1,000,000,000,000 and 1,000,000,000,100 without explaining the method; or, having discovered the nature and origin of comets, one might present a table of all comets that would appear and be visible to the naked eye in the next century; in neither case is anything divulged about the basic principles that permit the factoring or the predictions. Or, in Descartes' time, the secret information might even be sold to someone else who would use it in one of these ways. Thus, information in mathematics or in the sciences was frequently treated as a trade secret before such a practice was discouraged by the development of patent protection.

The suggestion that Descartes might deliberately have concealed his rules remains only speculative, of course. It is entirely possible that the change of plans was merely a normal tiring of one project and the undertaking of another which has happened to many writers, and frequently to Descartes himself. Or we may speculate that there was another reason for the change of plan: Descartes intended to develop a universal method for solving all problems, but as the method was developed in the *Rules,* the emphasis seemed to fall definitely upon mathematics and upon quantitative problems which reduce readily to mathematics. This emphasis might well have become even more evident in the uncompleted portion. Descartes could have been discontent with this, especially since he was concerned with the several metaphysical problems discussed in the *Discourse* and *Meditations,* and he may therefore have turned from his manuscript of the *Rules* because it was inadequate in scope. To clear Descartes further of the imputation of ignoble motives, we quote his statement in the *Discourse:*

As for the experiments which others have already made, even if they were willing to communicate them, which those who call them secrets never do, they are for the most part so complicated with unneeded details and superfluous ingredients that it would be very difficult for the investigator to discover their core of truth.[4]

In the *Rules,* we also find the following passage:

Indeed, I could readily believe that this mathematics was suppressed by these writers with a certain pernicious craftiness, just as we know many inventors have suppressed their discoveries, being very much afraid that to publish the method, since it was quite easy and simple, would make it seem worthless. And I believe they preferred to show us in its place, as the product of their art, certain barren truths which they cleverly demonstrate deductively so that we should admire them, rather than teach us the method itself, which would indeed detract from the admiration.[5]

Discourse on Method

Let us repeat once more that, though the titles of *Rules* and the *Discourse* suggest that they deal with the same topic, they do so in very different ways. The *Discourse on Method* includes only four sentences concerning the method itself, which is in contrast to the extensive discussion of the method contained in the *Rules.* The *Discourse* could therefore be viewed as a sort of preface to the *Rules,* advising the reader to study them carefully with the expectation of being able to achieve things of the same value as Descartes reports he was able to accomplish with them. These achievements are indeed astonishing, for, in the *Discourse* and the three appended illustrations which appeared in 1637, he exhibits the most remarkable list of accomplishments which have ever been given to the world by one man at one time.

A good part of the *Discourse* itself is devoted to an outline of the philosophy which he later gave to the world as *Meditations Concerning First Philosophy*—perhaps the most influential philosophical work since Aristotle. The *Discourse* also contains a treatment of physiology, probably the least important of Descartes' scientific works. His anatomy is ac-

4 Below, p. 53.
5 Below, p. 160.

curate enough, but he makes heat the cause, rather than the result, of bodily motion. Nevertheless, though Descartes is so mistaken in the functioning of the body, his picture is not altogether impossible, and foreshadows to some extent the principle of the steam engine and the internal combustion engine.

The principal achievements presented by Descartes in the second essay, *Optics,* are the following: the statement of the wave theory of light; the vector analysis of motion; the law of sines in refraction; the first theoretical account of farsightedness and nearsightedness; the first adequate account of space perception; the first adequate account of the theory of lenses; the first recognition of spherical aberration and of the method of correcting it; the determination of light-gathering power in a telescope; the principle of the iris diaphragm; the drawtube; the telescopic finder; the use of illuminating equipment in conjunction with the microscope; and the parabolic mirror.

His achievements as set forth in the third essay, *Meteorology,* include the following: he rejects Divine intervention as the explanation of events; he states the kinetic theory of heat and foreshadows Charles' law and the concept of specific heat; he gives the first outline of a scientific meteorology in his treatment of winds, clouds, and precipitation; he gives a correct and accurate description and explanation of the primary, secondary, and reflection rainbows; and he describes the division of white light into colors by a prism, and sets up the apparatus of the slit spectroscope.

The final essay is *Geometry,* in which Descartes combined the methods of algebra and geometry to produce the new field of analytic geometry. The importance of this achievement is difficult to overestimate, for it not only served as an example of the possibilities of the new scientific method and as a spur to men's enthusiasm for it, but also laid the foundation for the growth of mathematics in modern times. From analytic geometry came the simultaneous discovery of the calculus by Leibniz and Newton, and on the calculus is based the whole superstructure of modern developments in mathematics and of its application to the understanding of nature.

If it was indeed true, as Descartes professed, that all these achievements were the fruit of his method rather than of any good fortune or native ability, then the revelation of that method must certainly be the most valuable contribution to knowledge found in all of literature. If such a method exists, and if Descartes did in fact describe it, then the *Rules* is the only possible place where we may look for it. But in view of Descartes' failure to complete the work, it does seem more likely that we will find in the *Rules* no more than suggestions of what that method would be.

Meditations

Only the first of the essays of 1637, the *Discourse*, is included here, for in its fourth part and to some extent in the remainder, Descartes presents his metaphysical ideas. These give a foretaste of what he developed at considerably greater length in the *Meditations Concerning First Philosophy*, first published four years after the appearance of the *Discourse*, and at the same time are connected with the ideas presented in the *Rules*, as an illustration of method.

As far as the metaphysical content is concerned, *Meditations* is a longer and consequently more detailed treatment of the problem than that in the *Discourse*. The other differences are more subtle. For example, the problem of what we can surely know about the universe is the primary problem for the *Meditations*, whereas in the *Discourse* it is ostensibly subordinated to the epistemological problem of how we can know it. This and other differences result from an apparent change in attitude that took place in the interval between the writing of the two essays. For the four-year interval in the time of publication represents a much longer interval in the time of writing, and though the differences in the doctrines proclaimed by Descartes before and after this interval are very few, there is a world of difference in the form his proclamations take.

Descartes is not only the father of modern philosophy, of modern mathematics, and of modern physics, optics, meteorology, and science generally, but also the child of the Middle Ages. The ideas of Aristotle and of Medieval philosophy are so deeply ingrained in him that they are never really questioned; they govern the pattern of his thinking even when he does not consciously admit them and they are openly espoused during the development of his thought as the dictates of the light of nature.[6] So in Descartes there were two competing tendencies: he was at once the progressive, or rather the radical intellectual rebel, ready to break away from Medievalism and the Church to lay the foundation of a new philosophy and to build his hopes for the future of mankind on the development of science in general and of medicine in particular; and at the same time he was the conservative, educated in the Medieval tradition by the monks of the Jesuit order.

It is a matter of common experience that older persons tend more to conservatism; for this reason alone it is not strange that the Descartes of 1641 should have been more conservative than the Descartes of 1637 and earlier. But there was a more telling reason for the change. The Descartes of 1637 and before, while not actually unknown, had published nothing. His teachers, friends, and acquaintances recognized his abilities and expected great things of him, but as much can be said of countless men in every generation. Would this expectation be fulfilled? Born in 1596, Descartes was not so young any more, and doubts may have arisen in the minds of his friends and perhaps even in his own. Under the circumstances, Descartes willingly faced intellectual dangers to avoid losing not only his reputation but also his self-esteem.

[6] The "light of nature" was to Descartes and to writers of the Renaissance generally a mental faculty given to man by God for the immediate apprehension of truth.

In 1641 the situation was completely changed; the writings of 1637 had achieved a tremendous *éclat* and had established Descartes' reputation throughout Europe. He was honored and deferred to in philosophic, scientific, and theological circles. From having everything to gain and nothing to lose, his position had changed to that of having nothing to gain and everything to lose. Why antagonize the Church, the most powerful force in Europe, and the most terrible adversary?

Thus Descartes' later work shows important differences from his earlier. Not that his philosophy had changed, but the emphasis had shifted. Those issues in which he was in agreement with the Church were stressed, and the points of disagreement completely overlooked.

By comparison with other works written at the same time, we observe that a similar change had occurred in science. The later Descartes had few new theories to offer—nothing certainly to compare with his great fecundity of earlier years—and even these were largely developments of ideas that appeared in his earlier work. Of his later theories, the most important is the statement of what is now known as Newton's first law of motion. Next in importance is the theory of vortices, which was scientifically inaccurate and apparently conceived in the hope of reconciling Galileo's concept of the solar system with the *homo*-centric position of the Church, by means of a primitive theory of relativity. At the same time Descartes affirms the nonexistence of void, which logically leads to the conclusion that the propagation of light is instantaneous, in contradiction to his earlier view.

Thus the Descartes of the *Meditations* is both philosophically and scientifically less advanced than the Descartes of the *Discourse on Method*. Yet, while the *Method* is historically more significant, the *Meditations* have been traditionally rated Descartes' most important philosophic work, and from the point of view of philosophical content rather than historical significance, this is undoubtedly the case. The *Meditations* contain the most thorough exposition and defense of Des-

cartes' philosophy, and it is in this work that he most clearly
indicates the presuppositions, mainly taken from scholasti-
cism, upon which his reasoning is based.

The exposition of Descartes' philosophy rested with the
Meditations, as far as works of principal importance are concerned, until his undertaking to rewrite his philosophy in a
form more like the one traditionally used in pedagogy. He
therefore presents in his latest work, the *Principles of Philosophy,* the same philosophical and scientific doctrines that
were presented earlier, but divided into numbered steps and
presenting an argument for each step. The length of this
work rules it out for our purposes, and even if we desired to
present only the philosophical portions, it appears less in-
spiring than the three other works. The *Principles of Philosophy* will appeal to those who wish an exposition of all of
Descartes' ideas, scientific as well as philosophical, and who
do not wish to consult the more extensive but more vital
original documents.

Our choice, therefore, is to present the *Discourse on
Method,* the *Meditations Concerning First Philosophy,* and
the *Rules for the Direction of the Mind.* The first suggests
the existence of a method, gives some hints about it, and scientific and metaphysical examples of its application. The second expands upon the metaphysical principles proposed in
the first, laying the foundations of all modern philosophy; and
the third represents the attempt to give a specific account of
the method.[7]

LAURENCE J. LAFLEUR

[7] Readers who wish to have a similar expansion of the scientific side of
the method would be well advised to read the better example found in
Optics, and those looking for the mathematical side, *Geometry.*

NOTE ON THE TEXT

The translation of the *Discourse on Method* was made from the original French text and later revised to take into consideration the Latin text of 1644. In fact, it seemed advisable to adhere rather more closely to the Latin than the French, since Descartes wrote of it:

> These treatises, which I wrote in French and published seven years ago, were recently translated into Latin by a friend of mine [1] and his version intrusted to me so that I might alter anything that did not suit me. This I have done in several places, but I may have missed many others. My changes may be distinguished from his by the fact that he has everywhere tried to give a faithful word-for-word translation, whereas I have often changed the meanings themselves, and have everywhere attempted to improve, not his words, but my meaning.

The half-brackets and half-parentheses appearing in the text apply to the French and Latin versions respectively, and are explained below in reference to the *Meditations*.

The headings for the Parts of the *Discourse* were inserted by the translator and were taken from the first paragraph of the *Discourse,* where Descartes enumerates the parts of his work.

The translation of the *Meditations* is taken from three sources: the second Latin edition of 1642, which was the first one printed from Descartes' own manuscript and under his own supervision, the first French translation of 1647 by the Duc de Luynes, but read and approved by Descartes, and the second French translation by Clerselier. An attempt has been made in this translation to integrate these three versions into one complete and accurate edition by the use of brackets and parentheses. The reader may, by omitting the parentheses and

[1] Etienne De Courcelles.

brackets, have a translation which contains all ideas in the three versions. By omitting bracketed material, he will have a translation essentially that of the original Latin, and by omitting material in parentheses, that of the first French edition.

⟨ ⟩   indicates where the Latin adds a word or phrase not found in the French.

⌈ ⌉   indicates where the first French version adds a word or phrase not found in the Latin.

⟨ ⟩⌈ ⌉   indicates where the two versions differ: the Latin enclosed in the parentheses, the first French enclosed in square brackets. A connective such as "and" or "or" is occasionally supplied and the brackets and parentheses overlap so as to include it.

⌈⟨ ⟩⌉   indicates material occurring for the first time in the second French edition.

The numbers enclosed in brackets and parentheses refer to the corresponding pages in the French and Latin texts of the Adam and Tannery editions. For the *Discourse,* the numbers enclosed in parentheses refer to the Latin edition of 1644; the numbers enclosed in brackets, to the first French edition. For the *Meditations,* the numbers enclosed in parentheses refer to the second Latin text; the numbers enclosed in brackets, to the first French text.

The separate edition of *Meditations* previously published in the Library of Liberal Arts may be referred to for a discussion of some of the problems of interpretation and translation.

The translation of *Rules for the Direction of the Mind* is based on Volume X of the Adam and Tannery edition of *Œuvres de Descartes* which includes the three principal sources of Descartes' *Rules: Opuscula posthuma* (1701), the so-called Hanover manuscript purchased by Leibniz (1670), and *La logique ou l'art de penser (Port-Royal Logic).* This volume also contains comments by Baillet and Poisson.

The translator has supplied the division of the *Rules* into books, and has furnished titles for Books Two and Three, by following Descartes' indication of his planning in Rules VIII and XII. According to the translator's arrangement there are twenty-four rules; Rules XIX through XXI exist only as titles in Descartes' manuscripts; Rules XXII, XXIII, and XXIV do not have titles. The title for Book Three, which was to have contained twelve rules, XXV through XXXVI, is furnished by the translator.

All footnotes have been supplied by the translator, for identification, to fill gaps in the text, or to indicate points of difference among the different editions.

L. J. L.

SELECTED BIBLIOGRAPHY

Descartes' Major Works

Discours de la méthode (1637).

La Dioptrique (1637).

La Géométrie (1637).

Les Météores (1637).

Meditationes de prima philosophia (1641).

Principia philosophiae (1644).

Règles pour la direction de l'esprit (1628).

ADAM, CHARLES and PAUL TANNERY, eds. *Œuvres de Descartes*. Paris, 1897-1913.

Collateral Reading

BALZ, A. G. *Descartes and the Modern Mind*. Yale University, 1952.

————. *Cartesian Studies*. Columbia University, 1951.

BAILLET, A. *La vie de Monsieur Des Cartes*. Paris, 1691.

BRUNSCHWICG, LÉON. *Descartes et Pascal, lecteurs de Montaigne*. Paris and New York, 1944.

————. *René Descartes*. Paris, 1937.

CAJORI, FLORIAN. *Ce que Newton doit à Descartes*. Paris, 1926.

CRESSON, ANDRÉ. *Descartes; sa vie, son œuvre*. Paris, 1942.

FISCHER, KUNO. *Descartes and His School*. London, 1887.

GIBSON, A. BOYCE. *The Philosophy of Descartes*. London, 1932.

GILSON, ETIENNE. *Etudes sur le rôle de la pensée médiévale dans la formation du système cartésien*. Paris, 1930.

————. *La doctrine cartésienne de la liberté et la théologie*. Paris, 1913.

IVERACH, JAMES. *Descartes, Spinoza and the New Philosophy*. New York, 1904.

JASCOLEVICH, ALEJANDRO A. *Three Conceptions of Mind. Their Bearing on the Denaturalization of the Mind in History*. New York, 1926.

KEELING, S. V. *Descartes*. London, 1934.

LABERTHONNIERE, LE P. *Etudes sur Descartes*. Paris, 1935.

LAPORTE, JEAN MARIE FRÉDÉRIC. *Le rationalisme de Descartes*. Paris, 1945.

LEWIS, GENEVIÈVE. *L'individualité selon Descartes*. Paris, 1950.

MARITAIN, JACQUES. *Three Reformers: Luther, Descartes, Rousseau*. New York, 1937.

MILHAUD, GASTON. *Descartes savant*. Paris, 1921.

MOUY, PAUL. *Le développement de la physique cartésienne, 1646-1712*. Paris, 1934.

ROY, JEAN H. *L'imagination selon Descartes*. Paris, 1944.

SCOTT, J. F. *The Scientific Work of René Descartes*. London, 1953.

SEGOND, J. *La sagesse cartésienne et la doctrine de la science*. Paris, 1932.

SMITH, NORMAN KEMP. *New Studies in the Philosophy of Descartes*. London, 1952.

TELLIER, AUGUSTE. *Descartes et la médecine*. Paris, 1928.

VARTANIAN, A. *Diderot and Descartes*. Princeton University, 1953.

VERSFELD, MARTHINUS. *An Essay on the Metaphysics of Descartes*. London, 1940.

DISCOURSE ON THE METHOD OF RIGHTLY CONDUCTING THE REASON AND SEEKING TRUTH IN THE FIELD OF SCIENCE

DISCOURSE ON THE METHOD
OF
RIGHTLY CONDUCTING THE REASON
AND SEEKING TRUTH IN
THE SCIENCES

If this discourse seems too long to be read at one sitting, it may be divided into six parts. In the first will be found various thoughts on the sciences; in the second, the principal rules of the method the author has used; in the third, some moral rules derived from this method; in the fourth, his proofs of the existence of God and of the human soul which form the basis of his philosophy; in the fifth are treated some questions of physics, especially the explanation of the heartbeat and of some other difficulties in medicine, as well as the difference between the souls of men and animals; and in the last, some prerequisites for further advances in the study of nature, as well as the author's reasons for writing this work.

PART ONE

SOME THOUGHTS ON THE SCIENCES

Good sense is mankind's most equitably divided endowment, for everyone thinks that he is so abundantly provided with it that [2] even those ʿwith the most insatiable appetites andʾ most difficult to please in other ways do not usually want more than they have of this. As it is not likely that everyone is mistaken, this evidence shows that the ability to judge correctly, and to distinguish the true from the false—which is really what is meant by good sense or reason—is the same by ⌈innate⌉ nature in all men; and that differences of opinion are not due to differences in intelligence, but merely to the fact that we use different approaches and consider different things. For it is not enough to have a good mind: one must use it well. The greatest souls are capable of the greatest vices as well as of the greatest virtues; and those who walk slowly can, if they follow the right path, go much farther than those who run rapidly in the wrong direction.

As for myself, I have never supposed that my mind was above the ordinary. On the contrary, I have often wished to have as quick a wit or as clear and distinct an imagination, or as ready and retentive a memory, as another person. And I know of no other qualities which make for a good mind, because as far as reason is concerned, it is the only thing which makes us men ⌈and distinguishes us from the animals⌉, and I am therefore satisfied that it is fully present in each one of us. In this I follow the general opinion (541) of philosophers, who say that there are differences in degree only in the [3] *accidental* qualities, and not in the *essential* qualities or natures of individuals of the same species.

But I do not hesitate to claim the good fortune of having stumbled, in my youth, upon certain paths which led me without difficulty ⌈to certain considerations and maxims from which I formed a method of gradually increasing my knowledge ⌈and of improving my abilities⌉ as much as the mediocrity of my talents and the shortness of my life will permit. For I have already had such results that although in self-judgment I try to lean toward undervaluation ⌈rather than to presumption⌉, I cannot escape a feeling of extreme satisfaction with the progress I believe I have already made in the search for truth. And although from the philosophers' viewpoint almost all the activities of men appear to me as vain and useless, yet I conceive such hopes for the future that if some single one of the occupations of men, as men, should be truly good and important, I dare to believe that it is the one I have chosen.

It is always possible that I am wrong, and that I am mistaking a bit of copper and glass for gold and diamonds. I know how subject we are to making false judgments in things that concern ourselves, and how much we ought to mistrust the judgments of our friends when they are in our own favor. But I should be glad to show in this *Discourse* [4] what are the paths I have taken 'to search for truth,' and to present a sketch of my 'whole' life, so that each one can form his own judgment of it. In this way I may learn from the opinions of those who read it, and thus add another to the methods of progress which I am accustomed to use.

So it is not my intention to present a method which everyone ought to follow in order to think well, but only to show how I have made the attempt myself. Those who counsel others must consider themselves superior to those whom they counsel, and if they fall short in the least detail they are 'much' to blame. I only propose this writing as an autobiography, or, if you prefer, as a story in which you may possibly find some examples of conduct which you might see fit to imitate, as well as several others which you would have no reason to follow. I hope that it will prove useful to some without being harmful to any, and that all will take my frankness kindly.

From my childhood I lived in a world of books, and since I was taught that by their help I could gain a clear and assured knowledge of everything useful in life, (542) I was eager to learn from them. But as soon as I had finished the course of studies which usually admits one to the ranks of the learned, I changed my opinion completely. For I found myself saddled with so many doubts and errors that I seemed to have gained nothing in trying to educate myself unless it was to discover more and more fully how ignorant I was.

Nevertheless [5] I had been in one of the most celebrated schools in 'all of' Europe, where I thought there should be wise men if wise men existed anywhere on earth. I had learned there everything that others learned, and, not satisfied with merely the knowledge that was taught, I had perused as many books as I could find which contained more unusual and recondite knowledge. I also knew the opinions of others about myself, and that I was in no way judged inferior to my fellow students, even though several of them were preparing to become professors. And finally, it did not seem to me that our own times were less flourishing and fertile than were any of the earlier periods. All this led me to conclude that I could judge others by myself, and to decide that there was no such wisdom in the world as I had previously hoped to find.

I did not, however, cease to value the disciplines of the schools. I knew that the languages which one learns there are necessary to understand the works of the ancients; and that the delicacy of fiction ⟨refines and⟩ enlivens the mind; that famous deeds of history ennoble it and, if read with understanding, aid in maturing one's judgment; that the reading of all the great books is like conversing with the best people of earlier times: it is even a studied conversation in which the authors show us only the best of their thoughts; that eloquence has incomparable powers and beauties; that poetry has [6] enchanting delicacy and sweetness; that mathematics has very subtle processes which can serve as much to satisfy the inquiring mind as to aid all the arts and to diminish man's labor; that treatises on morals contain very useful teachings and exhortations to virtue; that theology teaches us how to go to heaven; that philosophy teaches us to talk with an appearance of truth about all things, and to make ourselves admired by the less learned; that law, medicine, and the other sciences bring honors and wealth to those who pursue them; and finally, that it is desirable to have examined all of them, even to the most (543) superstitious and false, in order to recognize their real worth and avoid being deceived thereby.

But I thought that I had already spent enough time on languages, and even on reading the works of the ancients, and their histories and fiction. For conversing with the ancients is much like traveling. It is good to know something of the customs of various peoples, in order to judge our own more objectively, and so that we do not make the mistake of the untraveled in supposing that everything contrary to our customs is ridiculous and irrational. But when one spends too much time traveling, one becomes at last a stranger at home; and those who are too interested in things which occurred in past centuries are often remarkably ignorant of what is going on today. In addition, fiction makes us imagine a number of events [7] as possible which are really impossible, and even the most faithful histories, if they do not alter or embroider episodes to make them more worth reading, almost always omit the meanest and least illustrious circumstances so that the remainder is distorted. Thus it happens that those who regulate their behavior by the examples they find in books are apt to fall into the extravagances of the knights of romances, and undertake projects which it is beyond their ability to complete ⟨or hope for things beyond their destiny⟩.

I esteemed eloquence highly, and loved poetry, but I felt that both were gifts of nature rather than fruits of study. Those who reason most cogently, and work over their thoughts to make them clear and intelligible, are always the most persuasive, even if they speak only a provincial dialect and have never studied rhetoric. Those who have the most agreeable imaginations and can express their thoughts with the most grace and color cannot fail to be the best poets, even if the poetic art is unknown to them.

I was especially pleased with mathematics, because of the certainty and self-evidence of its proofs; but I did not yet see its true usefulness and, thinking that it was good only for the mechanical arts, I was astonished that nothing more noble had been built on so firm and solid a foundation. On the other hand, I compared the ethical writings of the ancient pagans to [8] very superb and magnificent palaces built only on mud and sand: they laud the virtues and ⟨rightly⟩ make them appear more desirable than anything else in the world; (544) but they give no adequate criterion of virtue, and often what they call by such a name is nothing but ⟨cruelty and⟩ apathy, parricide, pride or despair.

I revered our theology, and hoped as much as anyone else to get to heaven, but having learned on great authority that the road was just as open to the most ignorant as to the most learned, and that the truths of revelation which lead thereto are beyond our understanding, I would not have dared to submit them to the weakness of my reasonings. I thought that to succeed in their examination it would be necessary to have some extraordinary assistance from heaven, and to be more than a man.

I will say nothing of philosophy except that it has been studied for many centuries by the most outstanding minds without having produced anything which is not in dispute and consequently doubtful ⟨and uncertain⟩. I did not have enough presumption to hope to succeed better than the others; and when I noticed how many different opinions learned men may hold on the same subject, despite the fact that no more than one of them can ever be right, I resolved to consider almost as false any opinion which was merely plausible.

Finally, when it came to the other branches of learning, since they took their cardinal principles from philosophy, I judged [9] that nothing solid could have been built on so insecure a foundation. Neither the honor nor the profit to be gained thereby sufficed to make me study them, for I was fortunately not in such a financial condition as to make it necessary to trade upon my learning; and though I was not enough of a cynic to despise fame, I was little concerned with that which I could only obtain on false pretenses ⟨, that is, by claiming to know things that were in fact false⟩. And finally, I thought I knew enough of the disreputable doctrines not to be taken in by the promises of an alchemist, the predictions of an astrologer, the impostures of a magician, or by the tricks and boasts of any of those who profess to know that which they do not know.

This is why I gave up my studies entirely as soon as I reached the age when I was no longer under the control of my teachers. I resolved to seek no other knowledge than that which I might find within myself, or perhaps in the great book of nature. I ⟨then⟩ spent a few (545) years ⌈of my adolescence⌉ traveling, seeing courts and armies, living with people of diverse types and stations of life, acquiring varied experience, testing myself in the episodes which fortune sent me, and, above all, thinking about the things around me so that I could derive some profit from them. For it seemed to me that I might find much more of the truth in the cogitations which each man made on things which were important to him, and where [10] he would be the loser if he judged badly, than in the cogitations of a man of letters in his study, concerned with speculations which produce no effect, and which have no consequences to him except perhaps that the farther they are removed from common sense, the more they titillate his vanity, since then he needs so much more wit and skill to make them seem plausible. Besides, I was always eager to learn to distinguish truth from falsehood, so that I could make intelligent decisions about the affairs of this life ⟨and act with greater confidence⟩.

It is true that while I did nothing but observe the customs of other men, I found nothing there to satisfy me, and I noted just about as much difference of opinion as I had previously remarked among philosophers. The greatest profit to me was, therefore, that I became acquainted with customs generally approved and accepted by other great peoples that would appear extravagant and ridiculous among ourselves, and so I learned not to believe too firmly what I learned only from example and custom. Also I gradually freed myself from many errors which could ⌈obscure the light of nature and⌉ make us less capable of correct reasoning. But after spending several years in thus studying the book of nature and acquiring experience, I eventually reached the decision to study my own self, and to employ all my abilities to try to choose the right path. This produced much [11] better results in my case, I think, than would have been produced if I had never left my books and my country.

PART TWO

THE PRINCIPAL RULES OF THE METHOD

I was then in Germany, where I had gone because of ⸨the desire to see⸩ the wars which are still not ended; and while I was returning to the army from the coronation of the Emperor, I was caught by the onset of winter. There was no conversation to occupy me, and being untroubled by any cares or passions, I remained all day alone in a warm room. There I had plenty of leisure to examine my ideas. One of the first that occurred to me was that frequently there is less perfection in a work produced by several persons (546) than in one produced by a single hand. Thus we notice that buildings conceived and completed by a single architect are usually more beautiful and better planned than those remodeled by several persons using ancient walls ⸨of various vintages⸩ ⸢that had originally been built for quite other purposes⸣ ⸨along with new ones⸩. Similarly, those ancient towns which were originally nothing but hamlets, and in the course of time have become great cities, are ordinarily very badly arranged compared to one of the symmetrical metropolitan districts which a city planner has laid out on an open plain according to his own designs. It is true that when we consider their buildings one by one, there is often as much beauty in the first city as in the second, or even more; nevertheless, when we observe how they are arranged, here a large unit, there a small; and how the streets are crooked and uneven, one [12] would rather suppose that chance and not the decisions of rational men had so arranged them. And when we consider that there were always some officials in charge of private building, whose duty it was to see that they were conducive to the general good appearance of the city, we recognize that it is not easy to do a good job when using only the works of others. Similarly I supposed that peoples who were once half savage ⸨and barbarous⸩, and who became civilized by a gradual process and invented their laws one by one as the harmfulness of crimes and quarrels forced them to outlaw them, would be less well governed than those who have followed the constitutions of some prudent legislator from the time that their communities were founded. Thus it is quite certain that the condition of the true religion, whose rules were laid down by God alone, must be incomparably superior to all others. And, to speak of human affairs, I believe that Sparta was such a flourishing community, not because of the goodness of each of its laws in particular, seeing that many of them were very strange and even contrary to good morals, but because they were produced by a single legislator, and so all tended to the same end. And similarly I thought that the sciences found in books, at least those whose reasons were only probable and which had no proofs, have grown up little by little by the accumulation of the opinions of many different persons, and are therefore by no means as near to the truth as the simple and natural reasonings of a man [13] ⌈of good sense⌉ ⸜, laboring under no prejudice⸝ concerning the things which he experiences.

Likewise I thought that we were all children before (547) being men, at which time we were necessarily under the control of our appetites and our teachers, and that neither of these influences is wholly consistent, and neither of them, perhaps, always tends toward the better. It is therefore impossible that our judgments should be as pure and firm as they would have been had we the ⌈whole⌉ use of our ⌈mature⌉ reason from the time of our birth and if we had never been under any other control.

It is true that we never tear down all the houses in a city just to rebuild them in a different way and to make the streets more beautiful; but we do see that individual owners often have theirs torn down and rebuilt, and even that they may be forced to do so ⸜when the building is crumbling with age, or⸝ when ⌈the foundation is not firm and⌉ it is in danger of collapsing. By this example I was convinced that a private individual should not seek to reform a nation by changing all its customs and destroying it to construct it anew, nor to reform the body of knowledge or the system of education. Nevertheless, as far as the opinions which I had been receiving since my birth were concerned, I could not do better than to reject them completely for once in my lifetime, and to resume them afterwards, or perhaps accept better ones in their place, when I had [14] determined how they fitted into a rational scheme. And I firmly believed that by this means I would succeed in conducting my life much better than if I built only upon the old foundations and gave credence to the principles which I had acquired in my childhood without ever having examined them to see whether they were true or not. For though I noticed several difficulties in the way, they were neither insurmountable nor comparable to those involved in the slightest reform of public affairs. For public affairs are on a large scale, and large edifices are too difficult to set up again once they have been thrown down, too difficult even to preserve once they have been shaken, and their fall is necessarily catastrophic. It is certain that many institutions have defects, since their differences alone guarantee that much, but custom has no doubt inured us to many of them. Custom has perhaps even found ways to avoid or correct more defects than prudence could have done. Finally, present institutions are practically always more tolerable than would be a change in them; just as highways which twist and turn among the mountains become gradually so easy to travel, as a result of much use, that it is much better to follow them than to attempt to go more directly by climbing cliffs and descending to the bottom of precipices. (548)

That is why I cannot at all approve those mischievous spirits who, not being called either by birth or by attainments to a position of political power, are nevertheless constantly proposing some new [15] reform. If I thought the slightest basis could be found in this *Discourse* for a suspicion that I was guilty of this folly, I would be loath to permit it to be published. Never has my intention been more than to try to reform my own ideas, and rebuild them on foundations that would be wholly mine. If my building has pleased me sufficiently to display a model of it to the public, it is not because I advise anyone to copy it. Those whom God has more bountifully endowed will no doubt have higher aims; there are others, I fear, for whom my own are too adventurous. Even the decision to abandon all one's preconceived notions is not an example for all to follow, and the world is largely composed of two sorts of individuals who should not try to follow it. First, there are those who think themselves more able than they really are, and so make precipitate judgments and do not have enough patience to think matters through thoroughly. From this it follows that once they have taken the liberty of doubting their established principles, thus leaving the highway, they will never be able to keep to the narrow path which must be followed to go more directly, and will remain lost all their lives. Secondly, there are those who have enough sense or modesty to realize that they are ⌐less wise ⌐and⌐ less able to distinguish the true from the false⌐ than are others, and so should rather be satisfied to follow the opinions of these others than to search for better ones themselves. [16]

As for myself, I should no doubt have belonged in the last class if I had had but a single teacher or if I had not known the differences which have always existed among the most learned. I had discovered in college that one cannot imagine anything so strange and unbelievable but that it has been upheld by some philosopher; and in my travels I had found that those who held opinions contrary to ours were neither barbarians nor savages, but that many of them were at least as reasonable as ourselves. I had considered how the same man, with the same capacity for reason, becomes different as a result of being brought up among Frenchmen or Germans than he would be if he had been brought up among Chinese or ⌐Americans ⌐or⌐ cannibals⌐; and how, in our fashions, the thing which pleased us ten years ago and perhaps will please us again ten years in the future, now seems extravagant and ridiculous; (549) and felt that in all these ways we are much more greatly influenced by custom and example than by any certain knowledge. Faced with this divergence of opinion, I could not accept the testimony of the majority, for I thought it worthless as a proof of anything somewhat difficult to discover, since it is much more likely that a single man will have discovered it than a whole people. Nor, on the other hand, could I select anyone whose opinions seemed to me to be preferable to those of others, and I was thus constrained to embark on the investigation for myself.

Nevertheless, like a man who walks alone in the darkness, I resolved to go so slowly and [17] circumspectly that if I did not get ahead very rapidly I was at least safe from falling. Also, ꞌjust as the occupants of an old house do not destroy it before a plan for a new one has been thought out,ꞌ I did not want to reject all the opinions which had slipped irrationally into my consciousness since birth, until I had first spent enough time planning how to accomplish the task which I was then undertaking, and seeking the true method of obtaining knowledge of everything which my mind was capable of understanding.

Among the branches of philosophy, I had, when younger, studied logic, and among those of mathematics, geometrical analysis and algebra; three arts or sciences which should have been able to contribute something to my design. But in examining them I noticed that as far as logic was concerned, its syllogisms and most of its other methods serve rather to explain to another what one already knows, or even, as in the art of Lully, to speak ꞌfreely andꞌ without judgment of what one does not know, than to learn new things. Although it does contain many true and good precepts, they are interspersed among so many others that are harmful or superfluous that it is almost as difficult to separate them as to bring forth a Diana or a Minerva from a block of virgin marble. Then, as far as the analysis of the Greeks and the algebra of the moderns is concerned, besides the fact that they deal with ⌜abstractions and⌝ ꞌspeculations whichꞌ appear to have no utility, the first is always so limited to the consideration of figures that it cannot exercise the [18] understanding without greatly fatiguing the imagination, and the last is so limited to certain rules and certain numbers that it has become a confused and obscure art which perplexes the mind instead of a science which educates it. In consequence I thought that some other method must be found (550) to combine the advantages of these three and to escape their faults. Finally, just as the multitude of laws frequently furnishes an excuse for vice, and a state is much better governed with a few laws which are strictly adhered to, so I thought that instead of the great number of precepts of which logic is composed, I would have enough with the four following ones, provided that I made a firm and unalterable resolution not to violate them even in a single instance.

The first rule was never to accept anything as true unless I recognized it to be ⟨certainly and⟩ evidently such: that is, carefully to avoid ⟨all⟩ precipitation and prejudgment, and to include nothing in my conclusions unless it presented itself so clearly and distinctly to my mind that there was no ⟨reason ⌐or⟩ occasion⌐ to doubt it.

The second was to divide each of the difficulties which I encountered into as many parts as possible, and as might be required for an easier solution.

The third was to think in an orderly fashion ⟨when concerned with the search for truth⟩, beginning with the things which were simplest and easiest to understand, and gradually and by degrees reaching toward more complex knowledge, even treating, as though ordered, [19] materials which were not necessarily so.

The last was ⟨, both in the process of searching and in reviewing when in difficulty,⟩ always to make enumerations so complete, and reviews so general, that I would be certain that nothing was omitted.

Those long chains of reasoning, so simple and easy, which enabled the geometricians to reach the most difficult demonstrations, had made me wonder whether all things knowable to men might not fall into a similar logical sequence. If so, we need only refrain from accepting as true that which is not true, and carefully follow the order necessary to deduce each one from the others, and there cannot be any propositions so abstruse that we cannot prove them, or so recondite that we cannot discover them. It was not very difficult, either, to decide where we should look for a beginning, for I knew already that one begins with the simplest and easiest to know. Considering that among all those who have previously sought truth in the sciences, mathematicians alone have been able to find some demonstrations, some certain and evident reasons, I had no doubt that I should begin where they did, although I expected no advantage (551) except to accustom my mind to work with truths and not to be satisfied with bad reasoning. I do not mean that I intended to learn all the particular branches of mathematics; for [20] I saw that although the objects they discuss are different, all these branches are in agreement in limiting their consideration to the relationships or proportions between their various objects. I judged therefore that it would be better to examine these proportions in general, and use particular objects as illustrations only in order to make their principles easier to comprehend, and to be able the more easily to apply them afterwards, without any forcing, to anything for which they would be suitable. I realized that in order to understand the principles of relationships I would sometimes have to consider them singly, and sometimes ʿcomprehend and remember themʾ in groups. I thought I could consider them better singly as relationships between lines, because I could find nothing more simple or more easily pictured to my imagination and my senses. But in order to remember and understand them better when taken in groups, I had to express them in numbers, and in the smallest numbers possible. Thus I took the best traits of geometrical analysis and algebra, and corrected the faults of one by the other.

The exact observation of the few precepts which I had chosen gave me such facility in clarifying all the issues in these two sciences that it took only two or three months to examine them. I began with the most simple and general, and each truth that I found was a rule which [21] helped me to find others, so that I not only solved many problems which I had previously judged very difficult, but also it seemed to me that toward the end I could determine to what extent a still unsolved problem could be solved, and what procedures should be used in solving it. In this I trust that I shall not appear too vain, considering that there is only one true solution to a given problem, and whoever finds it knows all that anyone can know about it. Thus, for example, a child who has learned arithmetic and performed an addition according to the rules may feel certain that, as far as that particular sum is concerned, he has found everything that a human mind can discover. For, after all, the method of (552) following the correct order and stating precisely all the circumstances of what we are investigating is the whole of what gives certainty to the rules of arithmetic.

What pleased me most about this method was that it enabled me to reason in all things, if not perfectly, at least as well as was in my power. In addition, I felt that in practicing it my mind was gradually ⟨dissipating its uncertainties and⟩ becoming accustomed to conceive its objects more clearly and distinctly, and since I had not directed this method to any particular subject matter, I was in hopes of applying it just as usefully to the difficulties of other sciences as I had already to those of ⟨geometry or⟩ algebra. Not that I would dare to undertake to examine at once all the difficulties that presented themselves, for that would have been contrary to the principle of order. But I had observed that all the basic principles of the sciences were taken from [22] philosophy, which itself had no certain ones. It therefore seemed that I should first attempt to establish philosophic principles, and that since this was the most important thing in the world and the place where precipitation and prejudgment were most to be feared, I should not attempt to reach conclusions until I had attained a much more mature age than my then twenty-three years, and had spent much time in preparing for it. This preparation would consist partly in freeing my mind from the false opinions which I had previously acquired, partly in building up a fund of experiences which should serve afterwards as the raw material of my reasoning, and partly in training myself in the method which I had determined upon, so that I should become more and more adept in its use.

PART THREE

SOME MORAL RULES DERIVED FROM THE METHOD

In planning to rebuild one's house it is not enough to draw up the plans for the new dwelling, tear down the old one, and provide 'stones and other\ materials 'useful for building,\ and obtain workmen for the task. We must see that we are provided with a comfortable place to stay while the work of rebuilding is going on. Similarly in my own case; while reason obliged me to be irresolute in my beliefs, there was no reason why I should be so in my actions. In order to live as happily as possible during the interval I prepared a provisional code of morality for myself, consisting of three or four maxims which I here set forth.

The first was to obey the laws and [23] customs of my country, constantly retaining the religion 'which I judged best, and\ in which, by God's grace, I had been brought up since childhood, and in all other matters to follow the most (553) moderate and least excessive opinions to be found in the practices of the more judicious part of the community in which I would live. For I was then about to discard my own opinions in order to re-examine them, and meanwhile could do no better than to follow those of the most reliable judges. While there may be, no doubt, just as reliable persons among the Persians or the Chinese as among ourselves, it seemed more practical to pattern my conduct on that of the society in which I would have to live. Furthermore, it seemed to me that to learn people's true opinions, I should pay attention to their

conduct rather than to their words, not only because in our
corrupt times there are few who are ready to say all that they
believe, but also because many are not aware of their own
beliefs, since the mental process of knowing a thing is 'good
or bad is' distinct from, and can occur without, the mental
process of knowing that we know it. Among a number of
opinions equally widely accepted, I chose only the most moderate, partly because these are always the most convenient in
practice and, since excess is usually bad, presumably the best;
but also so that I should stray a shorter distance from the true
road in case I should make a mistake, than I would in choosing one extreme when it was the other that should have been
followed. In particular, [24] I considered as 'extreme or' excessive all the promises by which we abandon some of our
freedom. Not that I disapproved of the laws which, to remedy
the inconstancy of vacillating spirits, permit them to make
bonds or contracts which oblige them to persevere with their
intentions, provided the intentions are good, or at least not
bad, but because I recognized that nothing is unchanging,
and that in my own case I was proposing to improve my judgment more and more, not to make it worse. It would therefore
have been a major violation of common sense if I obliged myself to continue to accept a thing I formerly approved after it
ceased to merit approval, or after I altered my opinion of it.

My second maxim was to be as firm and determined in my
actions as I could be, and not to act on the most doubtful decisions, once I had made them, any less resolutely than on the
most certain. In this matter I patterned my behavior on that
of travelers, who, finding themselves lost in a forest, must not
wander about, (554) now turning this way, now that, and still
less should remain in one place, but should go as straight as
they can in the direction they first select and not change the
direction except for the strongest reasons. By this method,
even if the direction was chosen at random, they will presumably arrive [25] at some destination, not perhaps where
they would like to be, but at least where they will be better
off than in the middle of the forest. Similarly, situations in life

often permit no delay; and when we cannot determine the course which is certainly best, we must follow the one which is probably the best; and when we cannot determine even that, we must nevertheless select one and follow it thereafter as though it were certainly best. If the course selected is not indeed a good one, at least the reasons for selecting it are excellent. This frame of mind freed me also from the repentance and remorse commonly felt by those vacillating individuals who are always seeking as worth while things which they later judge to be bad.

My third maxim was always to seek to conquer myself rather than fortune, to change my desires rather than the established order, and generally to believe that nothing except our thoughts is wholly under our control, so that after we have done our best in external matters, what remains to be done is absolutely impossible, at least as far as we are concerned. This maxim in itself should suffice to prevent me from desiring in the future anything which I could not acquire, and thus to make me happy. For it is our nature to [26] desire only that which we imagine to be somehow attainable, and if we consider all external benefits equally beyond our reach we will no more regret being unjustly deprived of our birthright than we regret not possessing the kingdoms of China or Mexico. Thus, making a virtue of necessity, we no more desire to be well when we are sick, or to be free when we are in prison, than we now desire bodies as incorruptible as diamonds, or wings to fly like the birds. (555) But I must admit that it takes much practice and frequently repeated meditations to become accustomed to view things in this manner, and I think that this must have been the principal secret of those philosophers of ancient times who were able to rise above fortune, and, despite pains and poverty, to vie with the gods in happiness. Being constantly occupied in considering the limits imposed upon them by nature, they were so perfectly convinced that nothing was really theirs but their thoughts that that alone was sufficient to keep them from any concern in other things. Their control of their thoughts, on the other hand, was so absolute ⟨, that is, they were so accustomed to regulate their desires and other passions,⟩ that they had some justification for considering themselves richer and more powerful, more free and happier, than any other man who did not have this philosophy, and who, however [27] much he might be favored by nature and fortune, had no such control over his desires.

Finally, I planned to make a review of the various occupations possible in this life, in order to choose the best. Without intending to disparage other occupations, I thought I could do no better than to continue in the one I was engaged in, employing my life in improving my mind and increasing as far as I could my knowledge of the truth by following the method that I had outlined for myself. I had experienced such periods of great happiness after I had begun to use this method, that I could hope for no greater or more innocent joys in this life. In discovering day after day truths which seemed fairly important and generally unknown to other men, I was filled with such satisfaction that other considerations did not affect me. Another reason for my decision was that the three maxims previously considered were based on my plan to continue the search for truth. For as God has given each one of us some ability to distinguish the true from the false, I should not have been content for one instant to rely on the opinions of others if I had not planned to use my own judgment at the proper time; nor could I have followed those opinions with a clear conscience if I had not hoped to take advantage of every opportunity to find better ones, if better ones [28] there were. And finally, I could not have limited my desires, nor been happy ⟨with the things within my power⟩, if I were not following a path by which I expected to obtain all the knowledge of which I was capable (556) and, by the same token, all the real values to which I might aspire. Besides, since our will neither seeks nor avoids anything except as it is judged good or bad by our reason, good judgment is sufficient to guarantee good behavior. Judging as best one can therefore implies that one acts as well as one can, or in other words, that one will acquire all the virtues and with them all other possible goods.

Once we are sure of this, we cannot well fail to be happy ⌐and blessed⌐.

After thus assuring myself of these maxims, and having put them aside with the truths of the Faith, which have always been most certain to me, I judged that I could proceed freely to reject all my other beliefs. And inasmuch as I hoped to obtain my end more readily by conversing with men than by remaining any longer ⌐alone⌐ in my ⌐warm⌐ retreat, ⌐where I had had all these thoughts,⌐ I proceeded on my way before winter was wholly passed. In the nine years that followed I wandered here and there throughout the world, trying everywhere to be spectator rather than actor in all the comedies that go on. I took particular pains in judging each thing to seek out whatever elements of uncertainty it contained, which might cause us to conceive false opinions about it. Meanwhile I tried to clear my mind of all the errors that had [29] previously accumulated. In this I did not wish to imitate the sceptics, who doubted only for the sake of doubting and intended to remain always irresolute; on the contrary, my whole purpose was to achieve greater certainty and to reject the loose earth and sand in favor of rock and clay. In all these things I seemed to succeed well enough, for, as I was trying to discover the falsity or uncertainty of the propositions I was examining, not by feeble conjectures but by clear and assured reasonings, I encountered nothing that did not lead me to some certain conclusions, even if it were only that the matter was wholly uncertain. And just as in tearing down a building we usually retain the debris to help build a new one, so in destroying all of my opinions which seemed to me ill-founded, I made many observations and acquired much experience which has since aided me in establishing more certain knowledge. In addition, I continued to practice the method which I had decided upon; and besides conducting all my thoughts according to its rules, I set aside a few hours now and then for practice upon mathematical difficulties. In some cases I even practiced upon some other difficulties (557) which could be made to parallel mathematical ones by rejecting those principles of the sciences in question which I did not find sufficiently well established, as I have explained in some of my other writings. Thus I lived, in [30] appearance, just like those who have nothing to do but to live a pleasant and innocent life and attempt to obtain the pleasures without the vices, to enjoy their leisure without ennui, and to occupy their time with all the respectable amusements available. But in reality I never desisted from my design and continued to achieve greater acquaintance with truth, perhaps more than I would have if I had only read books or sought the society of men of letters.

In any case, nine years passed before I reached my decision about the difficulties ordinarily in dispute among the learned, and before I sought to lay the groundwork of a philosophy more certain than popular belief. The example of several men of excellent abilities who had previously attempted my task and who, in my opinion, had failed, made me fear so many difficulties that I should perhaps not have dared to start so soon if I had not learned of a rumor that I had already completed my philosophy. I did not know on what such an opinion was based; if I contributed somewhat to it by my conversation, it must have been by confessing my ignorance more freely than is usually the case among those who have studied a little, and possibly also by presenting my reasons for doubting many things that others deemed certain. I am sure that I did not boast of any doctrines. But I did not want to be taken for more than I was, and so I thought that I should try by all means to make myself worthy of [31] my reputation. Just eight years ago, therefore, I decided to abandon those places where I would be among acquaintances, and retired to Holland, where the long duration of the war produced such conditions that the armies billeted there seemed but to guarantee the fruits of peace. There, in the midst of a great and busy people, more interested in their own affairs than curious about those of others, I was able to enjoy all the comforts of life to be found in the most populous cities while living in as solitary and retired a fashion as though in the most remote of deserts.

PART FOUR

PROOFS OF THE EXISTENCE OF GOD
AND OF THE HUMAN SOUL

I do not know whether I ought to touch upon my first meditations here, for they are so metaphysical and out (558) of the
ordinary that they might not be interesting to most people.
Nevertheless, in order to show whether my fundamental notions are sufficiently sound, I find myself more or less constrained to speak of them. I had noticed for a long time that
in practice it is sometimes necessary to follow opinions which
we know to be very uncertain, just as though they were indubitable, as I stated before; but inasmuch as I desired to
devote myself wholly to the search for truth, I thought that
I should take a course precisely contrary, and reject as absolutely false anything of which I could have the least doubt, in
order to see whether anything would be left after this procedure which could be called wholly certain. Thus, [32] as our
senses deceive us at times, I was ready to suppose that nothing
was at all the way our senses represented them to be. As there
are men who make mistakes in reasoning even on the simplest
topics in geometry, I judged that I was as liable to error as
any other, and rejected as false all the reasoning which I had
previously accepted as valid demonstration. Finally, as the
same percepts which we have when awake may come to us
when asleep without their being true, I decided to suppose
that nothing that had ever entered my mind was more real
than the illusions of my dreams. But I soon noticed that while
I thus wished to think everything false, it was necessarily true
that I who thought so was something. Since this truth, *I think,
therefore I am,* ⟨or exist,⟩ was so firm and assured that all the
most extravagant suppositions of the sceptics were unable to
shake it, I judged that I could safely accept it as the first principle of the philosophy I was seeking.

I then examined closely what I was, and saw that I could imagine that I had no body, and that there was no world nor any place that I occupied, but that I could not imagine for a moment that I did not exist. On the contrary, from the very fact that I doubted the truth of other things, ⸗or had any other thought,⸗ it followed ⸗very⸗ evidently ⸗and very certainly⸗ that I existed. On the other hand, if I had [33] ceased to think while ⸗my body and the world and⸗ all the rest of what I had ever imagined remained true, I would have had no reason to believe that I existed ⸗during that time⸗; therefore I concluded that I was a ⸗thing or⸗ substance whose whole essence or nature was only to think, and which, to exist, has no need of space nor of any material thing ⸗or body⸗. Thus it follows that this ego, ⸗this mind,⸗ ⸗this soul,⸗ by which I am what I am, (559) is entirely distinct from the body and is easier to know than the latter, and that even if the body were not, the soul would not cease to be all that it now is.

Next, I considered in general what is required of a proposition for it to be true and certain, for since I had just discovered one to be such, I thought I ought also to know of what that certitude consisted. I saw that there was nothing at all in this statement, "I think, therefore I am," to assure me that I was saying the truth, unless it was that I saw very clearly that to think one must exist. So I judged that I could accept as a general rule that the things which we conceive very clearly and ⸗very⸗ distinctly are always true, but that there may well be some difficulty in deciding which are those which we conceive distinctly.

After that I reflected ⸗upon the fact⸗ that I doubted ⸗many things⸗, and that, in consequence, my spirit was not wholly perfect, for I saw clearly that it was a greater perfection to know than to doubt. I decided to ascertain from what source I had learned to think of something more perfect than myself, and it appeared evident that it must have been [34] from some nature which was in fact more perfect. As for my ideas about many other things outside of me, as the sky, earth, light, heat, and thousands of other things, I was not so much troubled to discover where they came from, because I found nothing in them superior to my own nature. If they really existed, I could believe that whatever perfection they possessed might be derived from my own nature; if they did not exist, I could believe that they were derived from nothingness, that is, that they were derived from my own defects. But this could not be the explanation of my ⟨thought or⟩ idea of a being more perfect than my own. To derive it from nothingness was manifestly impossible, and it is no less repugnant to good sense to assume what is more perfect comes from and depends on the less perfect than it is to assume that something comes from nothing, so that I could not assume that it came from myself. Thus the only hypothesis left was that this idea was put in my mind by a nature that was really more perfect than I was, which had all the perfections that I could imagine, and which was, in a word, God. To this I added that since I knew some perfections which I did not possess, I was not the only being in existence—I will here use freely, if you will pardon me, the terms of the school—and that it followed of necessity that there was someone else more perfect upon whom I depended and from whom I had acquired all that I possessed. For if I had been alone and independent of anything else, so that I had (560) bestowed [35] upon myself all that limited quantity of value which I shared with the perfect Being, I would have been able to get from myself, in the same way, all the surplus which I recognize as lacking in me, and so would have been myself infinite, eternal, immutable, omniscient, omnipotent, and, in sum, I would possess all the perfections that I could discover in God.

For to know the nature of God, ⟨whose existence has been proved⟩, following the reasoning which I have just explained, as far as I was capable of such knowledge, I had only to consider each quality of which I had an idea, and decide whether it was or was not a perfection to possess that quality. I would then be certain that none of those which had some imperfection were in him, but that all the others were. I saw that doubt, inconstancy, sorrow and similar things could not be part of

God's nature, since I would be happy to be without them myself. In addition, I had ideas of many sensible and corporeal
entities, for although I might suppose that I was dreaming and
that all that I saw or imagined was false, I could not at any
rate deny that the ideas were truly in my consciousness. ⌜Since⌝
I had already recognized very clearly that intelligent nature is
distinct from corporeal nature ⌐, and that in every composite
one part depended upon another, and the whole upon its
parts, and that whatever depends upon something else is not
perfect⌐ ⌜, I considered that composition is an evidence of dependency and that dependency is manifestly a defect⌝. From
this I judged that it could not be a perfection in God to be
composed of these two natures, and that consequently he was
not so composed. But if there were in the world bodies, or
even intelligences or other natures that were not wholly [36]
perfect, their being must depend on God's power in such a
way that they could not subsist without him for a single moment.

At this point I wished to seek for other truths, and proposed
for consideration the object of the geometricians. This I conceived as a continuous body, or a space infinitely extended in
length, breadth, and ⌐height or⌝ depth; divisible into various
parts which can have different shapes and sizes and can be
moved or transposed in any way: all of which is presumed by
geometricians to be true of their object. I went through some
of their simplest demonstrations and noticed that the great
certainty which everyone attributes to them is only based on
the fact that they are ⌐clearly and⌝ evidently conceived, following the rule previously established. I noticed also that there
was nothing at all in them to assure me of the existence of
their object; it was clear, for example, that if we posit a triangle, its three angles must be (561) equal to two right angles,
but there was nothing in that to assure me that there was a
single triangle in the world. When I turned back to my idea
of a perfect Being, on the other hand, I ⌐immediately⌝ discovered that existence was included in that idea in the same
way that the idea of a triangle contains the equality of its

angles to two right angles, or that the idea of a ⌈sphere ⌐or⌉ circle⌐ includes the equidistance of all its parts from its center. Perhaps, in fact, the existence of the perfect Being is even more evident. Consequently, it is at least as certain that God, who is this perfect Being, exists, as any theorem of geometry could possibly be. [37]

What makes many people feel that it is difficult to know of the existence of God, or even of the nature of their own souls, is that they never ⌐withdraw their minds from their senses and⌐ consider things higher than corporeal objects. They are so accustomed never to think of anything without picturing it ⌐, that is, without picturing in their imagination some image, as though of a corporeal thing,⌐ ⌈—a method of thinking suitable only for material objects—⌉ that everything which is not picturable seems to them unintelligible. This is also manifest in the fact that even philosophers hold it as a maxim in the schools that there is nothing in the understanding which was not first in the senses, a location where it is clearly evident that the ideas of God and of the soul have never been. It seems to me that those who wish to use imagery to understand these matters are doing precisely the same thing that they would be doing if they tried to use their eyes to hear sounds or smell odors. There is even this difference: that the sense of sight gives us no less certainty of the truth of objects than do those of smell and hearing, while neither our imagery nor our senses could assure us of anything without the co-operation of our understanding ⌐or reason⌐.

Finally, if there are still some men who are not sufficiently persuaded of the existence of God and of their souls ⌐as really existing things considered apart from the body,⌐ by the reasons which I have given, I want them to understand that all the other things of which they might think themselves more certain, such as their having a body, or the existence of stars and of an earth, and other such things are less certain. For even though we have a moral assurance ⌐, as philosophers say,⌐ of these things, such that it seems [38] we cannot doubt them without extravagance, yet without being unreasonable we cannot deny that, as far as metaphysical certainty goes, there is sufficient room for doubt. For we can imagine, when asleep, that we have another body and see other stars and another earth without there being any such. How could one know that the thoughts which come to us in dreams are false rather than the others ⟨which we have when awake⟩, since they are often no less vivid and detailed? (562) Let the best minds study this question as long as they wish, I do not believe they can find any reason good enough to remove this doubt unless they presuppose the existence of God. The very principle which I took as a rule to start with, namely, that all those things which we conceived very clearly and very distinctly are true, is known to be true only because God exists, and because he is a ⟨supreme and⟩ perfect Being, and because everything in us ⟨necessarily⟩ comes from him. From this it follows that our ideas or notions, being real things which come from God insofar as they are clear and distinct, cannot to that extent fail to be true. Consequently, though we often have ideas which contain falsity, they can only be those ideas which contain some confusions and obscurity, in which respect they ⟨do not come from the supreme Being, but proceed from ⌈or⟩ participate in⌉ nothingness. That is to say, they are ⟨obscure and⟩ confused in us only because we ⟨lack something or⟩ are not wholly perfect. It is evident that it is no less ⟨impossible ⌈and⟩ repugnant to good sense⌉ to assume that falsity or [39] imperfection as such is derived from God, as that truth or perfection is derived from nothingness. But if we did not know that all reality and truth within us came from a perfect and infinite Being, however clear and distinct our ideas might be, we would have no reason to be certain that they were ⌈endowed with the perfection of being⌉ true.

After the knowledge of God and the soul has thus made us certain of our rule, it is easy to see that the ⟨errors of our⟩ dreams ⌈which we have when asleep⌉ do not in any way cast doubt upon the truth of our waking thoughts. For if it happened that we had some very distinct idea, even while sleeping, as for example when a geometrician dreams of some new proof, his sleep does not keep the proof from being good. As for the most common error of dreams, which is to picture various objects in the same way as our external senses represent them to us ⟨when awake⟩, it does not matter if this gives us a reason to distrust the truth of the impressions we receive ⟨, or think we receive,⟩ from the senses, because we can also be mistaken in them frequently without being asleep, as when jaundiced persons see everything yellow, or as the stars and other distant objects appear much smaller than they really are. For in truth, whether we are asleep or awake, we should never allow ourselves to be convinced except on the evidence of our reason. Note that I say of our *reason*, and not of our imagination or of our senses; for even though we see the [40] sun very clearly, we must not judge thereby that its size is such as we see it, and we can well imagine distinctly the head of a lion (563) mounted on the body of a goat, without concluding that a chimera exists in this world. For reason does not insist that all we see or visualize in this way is true, but it does insist that all our ideas or notions must have some foundation in truth, for it would not be possible that God, who is all-perfect and wholly truthful, would otherwise have given them to us. Since our reasonings ⟨or judgments⟩ are never as ⟨clear and distinct ⌈, as⟩ evident or as complete⌉ in sleep as in waking life, although sometimes our imaginations are then ⌈as⌉ lively and detailed ⌈as when awake, or even more so⌉, and since reason tells us also that all our thoughts cannot be true, as we are not wholly perfect; whatever of truth is to be found in our ideas will ⌈inevitably⌉ occur in those which we have when awake rather than in our dreams.

PART FIVE

SOME QUESTIONS OF PHYSICS

I would have been glad to continue my exposition and exhibit here the whole chain of other truths which I deduced from these basic ones, but for the fact that to do so I should have to speak of many questions which are in dispute among the learned. As I do not wish to embroil myself with them, I think it would be better to abstain, so I shall give only an outline of these views, and let wiser people judge whether the public should be informed in greater detail.

I have [41] always remained true to the resolution I made, never to suppose any other principle than that which I have just used to demonstrate the existence of God and the soul, and not to admit anything as true which did not seem to me clearer and more certain than the demonstrations of the geometricians previously seemed. Nevertheless, I have not only succeeded in satisfying myself in this short time on all the principal difficulties usually treated in philosophy, but have also discovered certain laws which God has so established in nature, and the notion of which he has so fixed in our minds, that after sufficient reflection we cannot doubt that they are exactly observed in all which exists or which happens in the world. Finally, in considering the implications of these laws I seem to have discovered several truths ⌈more useful and⌉ more important than anything I had previously learned or even hoped to learn.

Since I have tried to explain the most important of these laws in a work which certain considerations prevent my publishing, I see no better way to proceed than by summarizing its contents. I intended to include in it all that I thought I knew, before writing it, concerning the nature of material things. But I found myself in the same state as painters, who cannot equally well represent in a two-dimensional painting all the various faces of a solid body, and so choose one to bring to the light, and leave the others in shadow, [42] so that (564) they can be seen only while viewing the selected side. Therefore, fearing that I would not be able to put into any discourse all that I intended, I undertook solely to describe at length what I thought on the subject of light, and took that occasion to add something concerning the sun and the fixed stars, since they are almost the only sources of light; of the sky, since it transmits it; of the planets, the comets, and the earth, since they reflect it; and in particular of all the objects on earth, since they are either colored or transparent or luminous; and finally of man, since he is the observer of it. I even elected, as a painter might do, to place my object somewhat in the shadow, so that I could express my opinions more freely without being obliged to accept or to refute the opinions commonly held by the learned. I therefore resolved to leave this world for them to dispute about, and to speak only of what would happen in a new one, if God should now create, somewhere in imaginary space, enough matter to make one; and if he agitated the various parts of this matter without order, making a chaos as confused as the poets could imagine, but that afterward he did nothing but lend his usual support to nature, allowing it to behave according to the laws he had established.

So I first described this matter and tried to picture it in such a way that nothing in the world could be clearer or more intelligible except what has just been said about God and the soul. I even expressly supposed that this matter [43] had none of the forms or qualities concerning which one disputes in the schools, nor in general anything that we do not know so naturally that we cannot even pretend to ignore it. Furthermore, I showed what were the laws of nature, and without basing my reasons on anything more specific than the infinite perfection⌈s⌉ of God, I tried to demonstrate everything which might be doubtful, and to show that nature is such that even if God had created several worlds, there would have been none where these laws were not observed. After that, I showed how the greater part of the matter in this chaos would, in consequence of these laws, become arranged in a manner which would make it similar to our skies; and how nevertheless some of the parts must compose an earth, and some planets and comets, and others a sun and fixed stars. And here, enlarging upon the topic of light, I explained at considerable length its nature when contained in the sun and the stars, how from there it traverses in an instant the immense reaches of the heavens, and how it is reflected from the planets and comets toward the earth. I also added several things concerning the substance, situation, movements, and all the diverse qualities of these celestial objects and stars; (565) until I thought I had said enough to show that there were no phenomena ⟨in the sky or stars⟩ of this world which would not or at least could not occur similarly in the world [44] I was describing.

Thence I went on to speak particularly of the earth: how, even though I had expressly supposed that God had given no weight to the matter of which it was composed, all its parts would tend exactly toward its center; how the disposition of the celestial bodies and stars, principally the moon, would cause an ebb and flow in the water and air on its surface, similar in all respects to the tides of our seas, and in addition a certain current, as much of water as of air, from east to west, such as we find in the tropics; how mountains, seas, springs and rivers could naturally occur, metals come to be in mines, plants grow in the fields, and, in general, how the whole genus of mixed or composite objects would be formed.

Among other things, since outside of the stars I knew nothing but fire which produced light, I strove to explain quite clearly the whole of the nature of fire: how it is produced and maintained; how sometimes it has heat without light and sometimes light without heat; how it can produce different colors in different objects, and many other qualities; how it melts some objects and hardens others; how it can consume things entirely or convert them into ashes and smoke; and finally, how by the violence of its action it turns ashes into glass; for as this transmutation of [45] ashes into glass seemed as admirable as any that occurs in nature, I found a particular pleasure in describing it.

I did not wish to infer from all this that the world had been created in the manner I proposed, for it is much more likely that God created it in the beginning in the form it was to assume. But it is certain, and this is an opinion commonly held by theologians, that the action by which the world is now conserved is precisely the same as that by which it was created. Even therefore, if God had given the world in the beginning no other form but chaos, and had only established the laws of nature and given his concurrence for the world to behave as it usually does, one can believe, without injustice to the miracle of creation, that all material objects could have become, in time, such as we see them at present. Their nature is much easier to conceive when one pictures their gradual growth in this manner rather than considering them as produced in their completed state.

From the description of inanimate objects and plants I passed (566) to ⌜that of⌝ animals, and particularly ⌜of⌝ man. But I did not as yet know enough to speak of these in the same style as of the rest, in showing the causes of their existence and showing from what origins and in what manner nature must have produced them. I was therefore satisfied to assume that God formed the body of a man just like [46] our own, both in the external configuration of its members and in the internal configuration of its organs, without using in its composition any matter but that which I had described. I also assumed that God did not put into this body, to start with, any rational soul or any other entity to serve as a vegetable or sensitive soul, beyond kindling in the heart one of those fires without light which I had already described and which I considered to be entirely similar to that which heats grain when it is stored before it is dry, or which warms new wines when they are allowed to ferment before being separated from the grapes. Examining the functions which such a body would have, I discovered everything that can exist without thinking; everything except that which is contributed by the soul: that part of us distinct from the body whose essence, as we have previously said, is only to think. These functions are the same as those in which the unreasoning animals resemble us, and do not include any of those which are dependent on thinking and which belong to us as men. These human qualities I discovered somewhat later, when I supposed that God created a rational soul and joined it to the body in a certain fashion which I described.

In order to show how I treated this matter, I wish to insert here the explanation of the function of the heart and arteries. As the first and most general function found in animals, it will serve to indicate what the reader should [47] think of all the rest. Those who are not well versed in anatomy will find less difficulty in understanding what I am going to say if they will take the trouble, before reading this, to have the heart of some large animal cut open before them, for the heart of an animal with lungs is quite similar to that of man. Let them then observe the two chambers, or ventricles, which it contains. First, the one on the right side connects with two very large tubes: the *vena cava,* which is the principal container of blood and resembles the trunk of a tree of which all the other veins are branches; and the *vena arteriosa,* misnamed since it is really an artery which starts in the heart, then divides into several branches, and spreads throughout the lungs. The left ventricle has two similar tubes at least as large as those just described: (567) the *arteria venosa,* likewise misnamed since it is purely a vein, coming from the lungs, where it is divided into a number of branches interlaced with those of the *vena arteriosa* and those of the windpipe, through which enters the air we breathe; and the aorta, which, starting from the heart, sends its branches everywhere throughout the body. I should suggest also that the reader observe the eleven little membranes which, like so many little valves, open and close the four openings in these two ventricles. [48] Three are at the entrance to the *vena cava,* where they are so disposed that they cannot stop the blood that it contains from flowing into the right

ventricle but prevent any of it from flowing back. Three, at
the entrance of the *vena arteriosa,* are disposed in precisely
the opposite fashion, permitting the blood in the heart to pass
to the lungs but not allowing the blood in the lungs to return. So also, there are two at the entrance to the *arteria
venosa,* which permit the blood to pass from the lungs to the
left ventricle and prevent its return, and three at the entrance
to the aorta, permitting the blood to leave the heart but not
to return. There is no need to seek any other reason for the
number of these membranes other than the fact that the opening of the *arteria venosa,* being oval because of its location,
can be conveniently closed with two, while the others are
round and can be more readily closed with three. I should
like the reader to notice also that the aorta and the *vena
arteriosa* are much harder and firmer than the *arteria venosa*
and *vena cava,* and that these last two are enlarged near the
heart, forming two sacs called the "ears" or auricles of the
heart, composed of a flesh resembling that of the ears. Notice
also that there is always more heat in the heart than in any
other part of the body, and that this heat is capable of causing any drop of blood which enters the ventricles to expand
immediately, [49] just as any liquid does when it falls drop by
drop into some very hot vessel.

After that, I need say nothing more to explain the functioning of the heart, except that when its ventricles are not full of
blood, some necessarily flows into it. The right ventricle is
filled from the *vena cava,* and the left ventricle from the
arteria venosa, since these two vessels are always full and their
entrances, opening toward the heart, cannot then be closed.
The portions of blood in each ventricle cannot fail to be very
large since the openings are very large and the vessels from
which they came full of blood; and as soon as these portions
enter the heart, they become rarefied and expand because of
the heat there. This (568) dilates the whole heart and pushes
upon and closes the five valvules at the entrance of the ⌈two⌉
vessels from which the blood comes, preventing any more
blood from entering the heart. As the blood continues to ex-

pand, it pushes upon and opens the six other valvules which
are at the entrance to the other two vessels through which the
blood leaves, and thus inflates all the branches of the *vena
arteriosa* and the aorta at almost the same instant as the heart.
A moment later the heart and these arteries are all deflated
because the blood which has entered them has cooled. The six
valvules close, and the five of the *vena cava* and *arteria venosa*
reopen permitting [50] two more portions of blood to enter
and dilate the heart and the arteries the same as before. And
since the blood which thus enters the heart comes through the
two ⌐sacs called⌐ auricles, it follows that the condition of the
latter is the opposite of that of the ventricles, and that the
former are deflated when the latter are inflated.

For the rest, so that those who do not appreciate the force
of mathematical demonstration and are not accustomed to distinguish between good and bad reasons should not make the
mistake of denying this without examining it, I must warn
them that the motion which I have just explained follows
necessarily from the mere disposition of the parts of the heart
visible to the naked eye, from the heat which one can feel
with the fingers, and from the nature of the blood, which one
can learn by experiment: just as the motions of a clock follow
from the weight, location, and configuration of its counterweights and wheels.

But if one asks why the blood in the veins does not become
exhausted by thus flowing continually into the heart, and why
the arteries do not become overfull, since all that passes
through the heart goes there, I need only point out what has
already been written by an English doctor [1] who has the glory
of having broken the ice in this matter. He was the first to
show that there are many small passages at the ends of the
arteries, by which the blood received from the heart enters
into the small branches of the veins, whence it returns again
to the heart; so that its path is nothing but a [51] perpetual
circulation. This he proved very adequately by the common
experience of surgeons, who, having applied a tourniquet to

[1] Harvey.

the arm, not too tightly, above the spot where they open a vein, make the blood flow more abundantly than it would without the tourniquet. On the other hand, quite the contrary occurs if they tie it below, between the hand and the opening, or even if they tie it very tightly above. For it is obvious that a tourniquet which is moderately tight can prevent the blood which is already in the arm from returning toward the heart through the veins, but cannot hinder that which is continually coming from the heart through the arteries, because the arteries are situated below the veins, and because their walls are stiffer (569) and less easy to compress, and also because the blood comes from the heart with greater pressure than it has when returning through the veins. Since this blood leaves the arm through an opening in one of the veins, there must necessarily be some passages below the tourniquet, that is, toward the hand, by which it comes from the arteries. He also proves his contention about the circulation of the blood by certain small membranes ⟨in the form of valvules,⟩ so disposed in various places along the veins that they do not permit the blood to flow from the middle of the body toward the extremities, but only to return from the extremities toward the heart; and further by the fact that all the blood in the body can be lost in a very short time when a single artery is cut, even if it is tightly constricted close to the heart and cut between the constriction and the heart, so that there [52] is no imaginable way that the blood which escapes comes from another source than the heart.

There are several other considerations which prove that the real cause of this movement of the blood is the one which I have given; such as, first, the difference between that which comes from the veins and that which comes from the arteries: a difference only to be explained by the fact that the blood is rarefied, as though it were distilled, in passing through the heart, and is therefore thinner, more active, and warmer when it has just come from there and is in the arteries, than just before it enters and is in the veins. Careful observation shows that this difference is more apparent near the heart, and is not

so noticeable at points far removed from it. Then the hardness of the membranes of which the *vena arteriosa* and the
aorta are composed shows well enough that the blood passes
through them with greater pressure than through the veins.
Furthermore, why should the left ventricle and the aorta be
larger and broader than the right ventricle and the *vena
arteriosa,* if it is not that the blood of the *arteria venosa,* not
having been in the lungs since it passed through the heart, is
thinner and becomes more rarefied more readily than that
which comes directly from the *vena cava?* And what could
doctors tell by feeling the pulse, if they did not know that as
the nature of the blood changes, it can be rarefied by the heat
of the heart more or less strongly and more or less rapidly
than before? And if we examine how this heat is communicated to the other parts of the body, must we not admit that it
is [53] through the blood which is warmed in passing through
the heart and spreads this heat through the whole body? From
this it results that if the blood is withdrawn from any part of
the body, heat is withdrawn by the same token. Even if the
heart were as hot as glowing iron, it could not warm the hands
and feet as it does unless it continually sent new blood to
those parts. We also recognize from these considerations that
the true purpose of respiration (570) is to bring enough fresh
air into the lungs to condense the blood which was rarefied
in the right ventricle before it returns to the left; to take
blood which has almost been converted into vapor and recon-
vert it into blood. If this were not done, the blood would not
be suitable for the nourishing of the heart's fire. This is confirmed by seeing that animals that have no lungs have only
one ventricle, and that unborn children, who cannot use their
lungs while enclosed in their mothers' wombs, have an opening through which blood flows directly from the *vena cava*
into the left ventricle, and a ʹshortʹ tube by which it passes
from the *vena arteriosa* into the aorta without passing through
the lungs. Then, how could digestion take place in the
stomach if the heart did not send heat there through the
arteries, together with some of the most fluid parts of the

blood which help to dissolve the food which is placed there? Is it not easy to understand the action which converts the liquid part of these foods into blood if we consider that the blood is distilled possibly more than a hundred or two hundred times each day when passing through the heart? And we need say nothing more [54] to explain nutrition and the production of the several humors of the body, except that the force of the blood, expanding while passing from the heart to the ends of the arteries, brings it about that some of its parts come to rest in certain organs of the body, taking the place of others which they expel; and that certain parts of the blood come to rest in certain places rather than others, according to the location, shape, or size of the pores encountered; just as sieves with holes of different sizes serve to separate different grains from each other. The most remarkable aspect of all this is the production of animal spirits, which are like a very subtle wind, or rather a very pure ⌈and lively⌉ flame, which continuously rises in great abundance from the heart to the brain, and thence through the nerves into the muscles, where it produces the movement of all parts of the body. The most agitated and penetrating parts of the blood compose these animal spirits, and no other reason need be sought why these parts go to the brain rather than elsewhere than the fact that the arteries which conduct them are the straightest of all. According to the rules of mechanics, which are the same as the rules of nature, when several objects tend to move toward a place where there is not room enough for all, as is the case when parts of the blood leave the left ventricle and tend toward the brain, [55] the weakest and least agitated of them must ⌈necessarily⌉ be turned aside by the strongest, which thus are the only ones to arrive at their destination. (571)

I had explained all these things in sufficient detail in the treatise which I previously intended to publish. And I continued by showing what the nature of the network of nerves and muscles of the human body must be to enable the animal spirits within to move its members, as one sees when freshly severed heads still move and bite the earth although they are

no longer alive. I showed what changes must take place in
the brain to cause wakefulness, sleep, and dreams; how light,
sounds, odors, tastes, heat, and all the other qualities of external objects can implant various ideas through the medium
of the senses; and how hunger, thirst, and the other internal
passions are communicated. I explained what must be understood by that animal sense which receives these ideas, by
memory which retains them, and by imagination which can
change them in various ways and build new ones from them,
and thus, distributing the animal spirits in the muscles, move
the parts of the body, in response to the objects, which are
presented to the senses and the passions which are in the body,
in as great a variety of ways as our own bodies can move
without the guidance of volition. This will hardly seem
strange to those who know how many ⟨motions can be produced in⟩ automata ⎡or machines ⟨which⟩ can be⎤ made by
human industry, [56] although these automata employ very
few ⟨wheels and other⟩ parts in comparison to the large number of bones, muscles, nerves, arteries, veins, and all the other
component parts of each animal. Such persons will therefore
think of this body as a machine created by the hand of God,
and in consequence incomparably better designed and with
more admirable movements than any machine that can be
invented by man.

Here I paused to show that if there were any machines
which had the organs and appearance of a monkey or of
some other unreasoning animal, we would have no way of
telling that it was not of the same nature as these animals. But
if there were a machine which had such a resemblance to our
bodies, and imitated our actions as far as is morally possible,
there would always be two absolutely certain methods of
recognizing that it was still not truly a man. The first is that
it could never use words or other signs for the purpose of
communicating its thoughts to others, as we do. It is indeed
conceivable that a machine could be so made that it would
utter words, and even words appropriate to ⟨the presence of⟩
⎡physical acts ⟨or⟩ objects⟩ which cause some change in its

organs; (572) as, for example, if it was touched in some spot
that it would ask what you wanted to say to it; if in another,
that it would cry that it was hurt, and so on for similar things.
But it could never modify its phrases to [57] reply to the sense
of whatever was said in its presence, as even the most stupid
men can do. The second method of recognition is that, although such machines could do many things as well as, or
perhaps even better than, men, they would infallibly fail in
certain others, by which we would discover that they did not
act by ⌈understanding ⸍or⸌ reason⸥, but only by the disposition
of their organs. For while reason is a universal instrument
which can be used in all sorts of situations, the organs have
to be arranged in a particular way for each particular action.
From this it follows that it is ⌈morally impossible ⸍and⌉ clearly
incredible⸥ that there should be enough different devices in a
machine to make it behave in all the occurrences of life as our
reason makes us behave.

By these two methods we can also recognize the difference
between man and animals. For it is a very remarkable thing
that there are no men, not even the insane, so dull and stupid
that they cannot put words together in a manner to convey
their thoughts. On the contrary, there is no other animal,
however perfect and fortunately situated it may be, that can
do the same. And this is not because they lack the organs, for
we see that magpies and parrots can pronounce words as well
as we can, and nevertheless cannot speak as we do, that is, in
showing that they think what they are saying. On the other
hand, even those men born deaf and dumb, lacking the organs
which others make use of in [58] speaking, and at least as
badly off as the animals in this respect, usually invent for
themselves some signs by which they make themselves understood by those who are with them enough to learn their
language. And this proves not merely that animals have less
reason than men, but that they have none at all, for we see
that very little is needed in order to talk. Furthermore, we
notice variations among animals of the same species, just as
among men, and that some are easier to train than others.

It is therefore unbelievable that a monkey or a parrot which was one of the best of its species should not be the equal in this matter of one of the most stupid children, or at least of a child of infirm mind, if their soul were not of a wholly different nature from ours.

Note also that we should not confuse speech ⌐, and all those signs which in the practice of human beings convey thoughts,⌐ with the natural ⌐sounds and⌐ movements that indicate passions ⌐, and can be imitated by machines as well as by animals⌐; nor should we think, like some of the ancients, that animals speak although we (573) do not understand their language. For if it were true, they would make themselves understood by us as well as by their fellows, since they have several organs analogous to our own. It is another very remarkable fact that although there are many animals that show more industry than we in some of their behavior, these same animals show none at all in other ways; and so the fact that they do better than we do does not prove that they are rational, for on this basis they would be more rational than any of us, and [59] would surpass us in everything. It proves, on the contrary, that they are not rational, and that nature makes them behave as they do according to the disposition of their organs; just as a clock, composed only of wheels ⌐and weights⌐ ⌐and springs⌐, can count the hours and measure the time more accurately than we can with all our intelligence.

I then described the rational soul, and showed that it could not possibly be derived from the powers of matter, like the other things I have spoken about, but must have been specially created. I showed also that it would not suffice to place it in the human body, as a pilot in a ship, unless perhaps to move its parts, but that it must be more intimately joined and united with the body in order to have feelings and appetites like ours, and so constitute a real man. For the rest, I elaborated a little on the topic of the soul on account of its great importance; because, next to the error of those who deny God, which I think I have sufficiently refuted, there is none which is so apt to make weak characters stray from the path of virtue as the idea that the souls of animals are of the same nature as our own, and that in consequence we have no more to fear or to hope for after this life than have the flies and ants. Actually, when we know how different they are, we understand more fully the reasons which prove that our soul is by nature entirely independent of the body, and consequently does not have to die with it. Therefore, as long as [60] we see no ⌐other⌐ causes which might destroy it, we are naturally led to conclude that it is immortal.

PART SIX

SOME PREREQUISITES FOR FURTHER ADVANCES IN THE STUDY OF NATURE

Three years ago, when I had completed the treatise containing all these matters, and when I was beginning to review it for purposes of publication, I learned that people to whom I defer, and whose authority over my actions is hardly less than that of my own reason over my thoughts, had disapproved of a hypothesis in the field of physics that had been published somewhat earlier by another person.[1] I do not want to say that I had accepted that hypothesis, but at least before their censure I could not imagine that it was prejudicial to religion or to the state, and therefore I could see no ground for not professing it if reason (574) convinced me of its truth. This circumstance made me fear that there might be other opinions of mine in which I was misled, despite the great care I had always taken not to accept any new ones which were not very certainly demonstrated, and to write of none that might prove disadvantageous to anyone. This occurrence was enough to make me change my resolution to publish the treatise, for although the reasons for making it were very

[1] Galileo.

strong, my inclinations were always much opposed to writing books and I was quick to find other reasons to excuse myself for not publishing. These reasons, on both sides, are such that not [61] only have I some interest in relating them, but the ⟨reading⟩ public may also have some interest in learning them.

I have never entertained any pretensions about the products of my thinking. When the result of the application of my methods was merely my own satisfaction concerning some speculative questions, or perhaps the regulation of my own behavior by the principles which it showed me, I did not feel obliged to write of them. For when it comes to morals, everyone is so convinced of his own good sense that there might be as many reformers as individuals if others than those whom God has established as sovereigns over his peoples, or to whom he has given enough grace and zeal to be prophets, were permitted to attempt reforms. So, even though my speculations pleased me very much, I believed that other persons had their own speculations which perhaps pleased them even more. As soon, however, as I had achieved some general notions about physics, and when, testing them in various critical problems, I noticed how far they might lead and how they differed from the principles accepted up to this time, I thought that I could not keep them hidden without gravely sinning against the rule that obliges us to promote as far as possible the general good of mankind. For they have satisfied me that it is possible to reach knowledge that will be of much utility in this life; and that instead of the speculative philosophy now taught in the schools we can find [62] a practical one, by which, knowing the nature and behavior of fire, water, air, stars, the heavens, and all the other bodies which surround us, as well as we now understand the different skills of our workers, we can employ these entities for all the purposes for which they are suited, and so make ourselves masters and possessors of nature. This would not only be desirable in bringing about the invention of an infinity of devices to enable us to enjoy the fruits of agriculture and all the wealth of the earth without labor, but even more so in (575) conserving

health, the principal good and the basis of all other goods
in this life. For the mind is so dependent upon the humors
and the condition of the organs of the body that if it is
possible to find some way to make men ⌈in general⌉ wiser and
more clever than they have been so far, I believe that it is
in medicine that it should be sought. It is true that medicine
at present contains little of such great value; but without
intending to belittle it, I am sure that everyone, even among
those who follow the profession, will admit that everything we
know is almost nothing compared with what remains to be
discovered, and that we might rid ourselves of an infinity of
maladies of body as well as of mind, and perhaps also of the
enfeeblement of old age, if we had sufficient understanding of
the causes ⌐from which these ills arise⌐ and of all the remedies
which nature has provided. It was my intention to [63] devote
my whole life to the pursuit of this much-needed service, and
I had found a method which, it seemed to me, should infallibly lead me to it unless I was prevented either by the
brevity of life or the paucity of experiments. I judged that the
best precaution against these two dangers would be to publish
faithfully to the world the little which I had discovered, and
to urge men of ability to continue the work by contributing,
each one according to his inclinations and abilities, to the
experiments which must be made. I hoped that each one
would publish whatever he had learned, so that later investiga-
tors could begin where the earlier had left off. In this way
mankind would combine the lives and work of many people,
and would go much further than any individual could go by
himself.

I noticed that experimentation becomes more necessary in
proportion as we advance in knowledge. In beginning an investigation it is better to restrict ourselves to our usual experiences, which we cannot ignore if we pay any attention to
them at all, than to seek rarer and more abstruse experiences.
The reason for this is that these latter are often deceiving
when the causes of the more common phenomena are still unknown, as the circumstances on which they depend are almost

always so particular and so minute that it is very difficult to discover them. My own procedure has been the following: I first tried to discover the general [64] principles or first causes of all that exists or could exist in the world, without taking any causes into consideration but God as creator, and without using any evidence save certain indications of the truth which we find in our own minds. After that I examined what were the first and commonest effects which could be deduced from these causes; and it seems (576) to me that by this procedure I discovered skies, stars, an earth, and even, on the earth, water, air, fire, minerals, and several other things which are the commonest of all and the most simple, and in consequence the easiest to understand. Then, when I wanted to descend to particulars, it seemed to me that there were so many different kinds that I believed it impossible for the human mind to distinguish the forms or species of objects found on earth from an infinity of others which might have been there if God had so willed. It thus appeared impossible to proceed further deductively, and if we were to understand and make use of things, we would have to discover causes by their effects, and make use of many experiments. In consequence, reviewing in my mind all the objects which had ever been presented to my senses, I believe I can say that I have never noticed anything which I could not explain easily enough by the principles I had found. But I must also admit that the powers of nature are so ample and vast, and that these principles are so simple and so general, that I hardly ever observed a particular effect without immediately recognizing [65] several ways in which it could be deduced. My greatest difficulty usually is to find which of these is the true explanation, and to do this I know no other way than to seek several experiments such that their outcomes would be different according to the choice of hypotheses.

For the rest, I have now reached the point, it seems to me, where I see clearly enough the direction in which we should go in this research; but I also see that the character and the number of experiments required is such that neither my time nor my resources, were they a thousand times greater than they are, would suffice to do them all. In proportion, therefore, to the opportunity I shall have in the future to do more or fewer of them, I will advance more or less in the understanding of nature. This I expected to convey in my treatise, and I hoped to show so clearly how useful my project might be that I would oblige all those who desire human benefit, all those who are truly virtuous and not merely so in ⌈affectation or⌉ reputation, both to communicate to me the experiments that they have already made and to assist me in the prosecution of what remained to be done.

But since then other reasons occurred to me which have made me change my mind. I still think that I should continue to write everything that I consider important as soon as I discover its truth, and do so with as much care as if I intended to publish it. In this way [66] I will have additional opportunities to examine my ideas, for doubtless we always scrutinize more closely that which we expect to be read by others (577) than that which we do for ourselves alone, and frequently the ideas which seemed true to me when I first conceived them have appeared false when I wished to put them on paper. Also, I would thus lose no opportunity to benefit humanity, if I am capable of it; and if my writings have any value, those into whose hands they fall after my death may use them as may be most appropriate. But I decided that I should never consent to have them published during my life, for fear that the opposition and controversy which they might arouse, and the reputation which they might possibly bring me, would cause me to waste time which I plan to use in research. For although it is true that each man is obligated to do as much as he can for the benefit of others, and that to be of no use to anyone is really to be worthless, yet it is also true that our interest should extend beyond the present time, and that it is well to avoid things which may bring some profit to the living when it is done with the intention of profiting our descendants still more. So I want it to be understood that the little I have learned thus far is a mere nothing compared to what I do not know and yet do not despair of learning. For it is much the same with those who gradually discover truth in the [67] sciences as with those who, beginning to be rich, find it less difficult to make important acquisitions than they formerly did, when poorer, to make much smaller ones. Or perhaps we should make the comparison with army chieftains, whose forces usually grow in proportion to their victories and who need more skill to maintain themselves after a defeat than they do to win cities and whole provinces after a victory. For to try to conquer all the difficulties and errors which stand in our way when we try to reach the truth is really to engage in battle; and to reach a false conclusion on an important issue is to lose the battle. After such a loss, much more ability is needed to reinstate ourselves in our former position than is required to make great progress when we have already acquired well-tested principles. For myself, if I have thus far found some truths in the sciences, and I trust that the treatises contained in this volume [1] will convince the reader that I have, I can say that these are only the ⌜results and⌝ consequences of five or six principal difficulties which I have surmounted. These I count as so many battles in which fortune has been on my side. I would even go so far as to say that I think that two or three further victories of equal importance would enable me to reach my goal, and I am not so old that I cannot look forward to enough leisure, in the ordinary course of nature, for this purpose. [68] But I feel the greater obligation (578) to make good use of the time remaining to me, the more hope I have of being able to do so effectively, and I would no doubt find many occasions to waste time if I published the foundations of my physics. For although my principles are almost all so evident that to hear them is to believe them, and although there are none that I do not believe I can demonstrate, nevertheless, as they could not possibly agree with all the various opinions held by men at large, I foresee that I would often be distracted by the opposition which they would arouse.

---

[1] Optics, Meteorology, and Geometry.

One might argue that this opposition would be useful, partly to show me my mistakes, partly so that if there were anything worth while in my ideas, others would learn of it; and as many can see more than one, they would assist me immediately by their insight. But while I recognize that I am extremely likely to make mistakes, and while I rarely have much confidence in the first thoughts that come to me, nevertheless my experience of the objections that may be raised against me does not lead me to expect much profit by them. For I have often been favored with the judgments both of those I took to be friends and of those whom I took to be indifferent, as well as of a few who were moved by malignity and envy to expose what affection would hide from ⟨the eyes of⟩ my friends. Yet it has rarely happened that an objection was offered which I had not foreseen, except when it was [69] very far-fetched; so that I have hardly ever met a critic of my opinions who did not appear to me to be either less rigorous or less equitable than myself. Nor have I noticed that the arguments carried on in the schools have ever brought to light a truth which was previously unknown, for when each person tries to win, he is more concerned to make his views prevail by appearing to be right than he is to weigh the evidence for both sides. Those who have long been good trial lawyers do not therefore make better judges afterwards.

As for the advantages which others might derive from hearing my ideas, they could not be so very great, especially since my ideas are still in a stage where much more has to be done before they can be applied to practice. And I think I may say without vanity that if anyone can accomplish this, it should be myself rather than any other person. Not that there may not be many minds incomparably superior to my own, but that we never understand a thing so well, and make it our own, when we learn it from another as when we have discovered it for ourselves. This is so true in this instance that although I have often explained some of my opinions (579) to very intelligent people, who seemed to understand them very distinctly while I was speaking, nevertheless when they retold them I have noticed that they have almost always so changed them that I could no longer accept them as my own. I should also like to take advantage of this occasion to [70] request posterity never to believe that any ideas are mine unless I have divulged them myself. I am not at all surprised at the extravagances attributed to the ancient philosophers whose writings we do not possess, nor do I judge in consequence that their ideas were unreasonable. They were the wisest men of their time, so I presume that their ideas have been badly reported. We notice, also, that it has rarely happened that one of their disciples has surpassed them, and I feel sure that the most devoted of the contemporary followers of Aristotle would consider themselves fortunate if they had as much knowledge of nature as he had, even on the condition that they would never have any more. They are like the ivy, which has no tendency to climb higher than the trees which support it, and often grows downward after it has reached the top. For it seems to me that followers also decline; that is, they make themselves somehow less wise than they would be if they abstained from study when they are not satisfied to understand what is intelligibly explained by their author, but insist on finding in him the solutions of many problems of which he says nothing, and of which he has perhaps never thought. Just the same, their manner of philosophizing is very convenient for those who have only very mediocre minds; for the obscurity of the distinctions and principles which they use enables them to talk of all things as bravely as though they understood them ⟨perfectly⟩, and to defend all they [71] say against the deepest and cleverest thinkers, as there is no way to convince them. In this they appear to me similar to a blind man who wishes to fight on even terms with one who can see, and so brings him to the back of some very dark cave. These people, I may say, are interested in my abstaining from the publication of my principles of philosophy; for since these are very simple and evident, I would be doing much the same to them as though I opened some windows and let the light of day enter into that cave where they had retired to fight. But even the best minds need not wish to know my principles; for if they want to be able to talk about all things and gain the reputation of being learned, they can accomplish this more easily by being satisfied with the appearance of truth, which can be found without much trouble in all sorts of matters, than by seeking truth itself. Truth can be discovered only little by little, and in a few subjects, so that he who pursues truth is often obliged to admit his ignorance when discussing a subject which he has not investigated. But if they prefer the knowledge of a little truth to the vanity of seeming to know everything, as is no doubt preferable, and (580) if they wish to pursue a plan similar to mine, it is not necessary for me to tell them anything more than I have already said in this Discourse, for if they are capable of going further than I have gone, they will be still more capable of finding for themselves everything which I think I have found. This is especially true because I have always proceeded in a natural order, so that it is certain that what remains to be discovered is [72] more difficult in itself and more recondite than what I have so far encountered. They would also experience much less pleasure in learning it from me than in discovering it for themselves. In addition, they would thus acquire the habit of discovery by seeking easy things first, and pass gradually and by degrees to more difficult ones—a habit which will prove much more useful than all my information could possibly be. As for myself, I am persuaded that if I had been taught in my youth all the truths of which I have since sought demonstrations, and if I could have learned them without difficulty, I might never have learned any others, or at least, I would never have acquired the habit and ability that I believe I possess, always to find new truths in proportion to the efforts I make to find them. In a word, if there is one task in the world that cannot be finished as well by another as by the one who started it, it is this one ⟨in which I am occupied and⟩ at which I am working.

It is true that as far as the related experiments are concerned, one man is not enough to do them all; but he could not usefully employ other hands than his own, unless those of workers or other persons whom he could pay. Such people would do, in the hope of gain, which is a very effective motive, precisely what they were told. As for those volunteers who might offer to do it out of curiosity or the desire to learn, besides the fact that ordinarily they are stronger in promises than in performance and that they make nothing but beautiful proposals of which none ever succeeds, they [73] would infallibly expect to be paid by the explanation of some difficulties, or at least in compliments and useless conversation, which would necessarily consume ⌈so⌉ much of the time needed for investigation ⌈that the assistance would be at a net loss⌉. As for the experiments which others have already made, even if they were willing to communicate them, which those who call them secrets never do, they are for the most part so complicated with unneeded details and superfluous ingredients that it would be very difficult for the investigator to discover their core of truth. Besides this, he would find almost all these experiments so poorly explained or even false, because those who performed them forced themselves to make them appear conformable to their principles, that if some of them were useful, they could not counterbalance the time that would be lost in picking them out. So even if there were someone in the world who (581) could be recognized without question as capable of making the greatest and the most beneficial discoveries, and even if in consequence all other men attempted by every means to aid him in the accomplishment of his designs, I do not see that they could do anything except contribute to the costs of the necessary experiments, and see that his leisure is not interrupted by the importunities of anyone. But I am not so presumptuous as to promise anything extraordinary, nor do I indulge in such vain fancies as to imagine that the public ought to be much interested in my plans. Finally, I am not so base in spirit that I would be willing to accept from anyone [74] any favor which it might be thought I had not deserved.

All these considerations taken together made me decide, three years ago, that I did not wish to publish the treatise which I had on hand, and I even resolved never during my lifetime to permit others to read any paper of such a general nature that they might understand the foundations of my physics. But two other reasons have occurred since which have obliged me to submit herewith some detailed essays, and to give the public some account of my doings and my plans. The first reason is that if I did not do so, several people who knew of my previous intention to publish several essays might suppose that my reasons for abstaining were less honorable than they really are. For although I do not care too greatly for reputation—I might even say that I dislike it insofar as I consider it destructive of peace of mind, which I esteem above all things—nevertheless I have never tried to hide my actions as though they were criminal. Neither have I made much effort to remain unknown, partly because I would have thought I was doing myself an injustice, partly because that would have produced a certain disquiet unfavorable to that perfect peace of mind which I desire. I have always tried to remain indifferent to having or not having a reputation, but since I could not avoid having some kind, I thought I should at least do my best to avoid a bad one. The other reason which has obliged me to write [75] this is that I observe a constantly greater retardation in my plan to enlighten myself, because of an infinity of experiments which I must do, so that it is impossible for me to succeed without the aid of others. And although I do not ‹, like Suffenus,› flatter myself enough to hope that the public would be much interested in what I am doing, nevertheless I do not wish to be so remiss in upholding my own interests as to give occasion to those who survive me to reproach me, some day, on the ground that I might have accomplished many much better things than I did if I had not been too negligent to explain how others could contribute to my designs. (582)

And I thought that it would be easy to choose some topics which would not be too controversial, which would not force me to divulge more of my principles than I wish to, and which would demonstrate clearly enough what I could or could not

do in the sciences. It is not for me to say whether I have succeeded ⌐, and I do not wish to influence anyone's decisions by
speaking of my own writings⌐; nevertheless I should like to
request the reader to examine them. In order to add to the
opportunities of judging, I also request all who find some objections to my ideas to take the trouble to send them to my
publisher. He will inform me, and I shall try to have my replies published at the same time as the objections. By this
means the reader, seeing both together, will more easily judge
of the truth. For I do not promise ever to make lengthy replies, but only to admit my mistakes ⌐very⌐ frankly if I recognize them; or, [76] if I cannot recognize them, to say simply
what I believe to be required for the defense of what I have
written. But I shall not go on to explain any new material,
for fear of engaging in an endless chain of tasks.

If some of the matters I deal with at the beginning of *Optics*
and *Meteorology* should at first sight appear offensive, because
I call them hypotheses and do not try to prove them, let the
reader have the patience to read all of it with attention, and I
hope that he will be satisfied with the result. For it seems to
me that the arguments follow one another in such a way that,
just as the last principles are demonstrated by the first ones
which are their causes, so these first ones are reciprocally
demonstrated by the last which are their effects. And one must
not suppose that I have here committed the fallacy which
logicians call circular reasoning; for as experience makes most
of the effects very certain, the causes from which I deduce
them serve not so much to prove as to explain them. On the
contrary, the truth of the hypotheses is proved by the actuality
of the effects. And I have called them hypotheses only to let
it be known that although I think I can deduce them from
the first truths which I have previously explained, I expressly
desired not to make the deduction. For there are certain people who imagine that they can learn in one day all that another has thought in twenty years, as soon as he has only spoken
two or three words, and who are only the more subject to err
and less capable of truth as they are more penetrating and

lively of spirit. I should like to prevent [77] these people from building some extravagant philosophy on what they believe to be my principles, for the fault might be attributed to me. As for my real opinions, I do not apologize for their novelty, especially since I am sure that anyone who attends to the argument will find them so simple and so conformable to common sense that they will seem less extraordinary and strange than any other opinions that can be held on the same subjects. I do not claim, either, that I am original in any of these ideas, but only that I have never accepted them (583) because they were maintained by others, nor because they were not so maintained, but only because reason persuaded me of their truth.

And if the invention described in *Optics* cannot immediately be built, I do not think it is therefore faulty. Since much skill and practice are necessary in order to make and adjust the machines which I have described, without their having any defects, I would not be less astonished to find it successful on the first attempt than I would be if someone could learn to play the lute excellently in a single day, for the sole reason that he had been given some excellent sheet music. ⌈And if I write in French, which is the language of my country, rather than in Latin, which is that of my teachers, it is because I hope that those who rely purely on their natural intelligence will be better judges of my views than those who believe only what they find in the writings of antiquity. And those who combine good sense with studiousness, whom alone I wish for [78] my judges, will not, I am sure, be so partial to Latin that they will refuse to accept my reasons because I explain them in the vulgar tongue.⌉

For the rest, I do not wish to speak here in detail of the progress in the sciences which I hope to make in the future, nor to commit myself to any promise to the public which I am not sure of fulfilling. I shall therefore only say that I have resolved to employ as much of my life as remains wholly in trying to acquire some knowledge of nature, of such a sort that we may derive rules of medicine more certain than those which we have had up to the present. My inclinations are so far removed from any other plans, especially those which can be useful to some only by harming others, that if circumstances forced me to employ those plans, I do not think I would be capable of carrying them to a successful conclusion. The declaration I am here making will not, I well know, procure me any worldly advantages, but I have no desire for them; and I shall always consider myself more obligated to those by whose favor I shall enjoy uninterrupted leisure than I would be to those who offered me the most honorable office on earth.

THE MEDITATIONS CONCERNING FIRST PHILOSOPHY

In which the existence of God and the [Real] distinction between the Human Soul and the Body are demonstrated.

To ⌈those most learned and most illustrious
men,⌉ the Dean and Doctors of the Sacred
Faculty of Theology of Paris

Gentlemen:

My reason for offering you this work is so logical, and after
you have learned its plan you will also, I am sure, have so
logical a reason to take it under your protection, that I believe nothing will recommend it to you more than a brief
statement of what I herein propose to do.

I have always thought that the two questions, of God and
of the soul, were the principal questions among those that
should be demonstrated by ⌈rational⌉ philosophy rather than
theology. For although it may suffice us faithful ones to believe by faith that there is a God and that the human soul
does not perish with the body, (2) certainly it does not seem
possible ever to persuade those without faith to accept any religion, nor even perhaps any moral virtue, unless they can first
be shown these two things by means of natural reason. And
since in this life one frequently finds greater rewards offered
for vice than for virtue, few persons would prefer the just to
the useful if they were not restrained either by the fear of
God or by the expectation of another life. It is absolutely
true, both that we must believe that there is a God because it
is so taught in the Holy Scriptures, and, on the other hand,
that we must believe the Holy Scriptures because they come
from God. The reason for this is that faith is a gift of God,
and the very God that gives us the faith to believe other
things can also give us the faith to believe that he [5] exists.
Nevertheless, we could hardly offer this argument to those
without faith, for they might suppose that we were committing the fallacy that logicians call circular reasoning.

And truly I have noticed that you, ⌈gentlemen,⌉ along with
all other theologians, assure us not only that the existence of

God can be proved by natural reason, but also that we can infer from the Holy Scriptures that our knowledge of God is
much ⌈clearer ⌐and⌐ easier⌐ than our knowledge of various
created things, ⌈so clear⌐ in fact, ⌐so absolutely easy to attain,⌐
that those who do not possess it are blameworthy. This is evidenced in the words of the Book of the Wisdom of Solomon,
Chapter XIII, where it is said: "Howbeit they are not to be
excused; for if their understanding was so great that they
could discern the world and the creatures, why did they not
rather find out the Lord thereof?" And in the Epistle to the
Romans, Chapter I, where it is said that they are "without
excuse," and again in the same place in these words: "That
which may be known of God is manifest in them." It seems
that we are being told that all that can be known of God can
be demonstrated by reasons that we do not need to seek elsewhere than in ourselves, and that our minds alone are capable
of furnishing us. That is why I have believed that it would
not be inappropriate if I showed here how that can be done,
and by what means we can know God more easily and more
certainly than we know the things of the world.

And as for the soul, many have believed that it is not easy
to understand its nature, (3) and some have even dared to say
that human reasoning would convince us that it perishes with
the body, and that faith alone can teach us the contrary.
Nevertheless, as the Lateran Council, held under Leo X, Ses-
sion 8, condemns these persons, and expressly orders Christian
philosophers to refute their arguments and to employ all their
intellectual abilities to make the truth known, I have decided
to make the attempt in this work.

Moreover, the principal reason why many outside the Church
do not wish to believe that there is a God and that the human
soul is distinct from the body is that they claim that no one
has so far been able to demonstrate these two things. I do not
share their opinion; on the contrary, I hold that almost all of
the arguments brought to bear on these two questions by so
many illustrious men [6] are valid demonstrations when they
are properly understood, and that it is practically impossible

to invent new ones. So I believe that there is nothing more useful to be done in philosophy than ⌈critically and⌉ carefully to seek out, once and for all, the best ⌈and most reliable⌉ of such arguments, and to give them so clear and exact a presentation that it would thenceforward be evident to everyone that they are valid demonstrations. And finally, several persons have urged me to do this, since they knew that I have been practicing a certain method of solving all sorts of difficulties in the sciences—a method which really is not new, for nothing is older than the truth, but which they knew I was using rather successfully in other matters. I have therefore considered it my duty to see what I could achieve in this field. (4)

I have put in this treatise everything that I was able to discover about this subject. That is not to say that I have collected here all the various arguments which might be adduced as proofs in our subject, for I have never thought that that would be necessary unless no certain proof existed. I have only treated here of the most basic and principal ones in such a way that I can reasonably venture to maintain that they are very evident and very certain demonstrations. And I shall say further that they are such that I do not think there is any way in which the human mind can ever find better ones; for the importance of the subject, and the glory of God, to which all this relates, constrain me to speak somewhat more freely of myself here than I usually do. Nevertheless, whatever certainty and obviousness I find in my own arguments, I cannot convince myself that everyone will be able to understand them. There is a similar situation in geometry, where there are several proofs, left to us by Archimedes, Apollonius, Pappus, and several others, that are accepted by everyone as very certain and evident because they contain nothing but what, considered separately, is very easy to understand, and because there is no place where the consequences do not have an exact connection with and dependence upon their antecedents. Nevertheless, because these proofs are rather long and demand undivided attention, they are comprehended and understood by only a very few persons. In the same way, although I consider that the arguments I use here equal or even surpass in certainty and obviousness the [7] demonstrations of geometry, I nevertheless appreciate that they cannot be sufficiently well understood by many persons, partly because they also are somewhat lengthy and involved, but principally because they require a mind entirely free of all prejudice and one that can readily free itself from its attachment to the senses. And to tell the truth, there are not so many people in the world who are fitted for metaphysical speculations as there are those who are fitted for geometry. (5) There is this further difference, that in geometry everyone is persuaded that nothing should be written for which there is no certain proof. Therefore, those who are not well versed in the field are much more apt to make the mistake of accepting false demonstrations in order to make others believe that they understand them than they are to make the mistake of rejecting good ones. It is different in philosophy, where it is believed that there is nothing about which it is not possible to argue on either side. Thus few people engage in the search for truth, and many, who wish to acquire a reputation as clever thinkers, bend all their efforts to arrogant opposition to the most obvious truths.

That is why, ⌜gentlemen,⌝ since my arguments belong to philosophy, however strong they may be, I do not suppose that they will have any great effect unless you take them under your protection. But the esteem which everyone has for your Faculty is so great, and the name of the Sorbonne carries such authority, that not only is it more deferred to in matter of faith than any other group except the sacred councils, but even in human philosophy everyone agrees that it is impossible to find anywhere else so much reliability and knowledge, as well as prudence and integrity in the pronouncement of a judgment. Therefore, I do not doubt that if you will deign to give enough attention to this work so as to correct it—for, knowing not only my human fallibility but also my ignorance, I would not dare to affirm that it was free of error—and then to add to it whatever it lacks, to complete whatever is imperfect, and yourselves either to take the trouble to give a more adequate explanation of those points that need it or at least to advise me of them so that I may work on them; and finally, after the reasons by which I prove that there is a God and that the human soul differs from the body have been brought [8] to such a degree of clarity and obviousness, which I am sure is possible, (6) that they should be considered very exact demonstrations, if you then will deign to give them the authority of your approbation and publicly testify to their truth and certitude—I do not doubt, I say, that when this has been done, all the errors and false opinions which have ever been entertained on these two questions will soon be effaced from the minds of men. For the expression of the truth will cause all learned and wise men to subscribe to your judgment, and your authority will cause the atheists, who are ordinarily more arrogant than learned and judicious, to set aside their spirit of contradiction, or perhaps themselves defend the arguments which they see being accepted as demonstrations by all intelligent people, for fear of appearing not to understand them. And finally, everyone else will easily accept the testimony of so many witnesses, and there will no longer be anyone who dares to doubt the existence of God and the real and true distinction between the human soul and the body.

It is for you, ⌐who now see the disorders which doubt of these things produces,⌐ ⌐in your great wisdom⌐ to judge the fruit which would grow out of such belief, once it were well established; but it would not be fitting for me further to commend the cause of God and religion to those who have always been the firmest supporters ⌐of them ⌐and⌐ of the Catholic Church⌐. (7) [9]

PREFACE

I have already touched upon these two questions of God and of the human soul in the *Discourse on the Method of Rightly Conducting the Reason and Seeking Truth in the Sciences,* which I published in French in the year 1637. Then I was not concerned to give a complete discussion of the subjects, but only to treat of them in passing, in order to learn from the judgments of the readers in what way I should treat them afterward. For these questions have always seemed to me so important that I judged it appropriate to deal with them more than once. And the road I take to explain them is so little traveled and so far from the ordinary route that I did not think it would be useful to explain it in French in a discourse that might be read by anyone, for fear that those of feeble intellect would think it permissible for them to make the same attempt.

In the *Discourse on Method,* I requested everyone who found in my writings something worthy of criticism to do me the favor of informing me thereof. There were no noteworthy objections concerning these subjects except two, to which I shall here make a short reply before undertaking a more detailed presentation of them later.

The first objection is that it does not follow from the fact that the human mind, reflecting upon its own nature, (8) knows itself solely as a thinking being, that its nature or essence is only to think. The trouble is that this word "only" excludes all those other qualities that might perhaps also pertain to the nature of the mind.

To this objection I reply that it was not my intention at this point to exclude those qualities from the realm of objective reality, with which I was not then concerned, but only from the realm of my thought. My intention was to say that I knew nothing to pertain to my essence except that I was a being which thinks, that is, a being having in itself the faculty of thinking. Nevertheless, I shall show further on how it follows from the fact that I know nothing else which belongs to my essence that nothing else really does belong to it.

The second objection is that it does not follow from the fact that I have in my mind the idea of a thing more perfect than I am that this idea is more perfect than myself, much less that what is represented by this idea exists.

But I reply that in this word "idea" there is here an equivocation. For it can be taken materially, as an operation of my intellect, and in this sense it cannot be said to be more perfect than myself; or it can be taken objectively for the body which is represented by this operation, which, even though it is not supposed to exist outside of my understanding, can nevertheless be more perfect than myself in respect to its essence. In the rest of this treatise I shall show more fully how it follows from the mere fact that I have in my mind an idea of something more perfect than myself that this thing really exists.

In addition, I have seen two other rather long works on this subject which did not so much oppose my reasons as my conclusions, and this by arguments drawn from the commonplaces of the atheists. (9) But since arguments of this type cannot make any impression in the minds of those who fully understand my reasoning, and since the judgment of many persons is so weak and irrational that they much more often let themselves be convinced by the first opinions they hear on a subject, however false and unreasonable they may be, than by a refutation of their opinions which is valid and true but which is heard later, I do not wish to reply to the arguments here, for fear of being obliged first to report them.

I shall only say, in general, that the arguments which atheists use to combat the existence of God always depend either upon the assumption that God has human characteristics, or else upon the assumption that our own minds have so much ability and wisdom that we presume to delimit and comprehend what God can and should do. Thus all that atheists allege will give us no difficulty if only we remind ourselves that we should consider our minds to be finite and limited, and God to be an infinite and incomprehensible Being.

Now, having paid sufficient attention to the opinions of men, I undertake directly to treat of God and of the human mind, and at the same time to lay the foundations of first philosophy. I do this without expecting any praise for it from the vulgar, and without hoping that my book will be read by many. On the contrary, I would not recommend it to any except to those who would want to meditate seriously along with me, and who are capable of freeing the mind from attachment to the senses and clearing it entirely of all sorts of prejudices; and I know only too well that there are very few people of this sort. But as for those who do not care much about the order and connection of my arguments, and who amuse themselves by making clever remarks on the several parts, as (10) some will do—those persons, I say, will not profit much from reading this work. And although they may find opportunities for caviling in many places, they will hardly be able to make any objections which are important or which are worthy of reply.

And since I do not promise others to satisfy them wholly at the first attempt, and since I do not so far presume as to believe that I can foresee all that may entail difficulties for some people, I shall first present in these *Meditations* the same thoughts by which I think I have reached a certain and evident knowledge of the truth, in order to see whether I will be able to persuade others by means of the same reasons that have persuaded me. After that I shall reply to the objections which have been offered to me by people of insight and learning to whom I sent my *Meditations* to be examined before committing them to the press. These have been so numerous and so varied that I feel secure in believing that it would be difficult for anyone else to find an objection of consequence that has not already been treated.

That is why I beg my readers to suspend their judgment upon the *Meditations* until they have taken the trouble of reading all these objections and the replies that I have made to them. (11)

SYNOPSIS OF THE SIX FOLLOWING
MEDITATIONS

In the First Meditation, I offer the reasons why we can doubt all things in general, and particularly material objects, at least as long as we do not have other foundations for the sciences than those we have hitherto possessed. And although it is not immediately apparent that so general a doubt can be useful, it is in fact very much so, since it delivers us from all sorts of prejudices and makes available to us an easy method of accustoming our minds to become independent of the senses. Finally, it is useful in making it subsequently impossible to doubt those things which we discover to be true after we have taken doubt into consideration.

In the Second, the mind,[1] which in its intrinsic freedom supposes that everything which is open to the least doubt is nonexistent, recognizes that it is nevertheless absolutely impossible that it does not itself exist. This is also of the highest utility, since by this means the mind can easily distinguish between those qualities which belong to it—that is to say, to its intellectual nature—and those which belong to the body.

But because it might happen that some persons will expect me to offer at this point reasons to prove the immortality of the soul, I think it my duty to warn them now (13) that, since I have tried to write nothing in this treatise for which I did not have very exact demonstrations, I have found myself obliged to follow an order similar to that used by geometricians, which is to present first all those things on which the proposition one is seeking to prove depends, before reaching any conclusions about the proposition itself.

But the first and principal thing required in order to recognize the immortality of the soul [2] is to form the clearest possi-

[1] Latin: *mens;* French: *esprit.*
[2] L. *anima;* F. *âme.*

ble conception of it, [10] and one which is entirely distinct from all the conceptions one can have of the body, which has been done in this Second Meditation. It is necessary, in addition, to know that all things which we conceive clearly and distinctly are true in the manner in which we conceive them, and this cannot be proved before the Fourth Meditation. Furthermore, we must have a distinct conception of corporeal nature, which we acquire partly in the Second, and partly in the Fifth and Sixth Meditations. And finally, we must conclude from all this that things which we clearly and distinctly perceive to be diverse substances, as we conceive the mind and the body, are in fact substances which are really distinct from each other; which is what we conclude in the Sixth Meditation. This is confirmed again, in the same Meditation, by the fact that we cannot conceive any body except as divisible, while the mind or soul of man can only be conceived as indivisible. For in reality we cannot conceive of half of any soul, as we can of the smallest possible body, so that we recognize that their natures are not only different but even in some sense contrary. I have not treated this subject further in this treatise, partly because we have already discovered enough to show with sufficient clarity that the corruption of the body does not entail the death of the soul, and so to give men the hope of a second life after death; and partly because the premises from which the immortality of the soul may be concluded depend upon the explanation of the whole of physics. First, (14) we must know that all substances in general—that is to say, all those things which cannot exist without being created by God—are by nature incorruptible and can never cease to be, unless God himself, by denying them his usual support, reduces them to nothingness. And secondly, we must notice that body, taken in general, is a substance, and that it therefore will never perish. But the human body, however much it may differ from other bodies, is only a composite, produced by a certain configuration of members and by other similar accidents, whereas the human soul is not thus dependent upon any accidents, but is a pure substance. For even if all its accidents change—as, for example, if it conceives of certain things, wills others, and receives sense impressions of still others—nevertheless it still remains the same soul. But the human body becomes a different entity from the mere fact that the shape of some of its parts has been changed. From this it follows that the human body may very easily perish, but that the mind ⌈or soul of man, between which I find no distinction,⌉ is immortal by its very nature. [11]

In the Third Meditation, I have explained at sufficient length, it seems to me, the principal argument I use to prove the existence of God. Nevertheless, I did not want to use at that point any comparisons drawn from physical things, in order that the minds of the readers should be as far as possible withdrawn from the use of and commerce with the senses. There may, therefore, be many obscurities remaining, which I hope will be completely elucidated in my replies to the objections which have since been made to me. One of these obscurities is this: how can the idea of a supremely perfect Being, which we find in ourselves, contain so much objective reality, ⌈that is to say, how can it participate by representation in so many degrees of being and of perfection,⌉ that it must have come from a supremely perfect cause? This I have explained in these replies by means of a comparison with a very ⌈⟨in-genious and⟩⌉ artificial machine, the idea of which occurs in the mind of some worker. For as the real cleverness of this idea must have some cause, I conclude it to be either the knowledge of this worker or that of some other from whom he has received this idea. In the same way (15) it is impossible that the idea of God, which is in us, does not have God himself as its cause.

In the Fourth, it is proved that all things which we ⌈conceive ⟨or⌉ perceive⟩ very clearly and very distinctly are wholly true. At the same time I explain the nature of error or falsity, which nature we ought to discover, as much to confirm the preceding truths as to understand better those that follow. Nevertheless, it should be noticed that I do not in any way treat here of sin—that is, of error committed in the pursuit of good and evil—but only of that which occurs in the judgment and discernment of the true and the false; and that I do not intend to speak of beliefs which belong to faith or to the conduct of life, but only of those which pertain to speculative truth and which can be known by the aid of the light of nature alone.

In the Fifth Meditation, besides the explanation of corporeal nature in general, the existence of God is again demonstrated by a new argument. There may also be some difficulties in this argument, but the solution will be found in the replies to the objections which have been made to me. In addition, I show how it is true that even the certainty of geometrical demonstrations themselves depends on the knowledge of God.

Finally, in the Sixth, I distinguish the action of the understanding from that of the imagination, and the marks of this distinction are described. Here I show that the ⟨mind ⌈or⌉ soul⌉ of man is really distinct from the body, and that nevertheless it is so tightly bound and united with it that it [12] forms with it what is almost a single entity. All the errors which arise from the senses are here exposed, together with the methods of avoiding them. And finally, I here bring out all the arguments from which we may conclude the existence of material things; not because I judge them very useful, in that they prove what (16) they do prove—namely, that there is a world, that men have bodies, and other similar things which have never been doubted by any man of good sense—but because, in considering these arguments more closely, we come to recognize that they are not as firm and as evident as those which lead us to the knowledge of God and of our soul, so that the latter are the most certain and most evident truths which can become known to the human mind. That is all that I had planned to prove in these *Meditations,* which leads me to omit here many other questions with which I have dealt incidentally in this treatise. (17) [13]

FIRST MEDITATION

CONCERNING THINGS THAT CAN BE DOUBTED

There is no novelty to me in the reflection that, from my earliest years, I have accepted many false opinions as true, and that what I have concluded from such badly assured premises could not but be highly doubtful and uncertain. From the time that I first recognized this fact, I have realized that if I wished to have any firm and constant knowledge in the sciences, I would have to undertake, once and for all, to set aside all the opinions which I had previously accepted among my beliefs and start again from the very beginning. But this enterprise appeared to me to be of very great magnitude, and so I waited until I had attained an age so mature that I could not hope for a later time when I would be more fitted to execute the project. Now, however, I have delayed so long that henceforward I should be ⌈afraid that I was⌉ committing a fault if, in continuing to deliberate, I expended time which should be devoted to action.

The present is opportune for my design; I have freed my mind of all kinds of cares; (18) ⌈I feel myself, fortunately, disturbed by no passions;⌉ and I have found a serene retreat in peaceful solitude. I will therefore make a serious and unimpeded effort to destroy generally all my former opinions. ·In order to do this, however, it will not be necessary to show that they are all false, a task [14] which I might never be able to complete; because, since reason already convinces me that I should abstain from the belief in things which are not entirely certain and indubitable no less carefully than from the belief in those which appear to me to be manifestly false, it will be enough to make me reject them all if I can find in each some ground for doubt. And for that it will not be necessary for me to examine each one in particular, which would

be an infinite labor; but since the destruction of the foundation necessarily involves the collapse of all the rest of the edifice, I shall first attack the principles upon which all my
former opinions were founded.

Everything which I have thus far accepted as entirely true
⌈and assured⌉ has been acquired from the senses or by means
of the senses. But I have learned by experience that these
senses sometimes mislead me, and it is prudent never to trust
wholly those things which have once deceived us.

But it is possible that, even though the senses occasionally
deceive us about things which are barely perceptible and very
far away, there are many other things which we cannot reasonably doubt, even though we know them through the senses
—as, for example, that I am here, seated by the fire, wearing a
⟨winter⟩ dressing gown, holding this paper in my hands, and
other things of this nature. And how could I deny that these
hands and this body are mine, unless I am to compare myself
with certain lunatics (19) whose brain is so troubled and be-
fogged by the black vapors of the bile that they continually
affirm that they are kings while they are paupers, that they are
clothed in ⌈gold and⌉ purple while they are naked; or imagine
⟨that their head is made of clay, or⟩ that they are gourds, or
that their body is glass? ⌈But this is ridiculous;⌉ such men are
fools, and I would be no less insane than they if I followed
their example.

Nevertheless, I must remember that I am a man, and that
consequently I am accustomed to sleep and in my dreams to
imagine the same things that lunatics imagine when awake, or
sometimes things which are even less plausible. How many
times has it occurred that ⟨the quiet of⟩ the night made me
dream ⟨of my usual habits:⟩ that I was here, clothed ⟨in a
dressing gown⟩, and sitting by the fire, although I was in fact
lying undressed in bed! It seems apparent to me now, that I
am not looking at this paper with my eyes closed, that this
head that I shake is not drugged with sleep, that it is with design and deliberate intent that I stretch out this hand and
perceive it. What happens in sleep seems not at all as clear

and as distinct as all this. [15] But I am speaking as though I never recall having been misled, while asleep, by similar illusions! When I consider these matters carefully, I realize so clearly that there are no conclusive indications by which waking life can be distinguished from sleep that I am quite astonished, and my bewilderment is such that it is almost able to convince me that I am sleeping.

So let us suppose now that we are asleep and that all these details, such as opening the eyes, shaking the head, extending the hands, and similar things, are merely illusions; and let us think that perhaps our hands and our whole body are not such as we see them. Nevertheless, we must at least admit that these things which appear to us in sleep are like ⸗painted⸗ scenes ⸓and portraits⸔ which can only be formed in imitation of something ⸓real and⸔ true, and so, at the very least, these types of things—namely, eyes, head, hands, and the whole body—are not imaginary entities, but real and existent. For in truth painters, even when (20) they use the greatest ingenuity in attempting to portray sirens and satyrs in ⸓bizarre and⸔ extraordinary ways, nevertheless cannot give them wholly new shapes and natures, but only invent some particular mixture composed of parts of various animals; or even if perhaps ⸓their imagination is sufficiently extravagant that⸔ they invent something so new that nothing like it has ever been seen, and so their work represents something purely imaginary and ⸓absolutely⸔ false, certainly at the very least the colors of which they are composed must be real.

And for the same reason, even if these types of things—namely, ⸓a body,⸔ eyes, head, hands, and other similar things—could be imaginary, nevertheless, we are bound to confess that there are some other still more simple and universal concepts which are true ⸓and existent⸔, from the mixture of which, neither more nor less than in the case of the mixture of real colors, all these images of things are formed in our minds, whether they are true ⸓and real⸔ or imaginary ⸓and fantastic⸔.

Of this class of entities is corporeal nature in general and its extension, including the shape of extended things, their quantity, or size and number, and also the place where they are, the time that measures their duration, and so forth. [16] That is why we will perhaps not be reasoning badly if we conclude that physics, astronomy, medicine, and all the other sciences which follow from the consideration of composite entities are very dubious ⌜and uncertain⌝; whereas arithmetic, geometry, and the other sciences of this nature, which treat only of very simple and general things without concerning themselves as to whether they occur in nature or not, contain some element of certainty and sureness. For whether I am awake or whether I am asleep, two and three together will always make the number five, and the square will never have more than four sides; and it does not seem possible that truths ⌜so clear and⌝ so apparent can ever be suspected of any falsity ⌜or uncertainty⌝. (21)

Nevertheless, I have long held the belief that there is a God who can do anything, by whom I have been created and made what I am. But how can I be sure but that he has brought it to pass that there is no earth, no sky, no extended bodies, no shape, no size, no place, and that nevertheless I have the impressions of all these things ⌜and cannot imagine that things might be other than⌝ as I now see them? And furthermore, just as I sometimes judge that others are mistaken about those things which they think they know best, how can I be sure but that ⌜God has brought it about that⌝ I am always mistaken when I add two and three or count the sides of a square, or when I judge of something else even easier, if I can imagine anything easier than that? But perhaps God did not wish me to be deceived in that fashion, since he is said to be supremely good. But if it was repugnant to his goodness to have made me so that I was always mistaken, it would seem also to be inconsistent for him to permit me to be sometimes mistaken, and nevertheless I cannot doubt that he does permit it.

At this point there will perhaps be some persons who would prefer to deny the existence of so powerful a God, rather than to believe that everything else is uncertain. Let us not oppose them for the moment, and let us concede ⌜according to their point of view⌝ that everything which I have stated here about God is fictitious. Then in whatever way they suppose that I have reached the state of being that I now have, whether they attribute it to some destiny or fate or refer it to chance, or whether they wish to explain it as the result of a continual interplay of events ⌜or in any other manner⌝; nevertheless, since to err and be mistaken [17] is a kind of imperfection, to whatever degree less powerful they consider the author to whom they attribute my origin, in that degree it will be more probable that I am so imperfect that I am always mistaken. To this reasoning, certainly, I have nothing to reply; and I am at last constrained to admit that there is nothing in what I formerly believed to be true which I cannot somehow doubt, and this not for lack of thought and attention, but for weighty and well-considered reasons. Thus I find that, in the future, I should ⌜withhold and suspend my judgment about these matters, and⌝ guard myself no less carefully from believing them than I should from believing what is manifestly false (22) if I wish to find any certain and assured knowledge ⌜in the sciences⌝.

It is not enough to have made these observations; it is also necessary that I should take care to bear them in mind. For these customary and long-standing beliefs will frequently recur in my thoughts, my long and familiar acquaintance with them giving them the right to occupy my mind against my will ⌜and almost to make themselves masters of my beliefs⌝. I will never free myself of the habit of deferring to them and having faith in them as long as I consider that they are what they really are—that is, somewhat doubtful, as I have just shown, even if highly probable—so that there is much more reason to believe than to deny them. That is why I think that I would not do badly if I deliberately took the opposite position and deceived myself in pretending for some time that all these opinions are entirely false and imaginary, until at last I will have so balanced my former and my new prejudices that they cannot incline my mind more to one side than the other, and my judgment will not be ⌜mastered and⌝ turned by bad habits from the ⌐correct perception of things ⌜and the⌝ straight road leading to the knowledge of the truth⌝. For I feel sure that I cannot overdo this distrust, since it is not now a question of acting, but only of ⌜meditating and⌝ learning.

I will therefore suppose that, not ⌜a true⌝ God, ⌐who is very good and⌝ who is the supreme source of truth, but a certain evil spirit, not less clever and deceitful than powerful, has bent all his efforts to deceiving me. I will suppose that the sky, the air, the earth, colors, shapes, sounds, and all other objective things ⌜that we see⌝ are nothing but illusions and dreams that he [18] has used to trick my credulity. I will consider (23) myself as having no hands, no eyes, no flesh, no blood, nor any senses, yet falsely believing that I have all these things. I will remain resolutely attached to this hypothesis; and if I cannot attain the knowledge of any truth by this method, at any rate ⌜it is in my power to suspend my judgment. That is why⌝ I shall take great care not to accept any falsity among my beliefs and shall prepare my mind so well for all the ruses of this great deceiver that, however powerful and artful he may be, he will never be able to mislead me in anything.

But this undertaking is arduous, and a certain laziness leads me insensibly into the normal paths of ordinary life. I am like a slave who, enjoying an imaginary liberty during sleep, begins to suspect that his liberty is only a dream; he fears to wake up and conspires with his pleasant illusions to retain them longer. So insensibly to myself I fall into my former opinions; and I am slow to wake up from this slumber for fear that the labors of waking life which will have to follow the tranquillity of this sleep, instead of leading me into the daylight of the knowledge of the truth, will be insufficient to dispel the darkness of all the difficulties which have just been raised.

SECOND MEDITATION

OF THE NATURE OF THE HUMAN MIND, AND THAT IT IS MORE EASILY KNOWN THAN THE BODY

Yesterday's Meditation has filled my mind with so many doubts that it is no longer in my power to forget them. Nor do I yet see how I will be able to resolve them; I feel as though (24) I were suddenly thrown into deep water, being so disconcerted that I can neither plant my feet on the bottom nor swim on the surface. I shall nevertheless make every effort to conform precisely to the plan commenced yesterday and put aside every belief in which I could imagine the least doubt, just as though I knew that it was absolutely [19] false. And I shall continue in this manner until I have found something certain, or at least, if I can do nothing else, until I have learned with certainty that there is nothing certain in this world. Archimedes, to move the earth from its orbit and place it in a new position, demanded nothing more than a fixed and immovable fulcrum; in a similar manner I shall have the right to entertain high hopes if I am fortunate enough to find a single truth which is certain and indubitable.

I suppose, accordingly, that everything that I see is false; I convince myself that nothing has ever existed of all that my deceitful memory recalls to me. I think that I have no senses; and I believe that body, shape, extension, motion, and location are merely inventions of my mind. What then could still be thought true? Perhaps nothing else, unless it is that there is nothing certain in the world.

But how do I know that there is not some entity, of a different nature from what I have just judged uncertain, of which there cannot be the least doubt? Is there not some God or some other power who gives me these thoughts? But I need not think this to be true, for possibly I am able to produce them myself. Then, at the very least, am I not an entity myself? But I have already denied that I had any senses or any body. However, at this point I hesitate, for what (25) follows from that? Am I so dependent upon the body and the senses that I could not exist without them? I have just convinced myself that nothing whatsoever existed in the world, that there was no sky, no earth, no minds, and no bodies; have I not thereby convinced myself that I did not exist? Not at all; without doubt I existed if I was convinced ⌈or even if I thought anything⌉. Even though there may be a deceiver of some sort, very powerful and very tricky, who bends all his efforts to keep me perpetually deceived, there can be no slightest doubt that I exist, since he deceives me; and let him deceive me as much as he will, he can never make me be nothing as long as I think that I am something. Thus, after having thought well on this matter, and after examining all things with care, I must finally conclude and maintain that this proposition: *I am, I exist,* is necessarily true every time that I pronounce it or conceive it in my mind.

But I do not yet know sufficiently clearly what I am, I who am sure that I exist. So I must henceforth take very great care that I do not incautiously mistake [20] some other thing for myself, and so make an error even in that knowledge which I maintain to be more certain and more evident than all other knowledge ⌈that I previously had⌉. That is why I shall now consider once more what I thought myself to be before I began these last deliberations. Of my former opinions I shall reject all that are rendered even slightly doubtful by the arguments that I have just now offered, so that there will remain just that part alone which is entirely certain and indubitable.

What then have I previously believed myself to be? Clearly, I believed that I was a man. But what is a man? Shall I say a rational animal? Certainly not, for I would have to determine what an "animal" is and what is meant by "rational"; and so, from a single question, I would find myself gradually enmeshed in an infinity of others more difficult ⌈and more inconvenient⌉, and I would not care to waste the little time and leisure remaining to me in disentangling such difficulties. I shall rather pause here to consider the ideas which previously arose naturally and of themselves (26) in my mind whenever I considered what I was. I thought of myself first as having a face, hands, arms, and all this mechanism composed of ⌈bone and flesh ⌐and⌐ members⌐, just as it appears in a corpse, and which I designated by the name of "body." In addition, I thought of the fact that I consumed nourishment, that I walked, that I perceived and thought, and I ascribed all these actions to the soul. But either I did not stop to consider what this soul was or else, if I did, I imagined that it was something very rarefied and subtle, such as a wind, a flame, or a very much expanded air which ⌈penetrated into and⌐ was infused thoughout my grosser components. As for what body was, I did not realize that there could be any doubt about it, for I thought that I recognized its nature very distinctly. If I had wished to explain it according to the notions that I then entertained, I would have described it somewhat in this way: By "body" I understand all that can be bounded by some figure; that can be located in some place and occupy space in such a way that every other body is excluded from it; that can be perceived by touch or sight or hearing or taste or smell; that can be moved in various ways, not by itself but by some other object by which it is touched ⌈and from which it receives an impulse⌐. For to possess the power to move itself, and also to feel or to think, I did not believe at all that these are attributes of corporeal nature; on the contrary, rather, I was astonished [21] to see a few bodies possessing such abilities.

But I, what am I, on the basis of the present hypothesis that there is a certain spirit who is extremely powerful and, if I may dare to say so, malicious ⌈and tricky⌐, and who uses all his abilities and efforts in order to deceive me? Can I be sure that I possess the smallest fraction of all those characteristics which I have just now said belonged to the nature of body? (27) I pause to consider this attentively. I pass and repass in review in my mind each one of all these things—it is not necessary to pause to take the time to list them—and I do not find any one

of them which I can pronounce to be part of me. Is it characteristic of me to consume nourishment and to walk? But if
it is true that I do not have a body, these also are nothing but
figments of the imagination. To perceive? [1] But once more, I
cannot perceive without the body, except in the sense that I
have thought I perceived various things during sleep, which
I recognized upon waking not to have been really perceived.
To think? [2] Here I find the answer. Thought is an attribute
that belongs to me; it alone is inseparable from my nature.

I am, I exist—that is certain; but for how long do I exist?
For as long as I think; for it might perhaps happen, if I to-
tally ceased thinking, that I would at the same time completely cease to be. I am now admitting nothing except what
is necessarily true. I am therefore, to speak precisely, only a
thinking being, that is to say, a mind, an understanding,[3] or a
reasoning being, which are terms whose meaning was previously unknown to me.

I am something real and really existing, but what thing am
I? I have already given the answer: a thing which thinks. And
what more? I will stimulate my imagination ⌈to see if I am
not something else beyond this⌉. I am not this assemblage of
members which is called a human body; I am not a rarefied
and penetrating air spread throughout all these members; I
am not a wind, ⌈a flame,⌉ a breath, a vapor, or anything at all
that I can imagine and picture to myself—since I have supposed that all that was nothing, and since, without abandon-
ing this supposition, I find that I do not cease to be certain
that I am something.

But perhaps it is true that those same things which I suppose not to exist because I do not know them are really no
different from the self which I do know. As to that I cannot
decide; I am not discussing that question at the moment, since
I can pass judgment only upon those things which are known
to me: I know that I exist and I am seeking to discover what

1 L. *sentire;* F. *sentir.*
2 L. *cogitare;* F. *penser.*
3 L. *intellectus;* F. *entendement.*

I am, that "I" that I know to be. Now it is very [22] certain
that this notion ⌈and knowledge of my being⌉, thus precisely
understood, does not depend on things whose existence (28) is
not yet known to me; and consequently ⌈and even more cer-
tainly⌉, it does not depend on any of those things that I
⌈⌈can⌉⌉ picture in my imagination. And even these terms, "picture" and "imagine," warn me of my error. For I would be
imagining falsely indeed were I to picture myself as something; since to imagine is nothing else than to contemplate
the shape or image of a bodily entity, and I already know
both that I certainly exist and that it is altogether possible
that all these images, and everything in general which is involved in the nature of body, are only dreams ⌈and illusions⌉.
From this I see clearly that there was no more sense in saying
that I would stimulate my imagination to learn more distinctly what I am than if I should say: I am now awake, and
I see something real and true; but because I do not yet perceive it sufficiently clearly, I will go to sleep on purpose, in
order that my dreams will show it to me with more truth and
evidence. And thus I know manifestly that nothing of all that
I can understand by means of the imagination is pertinent to
the knowledge which I have of myself, and that I must remember this and prevent my mind from thinking in this fashion, in order that it may clearly perceive its own nature.

But what then am I? A thinking being.[4] What is a thinking
being? It is a being which doubts, which understands, ⌈which
conceives,⌉ which affirms, which denies, which wills, which rejects, which imagines also, and which perceives. It is certainly
not a trivial matter if all these things belong to my nature.
But why should they not belong to it? Am I not that same
person who now doubts almost everything, who nevertheless
understands ⌈and conceives⌉ certain things, who ⌈is sure of
and⌉ affirms the truth of this one thing alone, who denies all
the others, who wills and desires to know more about them,
who rejects error, who imagines many things, sometimes even
against my will, and who also perceives many things, as

---

[4] L. *res cogitans;* F. *une chose qui pense.*

through the medium of ⌐the senses ⌐or⌐ the organs of the body⌐? Is there anything in all that which is not just as true as it is certain that I am and that I exist, even though I were always asleep (29) and though the one who created me directed all his efforts to deluding me? And is there any one of these attributes which can be distinguished from my thinking or which can be said to be separable from my nature? For it is so obvious that it is I who doubt, understand, and desire, that nothing could be added to make it more evident. And I am also certainly the same one who imagines; [23] for once more, even though it could happen that the things I imagine are not true, nevertheless this power of imagining cannot fail to be real, and it is part of my thinking. Finally I am the same being which perceives—that is, which observes certain objects as though by means of the sense organs, because I do really see light, hear noises, feel heat. Will it be said that these appearances are false and that I am sleeping? ⌐Let it be so; yet at the very least⌐ it is certain that it seems to me that I see light, hear noises, and feel heat. This much cannot be false, and it is this, properly considered, which in my nature is called perceiving, and that, again speaking precisely, is nothing else but thinking.

As a result of these considerations, I begin to recognize what I am ⌐somewhat better ⌐and⌐ with a little more clarity and distinctness⌐ than heretofore. But nevertheless ⌐it still seems to me, and⌐ I cannot keep myself from believing that corporeal things, images of which are formed by thought and which the senses themselves examine, are ⌐much⌐ more distinctly known than that indescribable part of myself which cannot be pictured by the imagination. Yet it would truly be very strange to say that I know and comprehend more distinctly things whose existence seems doubtful to me, that are unknown to me and do not belong to me, than those of whose truth I am persuaded, which are known to me, and which belong to my real nature ⌐—to say, in a word, that I know them better than myself⌐. But I see well what is the trouble: my mind ⌐is a vagabond who⌐ likes to wander and is not yet able to stay

within the strict bounds of truth. Therefore, let us ⌐give it
the rein once more ⌐and⌐ allow it every kind of liberty,
(30) ⌐permitting it to consider the objects which appear to be
external,⌐ so that when a little later we come to restrain it
⌐gently and⌐ at the right time ⌐and force it to the consideration of its own nature and of the things that it finds in itself⌐,
it will more readily permit itself to be ruled and guided.

Let us now consider the ⌐commonest⌐ things, which are
commonly believed to be the most distinctly known ⌐⌐and the
easiest of all to know⌐⌐, namely, the bodies which we touch
and see. I do not intend to speak of bodies in general, for general notions are usually somewhat more confused; let us
rather consider one body in particular. Let us take, for example, this bit of wax which has just been taken from the
hive. It has not yet completely lost the sweetness of the honey
it contained; it still retains something of the odor of the
flowers from which it was collected; its color, shape, and size
are apparent; it is hard and cold; it can easily be touched;
and, if you knock on it, it will give out some sound. Thus
everything which can make a body distinctly known are found
in this example.

But now while I am talking I bring it close to the fire.
What remains of the taste evaporates; the odor vanishes; its
color changes; its shape is lost; its size increases; it becomes
liquid; it grows hot; one can hardly touch it; and although it
is knocked upon, it [24] will give out no sound. Does the same
wax remain after this change? We must admit that it does; no
one denies it ⌐, no one judges otherwise⌐. What is it then in
this bit of wax that we recognize with so much distinctness?
Certainly it cannot be anything that I observed by means of
the senses, since everything in the field of taste, smell, sight,
touch, and hearing are changed, and since the same wax
nevertheless remains.

The truth of the matter perhaps, as I now suspect, is that
this wax was neither that sweetness of honey, nor that ⌐pleas-
ant⌐ odor of flowers, nor that whiteness, nor that shape, nor
that sound, but only a body which a little while ago appeared

to my senses under these forms and which now makes itself
felt under others. But what is it, to speak precisely, that I
imagine ⌈when I conceive it⌉ in this fashion? Let us consider
it attentively (31) and, rejecting everything that does not belong to the wax, see what remains. Certainly nothing is left
but something extended, flexible, and movable. But what is
meant by flexible and movable? Does it consist in my picturing that this wax, being round, is capable of becoming
square and of passing from the square into a triangular shape?
Certainly not; ⌈it is not that,⌉ since I conceive it capable of
undergoing an infinity of similar changes, and I could not
compass this infinity in my imagination. Consequently this
conception that I have of the wax is not achieved by the faculty of imagination.

Now what is this extension? Is it not also unknown? For it
becomes greater in the melting wax, still greater when it is
completely melted, and much greater again when the heat increases still more. And I would not conceive ⌈clearly and⌉
truthfully what wax was if I did not think that even this bit
of wax is capable of receiving more variations in extension
than I have ever imagined. We must therefore agree that I
cannot even conceive what this bit of wax is by means of the
imagination, and that there is nothing but my understanding [5] alone which does conceive it. I say this bit of wax in
particular, for as to wax in general, it is still more evident.
But what is this bit of wax which cannot be comprehended
except by ⌈the understanding, or by⌉ the mind? Certainly it is
the same as the one that I see, that I touch, that I imagine;
and finally it is the same as I always believed it to be from the
beginning. But what is here important to notice is that perception [6] ⌈,or the action by which we perceive,⌉ is not a vision,
a touch, nor an imagination, and has never been that, even
though it formerly appeared so; [25] but is solely an inspec-
tion by the mind, which can be imperfect and confused as it

5 L. *mens;* F. *entendement.*
6 L. *perceptio;* F. *perception.*

was formerly, or clear and distinct as it is at present, as I attend more or less to the things ⌜which are in it and⌝ of which
it is composed.

Now I am truly astonished when I consider ⌜how weak my
mind is and⌝ how apt I am to fall into error. For even though
I consider all this in my mind without speaking, (32) still
words impede me, and I am nearly deceived by the terms of
ordinary language. For we say that we see the same wax if it is
present, and not that we judge that it is the same from the
fact that it has the same color or shape. Thus I might be
tempted to conclude that one knows the wax by means of eye-
sight, and not uniquely by the perception of the mind. So I
may by chance look out of a window and notice some men
passing in the street, at the sight of whom I do not fail to say
that I see men, just as I say that I see wax; and nevertheless
what do I see from this window except hats and cloaks which
might cover ⌜ghosts, or⌝ automata ⌜which move only by
springs⌝? But I judge that they are men, and thus I comprehend, solely by the faculty of judgment which resides in my
mind, that which I believed I saw with my eyes.

A person who attempts to improve his understanding beyond the ordinary ought to be ashamed to go out of his way
to criticize the forms of speech used by ordinary men. I prefer to pass over this matter and to consider whether I understood what wax was more evidently and more perfectly when
I first noticed it and when I thought I knew it by means of
the external senses, or at the very least by common sense, as
it is called, or the imaginative faculty; or whether I conceive
it better at present, after having more carefully examined
what it is and how it can be known. Certainly it would be
ridiculous to doubt the superiority of the latter method of
knowing. For what was there in that first perception which
was distinct ⌜and evident⌝? What was there which might not
occur similarly to the senses of the lowest of the animals? But
when I distinguished the real wax from its superficial appearances, and when, just as though I had removed its gar-

ments, I consider it all naked, it is certain that although there might still be some error in my judgment, I could not conceive it in this fashion without a human mind. (33)

And now what shall I say of the mind, that is to say, of myself? For so far I do not admit in myself anything other than the mind. Can it be that I, who seem to perceive this bit of wax [26] so ⌈clearly and⌉ distinctly, do not know my own self, not only with much more truth and certainty, but also much more distinctly and evidently? For if I judge that the wax exists because I see it, certainly it follows much more evidently that I exist myself because I see it. For it might happen that what I see is not really wax; it might also happen that I do not even possess eyes to see anything; but it could not happen that, when I see, or what amounts to the same thing, when I think I see, I who think am not something. For a similar reason, if I judge that the wax exists because I touch it, the same conclusion follows once more, namely, that I am. And if I hold to this judgment because my imagination, or whatever other entity it might be, persuades me of it, I will still reach the same conclusion. And what I have said here about the wax can be applied to all other things which are external to me.

Furthermore, if the idea or knowledge of the wax seems clearer and more distinct to me after I have investigated it, not only by sight or touch, but also in many other ways, with how much more ⌈evidence,⌉ distinctness ⌈and clarity⌉ must it be admitted that I now know myself; since all the reasons which help me to know and conceive the nature of the wax, or of any other body whatsoever, serve much better to show the nature of my mind! And we also find so many other things in the mind itself which can contribute to the clarification of its nature, that those which depend on the body, such as the ones I have just mentioned, hardly deserve to be taken into account.

And at last here I am, having insensibly returned to where (34) I wished to be; for since it is at present manifest to me that even bodies are not properly known by the senses nor by the faculty of imagination, but by the understanding alone; and since they are not known in so far as they are seen or touched, but only in so far as they are understood by thinking, I see clearly that there is nothing easier for me to understand than my mind. But since it is almost impossible to rid oneself so soon of an opinion of long standing, it would be wise to stop a while at this point, in order that, by the length of my meditation, I may impress this new knowledge more deeply upon my memory. [27]

THIRD MEDITATION

OF GOD: THAT HE EXISTS

Now I shall close my eyes, I shall stop my ears, I shall disregard my senses, I shall even efface from my mind all the images of corporeal things; or at least, since that can hardly be done, I shall consider them vain and false. By thus dealing only with myself and considering what is included in me, I shall try to make myself, little by little, better known and more familiar to myself.

I am a thing which thinks, that is to say, which doubts, which affirms, which denies, which knows a few things, which is ignorant of many, ⌈which loves, which hates,⌉ which wills, which rejects, which imagines also, and which senses. For as I have previously remarked, although the things which I sense and which I imagine are perhaps nothing at all apart from me ⌈and in themselves⌉, I am nevertheless sure that those modes of thought which I call sensations and imaginations, (35) only just as far as they are modes of thought, reside and are found with certainty in myself.

And in this short statement I think I have reported all that I truly know, or at least all that I have so far noticed that I know. Now, ⌈⌈in order to try to extend my knowledge fur-

ther,⌐1 I shall ⌐be circumspect and⌐ consider with care if I cannot still discover in myself some other bits of knowledge
which I have not yet observed. I am sure that I am a thinking
being; but do I not then know what is required to make me
sure of something? Certainly, in this first conclusion, there is
nothing else which assures me of its truth but the clear and
distinct perception of what I affirm. But this would really not
be sufficient to assure me that what I affirm is true if it could
ever happen that something which I conceived just as clearly
and distinctly should prove false. And therefore it seems to
me that I can already establish as a general principle that
everything which we conceive very clearly and very distinctly
is wholly true.

I have, however, previously accepted and admitted several
things as very certain and very obvious which I have nevertheless subsequently recognized to be doubtful and uncertain.
What, then, were those things? They were the earth, the sky,
the stars, and all the other things I perceived through the
medium of my senses. But [28] what did I conceive [1] clearly
⌐and distinctly⌐ in them? Nothing, certainly, unless that the
ideas or thoughts of those things were present to my mind.
And even now I do not deny the occurrence of these ideas in
me. But there was still another thing of which I was sure and
which, because of my habit of believing it, I thought I perceived very clearly, although in truth I did not perceive it at
all—namely, that there were things outside of myself from
which these ideas came and to which they were completely
similar. That was the point in which, perhaps, I was mistaken; or at any rate, even if my judgment was in accord with
the truth, it was no knowledge of mine which produced the
truth of my judgment.

But when I considered something very simple and very easy
concerning arithmetic and geometry, (36) as, for example, that
two and three joined together produce the number five, and
other similar things, did I not conceive them at least sufficiently clearly to guarantee that they were true? Certainly, if

1 L. *percipio;* F. *concevoir.*

I have since judged that these things might be doubted, it was for no other reason than that it occurred to me that some God might perhaps have given me such a nature that I would be mistaken even about those things that seemed most obvious to me. Every time that this idea of the supreme power of a God, as previously conceived, occurs to me, I am constrained to admit that it is easy for him, if he wishes it, to bring it about that I am wrong even in those matters which I believe I perceive ⌐with the mind's eye⌐ with the greatest ⌐possible⌐ obviousness. And on the other hand, every time I turn to the things I think I conceive very clearly, I am so convinced by them that I am spontaneously led to proclaim: "Let him deceive me who can; he will never be able to bring it about that I am nothing while I think I am something, or, it being true that I now am, that it will some day be true that I have never been, or that two and three joined together make more or less than five, or similar things ⌐in which I recognize a manifest contradiction ⌐and⌐ which I see clearly could not be otherwise than as I conceive them⌐."

And certainly, since I have no reason to believe that there is a God who is a deceiver, and since I have not yet even considered those reasons that prove that there is a God, the argument for doubting which depends only on this opinion is very tenuous and, so to speak, metaphysical. But in order to remove it altogether I must examine whether there is a God as soon as an opportunity occurs, and if I find that there is one I must also investigate whether he can be [29] a deceiver; for as long as this is unknown, I do not see that I can ever be certain of anything. And now, ⌐in order that I shall have an opportunity to examine this question without interrupting the order of thought which I have proposed for myself, which is to pass by degrees from the notions which I discover to be most basic in my mind to those that I can discover afterward,⌐ ⌐good order seems to demand that⌐ I should first classify all (37) my thoughts into certain types and consider in which of these types there is, properly, truth or error.

Among my thoughts some are like images of objects, and it

is to these alone that the name of "idea" properly applies, as when I picture to myself a man, or a chimera, or the sky, or an angel, or God ⌜himself⌝. Then there are others with different forms, as when I wish, or fear, or affirm, or deny. In these cases I do conceive something as the object of the action of my mind, but I also add something else by this action to the idea which I have of the entity; and of this type of thought, some are called volitions or emotions, and others judgments.

Now as far as ideas are concerned, if we consider them only in themselves and do not relate them to something else, they cannot, properly speaking, be false; for whether I imagine a sage or a satyr, it is no less true that I imagine the one than the other. Similarly, we must not fear to encounter falsity in the emotions or volitions; for even though I may desire bad things, or even things which never existed, nevertheless it is no less true on that account that I desire them. So there is nothing left but judgments alone, in which I must take very great care not to make a mistake. But the principal and most common error which can be encountered here consists in judging that the ideas which are in myself are similar to, or conformable to, things outside of myself; for certainly, if I considered the ideas only as certain modes ⌜or aspects⌝ of my thought, without intending them to refer to some other exterior object, they could hardly offer me a chance of making a mistake.

Among these ideas, some seem to be born with me, others to ⌜be alien to me and to⌝ come from without, (38) and the rest to be made ⌜and invented⌝ by myself. For I have the ability to conceive what is generally called a thing, or a truth, or a thought; and it seems to me that I do not conceive this from anything but my own nature. But if I now hear some noise, if I [30] see the sun, if I feel heat, I have hitherto judged that these feelings proceeded from some things which exist outside of myself; and finally, it seems to me that sirens, hippogriffs, and ⌜all other⌝ similar chimeras are fictions and inventions of my mind. Perhaps I might persuade myself that all these ideas are ⌜of the type of those I call⌝ alien ⌜and which come from without⌉, or perhaps they are all innate, or perhaps they might all be invented; for I have not yet clearly discovered their true origin. And what I must principally do at this point is to consider, concerning those which seem to me to come from objects outside of me, what evidence obliges me to believe that they resemble those objects.

The first of these reasons is that it seems to me that nature teaches me so, and the second that I have direct experience that these ideas are not dependent upon my will ⌐nor upon myself⌐. For often they come to me despite my wishes; just as now, whether I wish it or not, I feel heat, and for that reason I conclude that this sensation, or rather this idea, of heat is produced in me by something different from myself, namely, by the heat of the fire near which I am sitting. And I see nothing which appears more reasonable to me than to judge that this alien entity sends to me and imposes upon me its likeness rather than anything else.

Now I must see whether these reasons are sufficiently strong and convincing. When I say that it seems to me that nature teaches me so, I understand by this word "nature" only a certain inclination which leads me to believe it, and not the light of nature which makes me know that it is true. But these two expressions are very different from each other; for I could not doubt in any way what the light of nature made me see to be true, just as it made me see, a little while ago, that from the fact that I doubted I could conclude that I existed. And ⌐there is no way in which this could be doubted, because⌐ I have no other faculty or power to distinguish the true from the false which could teach me that what this light of nature shows me as true is not so, and in which I could trust as much as in the light of nature itself. (39) But as for inclinations, which also seem to me to be natural, I have often noticed, when it was a question of choosing between virtues and vices, that they led me to the bad no less than to the good; and for this reason I have not been inclined to follow them even in what concerns the true and the false. [31]

As for the other reason, which is that these ideas must come from elsewhere, since they do not depend upon my will, I do not find this convincing either. For just as the inclinations which we are now considering occur in me, despite the fact that they are not always in accord with my will, so perhaps there is in me some faculty or power adequate to produce these ideas without the aid of any external objects, even though it is not yet known to me; just as it has so far always seemed to me that when I sleep, these ideas are formed in me without the aid of the objects which they represent. And finally, even if I should agree that the ideas are caused by these objects, it does not necessarily follow that they should be similar to them. On the contrary, I have often observed in many instances that there was a great difference between the object and its idea. Thus, for example, I find in myself two completely different ideas of the sun: the one has its origin in the senses, and must be placed in the class of those that, as I said before, came from without, according to which it seems to me extremely small; the other is derived from astronomical considerations—that is, from certain innate ideas—or at least is formed by myself in whatever way it may be, according to which it seems to me many times greater than the whole earth. Certainly, these two ideas of the sun cannot both be similar to the same sun ⟨existing outside of me⟩, and reason makes me believe that the one which comes directly from its appearance is that which least resembles it.

All this makes me recognize sufficiently well that up to now it has not been by (40) a valid and considered judgment, but only by a blind ⌈and rash⌉ impulse, that I have believed that there were things outside of myself and different from my own being which, through the organs of my senses or by whatever other method it might be, sent into me their ideas or images ⌈and impressed upon me their resemblances⌉.

But there is still another path by which to seek if, among the things of which I possess ideas, there are some which exist outside of myself. If these ideas are considered only in so far as they are particular modes of thought, I do not recognize any ⌈difference or⌉ inequality among them, and all of them

appear to arise from myself in the same fashion. But considering them as images, of which some represent one thing and
some another, it is evident that they differ greatly among
themselves. For those that represent substances [32] are undoubtedly something more, and contain in themselves, so to
speak, more objective reality ⌜, or rather, participate by representation in a higher degree of being or perfection,⌝ than
those that represent only modes or accidents. Furthermore,
that by which I conceive a supreme God, eternal, infinite, ⌜im-
mutable,⌝ omniscient, omnipotent, and the universal creator of
all things that exist outside of himself—that idea, I say, certainly contains in itself more objective reality than do those
by which finite substances are represented.

Now it is obvious, according to the light of nature, that
there must be at least as much reality in the total efficient
cause as in its effect, for whence can the effect derive its
reality, if not from its cause? And how could this cause communicate reality to the effect, unless it possessed it in itself?

And from this it follows, not only that something cannot be
derived from nothing, but also that the more perfect—that is
to say, that which contains in itself more reality (41)—cannot
be a consequence of ⌜and dependent upon⌝ the less perfect.
This truth is not only clear and evident in regard to the effects which have ⌜what philosophers call⌝ actual or formal reality, but also in regard to the ideas where one considers only
⌜what they call⌝ objective reality. For example, the stone
which has not yet existed cannot now begin to be, unless it is
produced by a being that possesses in itself formally or eminently all that enters into the composition of stone ⌜—that is,
which contains in itself the same things as, or others more excellent than, those which are in stone⌝. Heat cannot be produced in a being that previously lacked it, unless by something which is of an order ⌜, a degree, or a type⌝ at least as
perfect as heat, and so forth. But still, in addition, the idea of
heat or of stone cannot be in me, unless it was put there by
something which contains in itself at least as much reality as I
conceive there is in heat or stone; for even though that cause

does not transfer to my idea anything of its actual or formal reality, we must not therefore suppose that such a cause is any less real, nor that the nature of an idea ⌐, since it is a work of the mind,⌐ is such that it does not require any other formal reality than what it receives and borrows from thought or mind, of which it is only a mode ⌐—that is, a way or manner of thinking⌐. In order that an idea should contain one particular objective reality rather [33] than another, it should no doubt obtain it from some cause in which there is at least as much formal reality as the idea contains objective reality. For if we suppose that there is some element in an idea which is not present in its cause, this element must then arise from nothing. However imperfect may be this mode of being, by which a thing exists objectively or is represented by a concept of it in the understanding, certainly we can nevertheless say that this mode and manner of being is not nothing, and consequently the idea cannot derive its origin from nothingness.

Nor must I imagine that, since the reality that I consider to be in my ideas is only objective, the same reality need not (42) be present formally ⌐or actually⌐ in the causes of these ideas, but that it is sufficient that it should be objectively present in them. For just as this manner of existing objectively belongs to ideas as part of their own nature, so also the manner or fashion of existing formally belongs to the causes of these ideas, or at the very least to their first and principal causes, as part of their own nature. And even though it might happen that one idea gives birth to another idea, that could not continue indefinitely; but we must finally reach a first idea, the cause of which is like an archetype ⌐or source⌐, in which is contained formally ⌐and in actuality⌐ all the reality ⌐or perfection⌐ that is found only objectively or by representation in the ideas. Thus the light of nature makes me clearly recognize that ideas in me are like paintings or pictures, which can, truly, easily fall short of the perfection of the original from which they have been drawn, but which can never contain anything greater or more perfect. And the longer and the more carefully I consider all these arguments, the more clearly and distinctly I know that they are true.

What, then, shall I conclude from all this evidence? Clearly, that if the objective reality ⌜or perfection⌝ of some one of my ideas is such that I recognize clearly that this same reality ⌜or perfection⌝ does not exist in me, either formally or eminently, and consequently that I cannot myself be its cause, it necessarily follows that I am not alone in the world, but that there is also some other entity that exists and is the cause of this idea. On the other hand, if I find no such idea in myself, I will have no argument which can convince me and make me certain of the existence of any entity other than myself; for I have diligently searched for all such arguments [34] and have been thus far unable to find any other.

Among all these ideas which exist in me, besides that which represents myself to myself, concerning which there can be no difficulty here, (43) there is another which represents a God, others corporeal and inanimate things, others angels, others animals, and still others which represent men similar to myself. But as far as the ideas which represent other men, or animals, or angels are concerned, I can easily imagine that they could be formed by the ⌜mixture and⌝ combination of my other ideas, ʿof myself,ʾ of corporeal objects, and of God, even though outside of me there were no other men in the world, nor any animals, nor any angels. And as far as the ideas of corporeal objects are concerned, I recognize nothing in them so great ⌜or so excellent⌝ that it seems impossible that they could arise from myself. For if I consider them more closely and examine them in the same way that I examined the idea of wax yesterday, I find that there are only a few elements in them which I conceive clearly and distinctly—namely, size, or extension in length, width and depth; shape, which results from the termination and limitation of this extension; location, which the variously shaped objects have with respect to one another; and movement, or the changing of this location. To this one may add substance, duration, and number. As for other elements, such as light, colors, sounds, odors, tastes, heat, cold, and the other qualities involved in the sense of touch, they occur in my thought with so much obscurity and confusion that I do not even know whether they are true or false and only apparent, that is, whether my ideas of these qualities are really ideas of actual bodies or of non-bodies ⌐, which are only chimerical and cannot exist⌐. For even though I have previously stated that true and formal falsity can characterize judgments only, there can exist nevertheless a certain material falsity in ideas, as when they represent that which is nothing as though it were something. For example, my ideas of cold and heat are so little clear (44) and distinct that I cannot determine from them whether cold is only the absence of heat or heat the absence of cold, or whether both of them are real qualities, or whether neither is such. Besides, ⌐since ideas are like pictures,⌐ there can be no ideas which do not [35] seem to us to represent objects; and if it is true to say that cold is nothing but an absence of heat, the idea of cold which represents it as something real and positive could, not inappropriately, be called false, and so for other similar ideas.

And assuredly, it is not necessary for me to attribute to such ideas any other source than myself. For if they are false—that is, if they represent entities which do not exist—the light of nature lets me know that they proceed from nothingness; that is, that they occur in me only because something is lacking in my nature and that the latter is not altogether perfect. And if these ideas are true, nevertheless, since they show me so little reality that I cannot even ⌐clearly⌐ distinguish the object represented from the nonexistent, I do not see why they could not be produced by myself ⌐and why I could not be their author⌐.

As for my clear and distinct ideas of corporeal things, there are some of them which, it seems to me, might have been derived from my ideas of myself, such as my ideas of substance, duration, number, and other similar things. For I think that stone is a substance, or a thing which is capable of existing by itself, and that I myself am also a substance, even though I

understand perfectly that I am a being that thinks and
that is not extended, and that stone, on the contrary, is an
extended being which does not think. Nevertheless, even
though there is a notable difference between these two conceptions, they seem to agree in this fact that both of them
represent substances. In the same way, when I think I exist
now and remember in addition having existed formerly, or
when I conceive various thoughts of which I recognize the
number, I acquire (45) the ideas of duration and number
which I afterward am able to apply to any other things I
wish. As for the other qualities of which the ideas of material
entities are composed—namely, extension, shape, location, and
movement—it is true that they are not formally in my nature,
since I am only a thinking being; but since these are only particular modes of substance, ⌐or, as it were, the garments in
which corporeal substance appears to us,⌐ and since I am myself a substance, it seems that they might be contained in my
nature eminently.

Thus there remains only the idea of God, in which we must
consider if there is something which could not have come
from myself. By the word "God" I mean an infinite substance,
⌐eternal, immutable,⌐ [36] independent, omniscient, omnipotent, and that by which I myself and all other existent things,
if it is true that there are other existent things, have been
created and produced. But these attributes are ⌐such ⌐—they
are⌐ so great and so eminent—⌐ that the more attentively I
consider them, the less I can persuade myself that I could
have derived them from my own nature. And consequently we
must necessarily conclude from all that I have previously said
that God exists. For even though the idea of substance exists
in me from the very fact that I am a substance, I would nevertheless have no idea of an infinite substance, I who am a finite
being, unless the idea had been placed in me by some substance which was in fact infinite.

And I must not imagine that I do not conceive infinity as a
real idea, but only through the negation of what is finite in
the manner that I comprehend rest and darkness as the nega-

tion of movement and light. On the contrary, I see manifestly that there is more reality in infinite substance than in finite substance, and my notion of the infinite is somehow prior to that of the finite, that is, the notion of God is prior to that of myself. For how would it be possible for me to know that I doubt and that I (46) desire—that is, that I lack something and am not all perfect—if I did not have in myself any idea of a being more perfect than my own, by comparison with which I might recognize the defects of my own nature?

And we cannot say that this idea of God might be materially false, and that in consequence I might derive it from nothingness, ⌐or, in other words, that it might be in me as a deficiency,⌐ as I have just now said about the ideas of heat and cold, and other similar things. For, on the contrary, this idea is very clear and very distinct and contains more objective reality than does any other, so that there is no other which is more true from its very nature, nor which is less open to the suspicion of error and falsity.

This idea, I say, of a supremely perfect and infinite being, is entirely true; for even though one might imagine that such a being does not exist, nevertheless one cannot imagine that the idea of it does not represent anything real, as I have just said of the idea of cold. It is also very clear and very distinct, since everything real and true which my mind conceives clearly and distinctly, and which contains some perfection, is contained and wholly included in this idea. [37] And this will be no less true even though I do not comprehend the infinite and though there is in God an infinity of things which I cannot comprehend, or even perhaps suggest in thought, for it is the nature of infinity that I, who am finite and limited, cannot comprehend it. It is enough that I understand this and that I judge that all qualities which I conceive clearly and in which I know that there is some perfection, and possibly also an infinity of other qualities of which I am ignorant, are in God formally or eminently. Then the idea which I have of God is seen to be the truest, the clearest, and the most distinct of all the ideas which I have in my mind.

But possibly I am something more than I suppose myself to be. Perhaps all the perfections which I attribute to the nature of a God are somehow potentially in me, although they ⌜are not yet actualized and⌝ do not yet appear (47) and make themselves known by their actions. Experience shows, in fact, that my knowledge increases and improves little by little, and I see nothing to prevent its increasing thus, more and more, to infinity; nor ⌜even⌝ why, my knowledge having thus been augmented and perfected, I could not thereby acquire all the other perfections of divinity; nor finally, why my potentiality of acquiring these perfections, if it is true that I possess it, should not be sufficient to produce the ideas of them ⌜and introduce them into my mind⌝.

Nevertheless, ⌜considering the matter more closely, I see that⌝ this could not be the case. For, first, even if it were true that my knowledge was always achieving new degrees of perfection and that there were in my nature many potentialities which had not yet been actualized, nevertheless none of these qualities belong to or approach ⌜in any way⌝ my idea of divinity, in which nothing is merely potential ⌜and everything is actual and real⌝. Is it not even a most certain ⌜and infallible⌝ proof of the imperfection of my knowledge that it can ⌜grow little by little and⌝ increase by degrees? Furthermore, even if my knowledge increased more and more, I am still unable to conceive how it could ever become actually infinite, since it would never arrive at such a high point of perfection that it would no longer be capable of acquiring some still greater increase. But I conceive God to be actually infinite in such a high degree that nothing could be added to the ⌜supreme⌝ perfection that he already possesses. And finally, I understand ⌜very well⌝ that the objective existence of an idea can never be produced by a being that [38] is merely potential and that, properly speaking, is nothing, but only by a formal or actual being.

And certainly there is nothing in all that I have just said which is not easily known by the light of nature to all those who will consider it carefully. But when I relax my attention somewhat, my mind is obscured, as though blinded by the images of sensible objects, and does not easily recall the reason why my idea of a being more perfect than my own must necessarily have been imparted to me by a being that is actually more perfect. (48)

That is why I wish to pass on now to consider whether I myself, who have this idea of God, could exist if there had been no God. And I ask, from what source would I have derived my existence? Possibly from myself, or from my parents, or from some other causes less perfect than God; for we could ⌐think of or⌐ imagine nothing more perfect, nor even equal to him. But if I were ⌐independent of anything else and were⌐ the author of my own being, I would doubt nothing, I would experience no desires, and finally I would lack no perfection. For I would have endowed myself with all those perfections of which I had any notion, and thus I would be God ⌐himself⌐.

And I must not imagine that what I lack might be more difficult to acquire than what I already possess; for, on the contrary, it is very certain that it was far more difficult for this ego—that is, this being or substance that thinks—to emerge from nothingness than it would be for me to acquire the ⌐insight into and⌐ knowledge of various matters about which I am ignorant, since this knowledge would only be an accident of this substance. And certainly if I had given myself all the qualities that I have just mentioned and more, ⌐that is, if I were myself the author of my birth and of my being,⌐ I would at least not have denied to myself those things which could be obtained with greater facility ⌐as are an infinity of items of information, of which my nature happens to be deprived⌐. I would not even have denied myself any of the qualities which I see are included in the idea of God, because there is no one of them which seems to me to be more difficult to create or acquire. And if there were one of them which was more difficult, certainly it would have appeared so to me, because, on the assumption that all my other qualities were self-given, I would see in this one quality a limitation of my power ⌐since I would not be able to acquire it⌐.

Even if I could suppose that possibly I have always been as I am now, still I could not evade the force [39] of this argument ⸢since it would not follow that no author of my existence need then be sought ⸢and⸥ I would still have to recognize that it is necessary that God is the author of my existence⸥. For the whole duration of my life can be divided into (49) an infinite number of parts, no one of which is in any way dependent upon the others; and so it does not follow from the fact that I have existed a short while before that I should exist now, unless at this very moment some cause produces and creates me, as it were, anew or, more properly, conserves me.

Actually it is quite clear and evident to all who will consider attentively the nature of time that a substance, to be conserved at every moment that it endures, needs the same power and the same action which would be necessary to produce it and create it anew if it did not yet exist. Thus the light of nature makes us see clearly that conservation and creation differ only in regard to our manner of thinking ⸢and not in reality⸥.

It is therefore only necessary here for me to question myself and consider my own nature to see whether I possess some power and ability by means of which I can bring it about that I, who exist now, shall still exist a moment later. For since I am nothing but a being which thinks, or at least since we are so far concerned only with that part of me, if such a power resided in me, certainly I should at least be conscious of it ⸢and recognize it⸥. But I am aware of no such thing, and from that fact I recognize evidently that I am dependent upon some ⸢other⸥ being different from myself.

But possibly that being upon whom I am dependent is not God, and I am produced either by my parents or by some other causes less perfect than he. Not at all, that cannot be the case. For, as I have already said, it is very evident that there must be at least as much reality in the cause as in the effect; and since I am a being who thinks and who has some idea of God, whatever turns out to be the cause of my existence must be admitted to be also a being who thinks and which has in itself the idea of all the perfections which I attribute to ⌜the divine nature ⌐of⌐ God⌝. Thus we can in turn inquire whether this cause derives its ⌜origin and⌝ existence from itself or from something else. For if it is self-caused, it follows, for the reasons that I have previously given, that this cause must be God ⌐himself⌝, (50) since, to have the capacity to be or exist by itself, it must also, without doubt, have the power to possess in actuality all the perfections which it can imagine, that is, all those that I conceive [40] to be in God. But if it derives its existence from something else, we ask once more, for the same reason, whether this second cause is caused by itself or by another, until ⌜step by step⌝ we finally arrive at an ultimate cause which will ⌜turn out to⌝ be God. And it is very obvious that in this case there cannot be an infinite regress, since it is not so much a question of the cause which produced me in the past as of that which conserves me in the present.

Nor can we pretend that possibly several ⌐partial⌝ causes have concurred to produce me, and that from one of them I received the idea of one of the perfections which I attribute to God, and from another the idea of some other, so that each of these perfections would actually be found somewhere in the universe, but would nowhere be joined together ⌜and assembled⌝ in one entity which would be God. For, on the contrary, the unity, simplicity, or inseparability of all the qualities which are in God is one of the principal perfections which I conceive to be in him. And certainly the idea of this unity of all God's perfections could not have been placed in me by any cause from which I had not also received the ideas of all the other perfections. For nothing could have brought it about that I understood these qualities as joined together and inseparable, without having brought it about at the same time that I know what qualities they were ⌜and that I knew something about each one of them⌝.

Finally, concerning my parents, ⌜from whom it seems that I derive my birth,⌝ even if all that I could ever have believed of them should be true, that would still not imply that it is they who conserve me, nor even that they made and produced me in so far as I am a thinking being ⌐/, there being no relation between the bodily activity by which I have been accustomed to believe I was engendered and the production of a thinking substance⌐⌐. The most that they can have contributed to my birth is that they have produced certain arrangements in the matter within which I have so far believed that the real I, that is, my mind, (51) is enclosed. Thus the existence of my parents is no objection to the argument, and we must necessarily conclude from the mere fact that I exist and that I have an idea of a supremely perfect Being, or God, that the existence of God is very clearly demonstrated.

The only task left is to consider how I received this idea ⌐from God⌐; for I did not get it through the senses, nor has it ever appeared to me unexpectedly, as the ideas of sensible objects are wont to do, when these objects are presented or seem to be presented [41] to my external sense organs. Nor is it only a product ⌐or fiction⌐ of my mind, for it is not in my power to diminish it or to add anything to it. No possibility remains, consequently, except that this idea is born and produced with me from the moment that I was created, just as was the idea of myself.

And truly it must not be thought strange that God, in creating me, put this idea in my nature in much the same way as an artisan imprints his mark on his work. Nor is it necessary that this mark be something different from the work itself. From the very fact that God has created me, it is very credible that he has made me, in some sense, in his own image and similitude, and that I conceive this similitude, in which the idea of God is contained, by the same faculty by which I conceive myself. In other words, when I reflect upon myself, I not only know that I am ⌐an imperfect being,⌐ incomplete and dependent upon some other being, and a being which strives and aspires incessantly to become something better and greater than I now am, but also and at the same time I know that the being upon which I depend possesses in itself all these great qualities ⌐to which I aspire and the ideas of which

I find in myself, and possesses these qualities⌉, not indefinitely and merely potentially, but ⌈really,⌉ actually, and infinitely, and so that it is God. And the whole force of the argument ⌈I have here used to prove the existence of God⌉ consists in the fact that I recognize that it would not be possible (52) for my nature to be what it is, possessing the idea of a God, unless God really existed—the same God, I say, the idea of whom I possess, the God who possesses all these ⌈high⌉ perfections of which my mind can have some ⟨slight⟩ idea, without however being able fully to comprehend them; who is subject to no defect ⌈and who has no part of all those qualities which involve imperfection⌉. And from this it is quite evident that he cannot be a deceiver, since the light of nature teaches us that deception must always be the result of some deficiency.

But before I examine this more carefully and pass on to the consideration of other truths which may follow from this one, it seems proper to pause for a while to contemplate this all-perfect God, to weigh at leisure his ⌈marvelous⌉ attributes, to consider, admire, and adore the ⌈incomparable⌉ beauty of this immense magnificence, as far at least as the power of my mind, which is somewhat overwhelmed by it, permits. [42]

For just as faith teaches that the supreme felicity of the next life consists only in this contemplation of divine majesty, so let us try from now on whether a similar contemplation, although incomparably less perfect, will not make us enjoy the greatest happiness that we are capable of experiencing in this life.

FOURTH MEDITATION

OF THE TRUE AND THE FALSE

In these last few days I have become so accustomed to ignoring my senses, and I have so carefully noticed that we know very little (53) with certainty about corporeal things and that we know much more about the human mind, and still more again about God himself, that it is easy for me now to turn my consideration from ⌜sensible or⌝ picturable things to those which, being wholly dissociated from matter, are purely intelligible. And certainly my idea of the human mind, in so far as it is a thinking being, not extended in length, breadth, and depth, and participating in none of the qualities of body, is incomparably more distinct than my idea of anything corporeal. And when I consider that I doubt, that is to say, that I am an incomplete and dependent being, the idea of a complete and independent being, that is, of God, occurs to my mind with very great distinctness and clearness. And from the very fact that such an idea occurs in me, or that I who possess this idea exist, I so evidently conclude that God exists and that my own existence depends entirely upon him every moment of my life that I am confident that the human mind can know nothing with greater evidence and certainty. And I already seem to have discovered a path that will lead us from this contemplation of the true God, in whom all the treasures of science and wisdom are contained, to the knowledge of all other beings ⌜in the universe⌝.

For first, I recognize that it is impossible for God ever [43] to deceive me, since in all fraud and deception there is some kind of imperfection. And although it seems that to be able to deceive is a mark of ⸌acumen,⸍ ⌜subtlety,⌝ or power, nevertheless to wish to deceive testifies without question to weakness or malice, which could not be found in God.

Then, I know by my own experience that I have some ability to judge, ⌜⸌or to distinguish the true from the false,⸍⌝ an ability which I have no doubt received from God just as I have received all the other qualities ⸌which are part of me ⌜and⸍ which I possess⌝. (54) Furthermore, since it is impossible that God wishes to deceive me, it is also certain that he has not given me an ability of such a sort that I could ever go wrong when I use it properly.

And no doubt on this subject would remain, except that we could apparently then draw the conclusion that I can never commit an error. For if everything in me is derived from God, and if he has not given me any ability to make errors, it seems that I should never be mistaken. It is true that when I consider ⌜⟨myself⟩⌝ only ⌜⟨as a creature of⟩⌝ God, ⟨and when I orient myself completely upon him,⟩ I discover ⌜in myself⌝ no cause of error or falsity. But when, a little later, I think of myself, experience convinces me that I am nevertheless subject to innumerable errors. And when I try to discover the reason for this, I notice that there is present in my thought not only a real and positive idea of God, or rather of a supremely perfect being, but also, so to speak, a certain negative idea of nothingness, or of what is infinitely removed from every kind of perfection. And I see that I am, as it were, a mean between God and nothingness, that is, so placed between the supreme Being and not-being that, in so far as a supreme Being has produced me, there is truly nothing in me which could lead me into error; but if I consider myself as somehow participating in nothingness or not-being, that is, in so far as I am not myself the supreme being ⟨and am lacking many things⟩, ⌜I find myself exposed to an infinity of defects, so that⌝ I should not be astonished if I go wrong.

Thus I ⟨clearly⟩ recognize that error as such is not something real which depends upon God, but only a deficiency. Thus, in order to err, I do not need a faculty [1] which God has given to me expressly for the purpose; mistakes on my part occur because the power that God has given me to discriminate between the true and the false is not infinite.

Nevertheless I am not yet altogether satisfied, for error is not (55) a pure negation ⌜—that is, it is not a simple deficiency or lack of some perfection which is not my [44] due⌝, but rather a privation ⟨or lack⟩ of some knowledge which it seems to me that I should possess. And in considering the nature of God, it does not seem possible that he should have endowed me with any faculty [2] which is not perfect of its kind, or which

[1] L. *facultas;* F. *puissance.*
[2] L. *facultas;* F. *faculté.*

lacks some perfection which is its due. For if it is true that the more expert the artisan, the more perfect ⌈and finished⌉ the artifacts produced by his hands, what could ⌈we imagine to⌉ have been produced by this supreme creator of the universe that is not ⌈perfect and⌉ entirely complete in all its parts? Certainly there is no doubt but that God could have created me such that I would never be mistaken; it is also certain that he always wills that which is best. Is it therefore a better thing to ⌈⌐be able to⌝⌉ make a mistake than not to ⌈⌐be able to⌝⌉ do so?

Considering this question with attention, it occurs to me, to begin with, that I should not be astonished at not being able to understand why God does what he does; and that I must not for this reason doubt his existence, since I may perchance observe in my experience many other beings that exist, even though I cannot understand why or how they were made. For, knowing by now that my nature is extremely weak and limited and that God's, on the contrary, is immense, incomprehensible, and infinite, I no longer have any difficulty in recognizing that there are an infinity of things within his power the causes of which lie beyond the powers of my mind. And this consideration alone is sufficient to persuade me that all causes of the type we are accustomed to call final are useless in physical ⌈or natural⌉ affairs, for it does not seem possible for me, without presumption, to seek and undertake to discover the ⌈impenetrable⌉ purposes of God.

Furthermore, it occurs to me that we should not consider a single creation separately when we investigate whether the works of God are perfect, but generally all created objects together. For the same thing which might perhaps, with some sort of justification, appear to be very imperfect if it were alone in the world (56) is seen to be very perfect when considered as constituting a part of this whole universe. And although, since I undertook to doubt everything, I have so far only learned with certainty of my existence and of God's, nevertheless, since I have recognized the infinite power of God, I could not deny that he has produced many other

things, or at least that he could produce them, in such a way
that I exist and am placed in the world as forming a part of
the universality of all beings. [45]

Consequently, when I come to examine myself more closely
and to consider what are my errors, which alone testify that
there is imperfection in me, I find that they depend upon two
joint causes, namely, the faculty of knowing which I possess
and the faculty of choice, or rather of free will—that is to say,
of my understanding together with my will. For by the understanding alone ⌐I neither assert nor deny anything, but⌐ I
only conceive the ideas of things which I may assert or deny.
Nor ⌐in considering the understanding thus precisely⌐ can we
say that any error is ever found in it, provided that we take
the word "error" in its proper sense. And even if there might
be in the world an infinity of things of which my understanding has no idea, we cannot therefore say that it is deprived of these ⌐ideas as of something which is owed to its
nature⌐, but only that it does not possess them, because in
reality there is no argument which can prove that God ought
to have given me a greater ⌐and more ample⌐ faculty of knowing than what he has given me; and however adroit ⌐and able⌐
a worker I consider him to be, I must not therefore think that
he ought to have put in each of his works all the perfections
which he is able to bestow upon some. Thus I cannot complain because God has not given me a sufficiently ample and
perfect free will or volition, since ⌐, as a matter of fact,⌐ I experience ⌐it to be so ample and extended⌐ that there are no
limits which restrict it.

And it appears to me to be very remarkable that, of all the
other qualities which I possess, there is none (57) so perfect or
so great that I do not ⌐clearly⌐ recognize that it could be even
greater or more perfect. Thus for example, if I consider my
faculty of conceiving, I ⌐immediately⌐ recognize that it is of
very small extent and greatly limited; and at the same time
there occurs to me the idea of another faculty, much more
ample, ‹indeed immensely greater› and even infinite, and from

the very fact that I can imagine this I recognize ⌜without diffi-
culty⌝ that it belongs to the nature of God. In the same way,
if I examine memory, imagination, or any other faculty of
mine, I find no one of them which is not quite small and
limited and which is not, in God, immense ⌜and infinite⌝.
There is only volition alone, ⌐or the liberty of the ⌜free⌝ will,⌐
which I experience to be so great in myself that I cannot conceive the idea of any other more ⌜ample and⌝ extended, so
that this is what principally indicates to me that I am made
in the image and likeness of God. For even though the will
may be incomparably greater in God than in myself, either
because of the [46] knowledge and the power which are joined
with it and which make it surer and more efficacious, or because of its object, since it extends to infinitely more things,
nevertheless it does not appear any greater when I consider it
formally and precisely by itself. For it consists only in the fact
that we can ⌜make a choice; we can⌝ do a given thing or not
do it—that is to say, we can affirm or deny, pursue or avoid.
Or more properly, our free will consists only in the fact that
in affirming or denying, pursuing or avoiding the things suggested by the understanding, we behave in such a way that we
do not feel that any external force has constrained us in our
decision.

For in order to be free, it is not necessary for me to be indifferent about the choice of one or the other of the two con-
traries, but rather, the more I lean to one, either because I
see clearly that it contains ⌐the preponderance (58) of⌐ both
goodness and truth or because God so guides my private
thoughts, the more freely do I choose ⌜and embrace⌝ it. And
certainly, divine grace and natural understanding, far from
diminishing my liberty, rather augment and strengthen it.
Moreover, that indifference which I feel when I am not more
moved toward one side than the other by ⌜the weight of⌝ some
reason is the lowest degree of liberty, and is rather a defect
in the understanding than a perfection of the will. For if I always understood clearly what is true and what is good, I

would never need to deliberate about what judgment and what choice I ought to make, and so I would be entirely free without ever being indifferent.

From all this I recognize, on the one hand, that the cause of my errors is not the power of willing ⟨considered by itself⟩, which I have received from God, for it is very ample and perfect in its own kind. Nor, on the other hand, is it the power of ⌐understanding or¬ conceiving; for since I conceive nothing except by means of this power which God has given me in order to conceive, no doubt everything I conceive I conceive properly, and it is not possible for me to be deceived in that respect.

Whence, then, do my errors arise? Only from the fact that the will is ⌐much¬ more ample and far-reaching than the understanding, so that I do not restrain it within the same limits but extend it even to those things which I do not understand. Being ⌐by its nature¬ indifferent about such matters, it very easily is turned aside from the true and the good ⌐and chooses the false and the evil¬. And thus it happens that I make mistakes and that I sin.

For example, when I recently examined the question whether anything in the world existed, and I recognized from the very fact that I examined [47] this question that it was very evident that I myself existed, I could not refrain from concluding that what I conceived so clearly was true. Not that I found myself forced to this conclusion by any (59) external cause, but only because the great clarity which was in my understanding produced a great inclination of my will, and I was led to this conviction all the more ⟨spontaneously and⟩ freely as I experienced in myself less indifference. Now, on the contrary, I know not only that I exist, in so far as I am something that thinks, but there is also present in my mind a certain idea of corporeal nature. In consequence, I wonder whether this nature that thinks, which is in me, or rather which is myself, is different from this corporeal nature, or if both are one and the same. I am supposing, here, that I do not yet know any argument to convince me of one possibility rather than the other, so it follows that I am entirely indifferent as to denying or affirming it, or even as to abstaining from making any judgment.

And this indifference extends not only to those things with which the understanding has no acquaintance, but also to all those generally that it does not comprehend with ⌜sufficient ⌐-ly⌐ perfect⌐ clarity at the moment when the will is deliberating the issue. For however probable may be the conjectures which incline me to a particular judgment, the mere recognition that they are only conjectures and not certain and indubitable reasons is enough to give me grounds for making the contrary judgment. I have had sufficient experience of this in these past few days when I assumed as false all that I had previously held to be very true, merely because I noticed that it was somehow possible to doubt it.

Now, if I abstain from making a judgment upon a topic when I do not conceive it sufficiently clearly and distinctly, it is evident that I do well and am not making a mistake; but if I decide to deny or affirm it, then I am not making a proper use of my free will. And (60) if in this situation I affirm what is not true, it is evident that I am making a mistake; and even when I judge according to the truth, it is only by chance, and I am not for that reason free of blame ⌜for misusing my freedom⌝. For the light of nature dictates that the understanding should always know before the will makes a decision.

It is in this improper use of the free will that we find the privation which [48] constitutes the essence of error. Privation, I say, is found in the operation in so far as it proceeds from me, but not in the faculty which I have received from God, nor even in the operation in so far as it depends upon him. For certainly I have no reason to complain because God has not given me a more ample intelligence or a more perfect insight than what he has bestowed upon me, since it is ⌜actually⌝ the nature of a finite understanding not to comprehend many things, and it is the nature of a created understanding to be finite. On the contrary, far from conceiving such unjust sentiments as to imagine that he has deprived me or unjustly

kept from me the other perfections with which he has not endowed me, I have every reason to give him thanks because,
never having any obligation to me, he has nevertheless given
me those ⌐few⌐ perfections that I have.

Nor have I any reason to complain because he has given me
a volition more ample than my understanding. For as the
volition consists of just one body, ⌐its subject being⌐ apparently indivisible, it seems that its nature is such that nothing
could be taken from it without destroying it. And, certainly,
the more ample it is, the more reason I have to give thanks
for the generosity of the One who has given it to me.

Nor, finally, have I any reason to complain that God con-
curs with me to perform the acts of this volition, that is, the
judgments in which I am mistaken. For those acts are entirely
true and absolutely good in so far as they depend upon God,
and there is somehow more perfection in my nature because I
can perform them than there would be if I could not. As for
privation, in which alone is found the formal cause (61) of
error and sin, it has no need of any concurrence on the part
of God, since it is not a thing ⌐or a being⌐ and since, if it is
referred to God as to its cause, it should not be called privation but only negation ⌐according to the significance attached
to these words in the schools⌐. For actually it is not an imperfection in God that he has given me the liberty of ⌐judging or
not judging, ⌐or⌐ giving or withholding my assent,⌐ on certain
matters of which he has given me no clear and distinct knowledge. It is, without doubt, an imperfection in myself not to
make proper use of this liberty, and ⌐rashly⌐ to pass judgment
on matters which I ⌐do not rightly understand ⌐and⌐ conceive
only obscurely and confusedly⌐.

I perceive, nevertheless, that it would have been easy for
God to contrive that I would never make mistakes, even
though I remained free and with limited knowledge. He
might, for example, have given my understanding [49] a clear
and distinct comprehension of all the things about which I
should ever deliberate, or he might simply have engraved so
deeply in my memory the resolution never to pass judgment

on anything without conceiving it clearly and distinctly that
I could never forget this rule. And I ⸢readily⸣ recognize ⸢in so
far as I possess the comprehension of any whole,⸣ that ⸢when I
consider myself alone, as if I were the only person in the
world,⸣ I would have been ⸢much⸣ more perfect than I am if
God had so created me ⸢that I never made a mistake⸣; nevertheless I cannot therefore deny that the universe may be somehow more perfect because some of its parts are not free from
defect ⸢while others are⸣, than it would be if all its parts were
alike.

And I have no right to complain because God, having put
me in the world, has not wished to place me in the ranks of
the noblest and most perfect beings. ⸢I indeed have reason to
rejoice because,⸣ even if I do not have the power of avoiding
error by the first method ⸢which I have just described⸣, which
depends upon a clear and evident knowledge of all the things
about which I can deliberate, the other method, at least, is
within my power. This is, (62) firmly to adhere to the resolution never to pass judgment upon things whose truth is not
clearly known to me. For even though I experience in myself
the weakness of not being able to keep my mind continuously
faithful to a fixed resolution, I can nevertheless, by attentive
and frequently repeated meditation, so strongly impress it
upon my memory that I will never fail to recollect it whenever there is need, and thus I can acquire the habit of not
erring. And since this comprises the greatest and principal
perfection of man, I consider that I have benefited not a little
by today's meditation, in having discovered the cause of error
and falsity.

And certainly, there can be no other cause than the one I
have just explained, for whenever I restrict my volition within
the bounds of my knowledge, whenever my volition makes no
judgment except upon matters clearly and distinctly reported
to it by the understanding, it cannot happen that I err. For
every clear and distinct conception is without doubt something ⸢real and positive⸣, and thus cannot derive its origin
from nothingness, but must have God for its author—God, I

say, who, [50] being supremely perfect, cannot be the cause of any error—and consequently we must conclude that such a conception ⌐or such a judgment⌐ is true.

For the rest, I have not only learned today what I must avoid in order not to err, but also what I ought to do to arrive at the knowledge of the truth. For I shall certainly achieve this goal if I hold my attention sufficiently fixed upon all those things which I conceive perfectly and if I distinguish these from the others which I conceive only confusedly and obscurely. And from now on I shall take particular care to act accordingly. (63)

FIFTH MEDITATION

OF THE ESSENCE OF MATERIAL THINGS AND, ONCE MORE, OF GOD: THAT HE EXISTS

There are many other questions for me to inquire into concerning the attributes of God and concerning my own nature, or the nature of my mind. I may, perhaps, pursue this investigation some other time; for the present, having noticed what must be done or avoided in order to arrive at the knowledge of the truth, my principal task is to attempt to escape from ⌐and relieve myself of all⌐ the doubts into which I have fallen in these last few days, and to see if we cannot know anything certain about material objects. But before examining whether such objects exist outside of myself, I must consider the concepts of these objects, in so far as they occur in my thought, and see which of them are distinct and which of them are confused.

In the first place, I picture distinctly that quantity which philosophers commonly call the "continuum," or extension in length, width, and depth which exists in this quantity, or rather in the body to which we attribute it. Furthermore, I can distinguish in it various different parts and attribute to each of these parts all sorts of sizes, shapes, positions, and movements; and, finally, I can assign to each of these movements all degrees of duration.

And I not only know these things distinctly when I consider them thus in general, but also, ⌈however little I am⌉ applying my attention to it, I ⌈⌐come to⌐⌉ recognize an infinity of details concerning [51] numbers, shapes, movements, and other similar things, the truth of which makes itself so apparent (64) and accords so well with my nature that when I discover them for the first time it does not seem ⌈to me⌉ as though I were learning anything new, but rather as though I were remembering what I had previously known—that is, that I am perceiving things which were already in my mind, even though I had not yet focussed my attention upon them.

And what I believe to be more important here is that I find in myself an infinity of ideas of certain things which cannot be assumed to be pure nothingness, even though they may perhaps have no existence outside of my thought. These things are not figments of my imagination, even though it is within my power to think of them or not to think of them; on the contrary, they have their own true and immutable natures. Thus, for example, when I imagine a triangle, even though there may perhaps be no such figure anywhere in the world outside of my thought, nor ever have been, nevertheless the figure cannot help having a certain determinate nature, or form, or essence, which is immutable and eternal, which I have not invented and which does not in any way depend upon my mind. This is evidenced by the fact that we can demonstrate various properties of this triangle, namely, that its three angles are equal to two right angles, that the greatest angle subtends the longest side, and other similar properties. Whether I wish it or not, I ⟨now⟩ recognize ⌈very⌉ clearly ⌈and evidently⌉ that these are properties of the triangle, even though I had never previously thought of them in any way when I first imagined one. And therefore it cannot be said that I have ⌈imagined or⌉ invented them.

Nor can I raise the objection here that possibly this idea of the triangle came to my mind ⸂from external things⸃ through the medium of my senses, since I have sometimes seen triangularly shaped objects; for I can picture in my mind an infinity of other shapes such that I cannot have the least suspicion that they have ever been present to my senses, and I am still (65) no less able to demonstrate various properties about their nature than I am about that of the triangle. These properties, certainly, must be wholly true, since I conceive them clearly. And thus they are something, and not pure negation, since it is quite evident that everything which is true is something ⌐, as truth is the same as being⌐⌐. I have already amply demonstrated that everything that I recognize clearly and [52] distinctly is true; and even if I had not demonstrated this, the nature of my mind is such that I can ⸂nevertheless⸃ not help believing things to be true while I am conceiving them clearly ⌐and distinctly⌐. And I recollect that even when I was still strongly attached to the objects of sense, I numbered among the most constant truths that which I conceived clearly ⌐and distinctly⌐ about the shapes, numbers, and other properties which belong to the fields of arithmetic and geometry ⸂or, in general, to pure and abstract mathematics⸃.

Now, if from the very fact that I can derive from my thoughts the idea of something, it follows that all that I clearly and distinctly recognize as characteristic of this thing does in reality characterize it, can I not derive from this an argument which will ⌐demonstratively⌐ prove the existence of God? It is certain that I find in my mind the idea of God, of a supremely perfect Being, no less than that of any shape or number whatsoever; and I recognize that an ⌐actual and⌐ eternal existence belongs to his nature no less clearly and distinctly than I recognize that all I can demonstrate about some figure or number actually belongs to the nature of that figure or number. Thus, even if everything that I concluded in the preceding Meditations were ⸂by chance⸃ not true, the existence of God should pass in my mind as at least as certain (66) as I have hitherto considered all the truths of mathematics ⌈, which deal only with numbers and figures⌉.

And this is true even though I must admit that it does not⌉ at first appear entirely obvious, but seems to have some appearance of sophistry. For since in all other matters I have become accustomed to make a distinction between existence and essence, I am easily convinced that the existence óf God can be separated from his essence, and that thus I can conceive of God as not actually existing. Nevertheless, when I consider this with more attention, I find it manifest that we can no more separate the existence of God from his essence than we can separate from the essence of a ⌈rectilinear⌉ triangle the fact that the size of its three angles equals two right angles, or from the idea of a mountain the idea of a valley. Thus it is no less self-contradictory to conceive of a God, a supremely perfect Being, who lacks existence—that is, who lacks some perfection—than it is to conceive of a mountain for which there is no valley.

But even though in fact I cannot conceive of a God without existence, any more than of a mountain without a valley, nevertheless, just as from the mere fact that I conceive a mountain with a valley, it does not [53] follow that any mountain exists in the world, so likewise, though I conceive of God as existing, it does not seem to follow for this reason that God exists. For my thought does not impose any necessity upon things; and just as I can at my pleasure imagine a winged horse, even though no horse has wings, so I could perhaps attribute existence to God, even though no God existed.

⌈This is far from the truth;⌉ it is here that there is sophistry hidden ⌈under the guise of a valid objection⌉. For from the fact that I cannot conceive a mountain without a valley it does not follow that there is a mountain or a valley anywhere ⌈in the world⌉, but only that the mountain (67) and the valley, whether they exist or not, are inseparable from each other. From the fact alone that I cannot conceive God except as existing, it follows that existence is inseparable from him, and consequently that he does, in truth, exist. Not that my thought can bring about this result or that it imposes any necessity upon things; on the contrary, the necessity which is in the thing itself—that is, the necessity of the existence of God—determines me to have this thought. For it is not in my power to conceive of a God without existence—that is to say, of a supremely perfect Being without a supreme perfection—as it is in my power to imagine a horse either with or without wings.

And it must not be said here that it is only necessary that I admit that God exists after I have supposed that he possesses all sorts of perfections, since existence is one of them, but that my first supposition was not really necessary. Thus it is not necessary to think that all four-sided figures can be inscribed in a circle; but if we suppose that I do have this idea, I am forced to admit that a rhombus can be inscribed in one, ⌈since it is a four-sided figure,⌉ and ⌈by⌉ this ⌈I will be forced to admit what⌉ is ⟨clearly⟩ false. We must not, I say, argue thus; for even though it is not necessary that I should ever have any thought about God, nevertheless, whenever I do choose to think of a first and supreme being and to derive ⌈, so to speak,⌉ the idea of God from the treasure house of my mind, it is necessary that I attribute to him all kinds of perfections, even though it does not occur to me to mention them all and to pay attention to each one of them severally. And this necessity is enough to bring it about that afterward, as soon as I come to recognize that existence is a perfection, I conclude ⟨very properly⟩ that this first and supreme Being ⌈truly⌉ exists; just as it is not necessary that I should ever imagine any triangle, but [54] every time that I wish to consider a rectilinear figure containing three angles only, it is absolutely necessary that I attribute to it everything that leads (68) to the conclusion that these three angles are not greater than two right angles, even if perhaps I do not then consider this matter in particular. But when I wish to determine what figures can be inscribed in a circle, it is in no way necessary that I think that all four-sided figures are of this number; on the contrary, I cannot even pretend that this is the case as long as I do not wish to accept anything but what I can conceive clearly and distinctly. Consequently, there is a vast difference between false suppositions, such as this one, and the true ideas which are inborn in me, of which the first and chief one is that of God. For actually I have several reasons for recognizing that this idea is not something ⌈imaginary or⌉ fictitious, depending only on my thought, but that it is the image of a true and immutable nature. The first reason is that I cannot conceive anything but God alone, to whose essence existence belongs ⌈with necessity⌉. Another reason is that it is not possible for me to conceive ⌈in the same way⌉ two or more gods ⌟such as he⌞. Again, assuming that there is now a God who exists, I see clearly that he must have existed before from all eternity and that he should be eternally in the future. And a final reason is that I conceive various other qualities in God, of which I can neither diminish nor change a particle.

For the rest, whatever proof or argument I use, I must always come back to this conclusion: that it is only the things that I conceive clearly and distinctly which have the power to convince me completely. And although among the things which I conceive in this way there are, in truth, some which are obvious ⌈-ly known⌉ to everyone, while others of them only become known to those who consider them more closely and examine them more carefully, nevertheless, after they have once been discovered, none of them can be esteemed less certain than the rest. Thus, for example, in every right-angled triangle, even though it is not so readily apparent (69) that the square of the hypotenuse is equal to the squares of the other two sides as it is that this hypotenuse is opposite the greatest angle, nevertheless, after this fact has once been recognized, we are as much convinced of the truth of the one proposition as of the other. And as for the question of God, certainly, if my mind were not prejudiced and if my thought were not distracted by the ⌈constant⌉ presence ⌟on all sides⌞ of images of sensible objects, [55] there would be nothing that I would recognize sooner or more easily than God. For is there anything ⌈clearer and⌉ more obvious in itself than ⌈to think⌉ that there is a God, ⌈that is to say,⌉ a supreme ⌈and perfect⌉ Being, in whom ⟨uniquely⟩ ⌈necessary or eternal⌉ existence is included in essence, and who consequently exists?

And although, in order thoroughly to understand this truth, I have had to make a great mental effort, nevertheless I find myself at present not only as certain of this as of everything which seems to me most certain, but even beyond that I notice that the certainty of all other things depends upon this so ⌈absolutely⌉ that, without this knowledge, it is impossible ever to be able to know anything perfectly.

For even though my nature is such that as soon as I understand anything very clearly and very distinctly I cannot help but believe it to be true, nevertheless, because I am also of such a nature that I cannot always confine my attention to one thing and frequently remember having judged a thing to be true when I have ceased considering the reasons which forced me to that conclusion, it can happen at such a time that other reasons occur to me which would easily make me change my mind if I did not know that there was a God. And so I would never have true and certain knowledge concerning anything at all, but only vague and fluctuating opinions.

Thus, for example, when I consider the nature of the ⌈⟨rectilinear⟩⌉ triangle, I recognize ⟨most⟩ evidently, I, who am somewhat skilled in geometry, that its three angles are equal to two right angles; nor can I disbelieve this while I am paying attention to (70) its demonstration. But as soon as I turn my attention away from the demonstration, even while I remember having clearly understood it, it can easily happen that I doubt its truth, if I do not know that there is a God. For I can persuade myself that I was so made by nature that I could easily make mistakes, even in those matters which I believe I understand with the greatest evidence ⌈and certainty⌉, especially because I remember having often judged many things true and certain, which, later, other reasons constrained me to consider absolutely false.

But after having recognized that there is a God, and having recognized at the same time that all things are dependent upon him and that he is not a deceiver, I can infer as a consequence that everything which I conceive clearly and distinctly is necessarily true. Therefore, even if I am no longer thinking of the reasons why [56] I have judged something to be true, provided only I remember having understood it clearly and distinctly, there can never be a reason on the other side which can make me consider the matter doubtful. Thus I have ⌐a¬ true and certain ⌐body of¬ knowledge ⌐on this matter⌐. And this same ⌐body of¬ knowledge extends also to all the other things which I remember having formerly demonstrated, such as the truths of geometry and other similar matters. For what reason can anyone give to make me doubt them? Would it be that my nature is such that I am ⌐very likely to be¬ ⌐frequently¬ deceived? But I know already that I cannot go wrong in judgments for which I clearly know the reasons. Would it be that I have formerly considered many things true and certain which I later recognized to be false? But I had not clearly or distinctly known any of those things; and not yet knowing this rule by which I am certain of truth, I had been led to believe them by reasons that I have since recognized to be less strong than I had then imagined them. What further objections could be raised? Would it be that possibly I am asleep, as I had myself argued earlier, or that all the thoughts that I now have are no more true than the dreams we imagine when asleep? But ⌐even so, nothing would be altered. For¬ (71) even if I were asleep, all that appears evident to my mind is absolutely true.

And thus I recognize very clearly that the certainty and truth of all knowledge depends solely on the knowledge of the true God, so that before I knew him I could not know any other thing perfectly. And now that I know him, I have the means of acquiring ⌐clear and certain ⌐and¬ perfect¬ knowledge about an infinity of things, not only about God himself ⌐and about other intellectual matters¬, but also about ⌐that which pertains to⌐ corporeal nature, in so far as it can be the object of ⸍pure mathematics ⌐—that is, of⸜ the demonstrations of geometricians who are not concerned with its existence⌐. [57]

SIXTH MEDITATION

OF THE EXISTENCE OF CORPOREAL THINGS AND OF THE REAL DISTINCTION BETWEEN THE MIND AND BODY ⌐OF MAN⌐

Nothing more is now left for me to do except to examine whether corporeal things exist; and I already know ⌐for certain⌐ that they can exist at least in so far as they are considered as the objects ⸍of pure mathematics, ⌐or⸜ of the demonstrations of geometry,⌐ since I conceive them in this way very clearly and very distinctly. For there is no doubt but that God has the power of producing everything that I am able to conceive with distinctness; and I have never supposed that it was impossible for him to do anything, except only when I found a contradiction in being able to conceive it well. Furthermore, my faculty of imagination, which I find by experience that I use when I apply myself to the consideration of material objects, is capable of persuading me of their existence. For when I consider attentively what the imagination is, (72) I find that it is nothing else than a particular application of the faculty of knowledge to a body which is intimately present to it and which therefore exists.

And to make this ⌐very⌐ obvious, I take note of the difference between imagination and pure intellection ⌐or conception⌐. For example, when I imagine a triangle, not only do I conceive that it is a figure composed of three lines, but along with that I envision these three lines as present, by the force ⌐and the internal effort⌐ of my mind; and it is just this that I call "imagination." But if I wish to think of a chiliogon, I recognize quite well, indeed, that it is a figure composed of a thousand sides, as easily as I conceive that a triangle is a figure composed of ⌜only⌝ three sides, but I cannot imagine the thousand sides ⌜of a chiliogon as I can the three of a triangle, nor, so to speak, look at them⌝ as though they were present ⌜to the eyes of my mind⌝. And although, following my habit of always using my imagination when I think of corporeal things, it may happen that in conceiving a chiliogon I confusedly picture some figure to myself, nevertheless it is ⌜quite⌝ evident that this figure is not a chiliogon, since it is in no way different from what I would picture to myself if I thought of a myriogon or of some other figure of many sides, and that it in no way serves [58] to bring out the properties which constitute the difference between the chiliogon and the other polygons. But if it is a question of considering a pentagon, ⌜it is quite true that⌝ I can conceive its shape, just as well as that of a chiliogon, without the aid of the imagination; but I can also imagine it by applying my mind attentively to each of its five sides, and ⟨at the same time⟩ ⌜collectively⌝ to the area ⌜or space⌝ that they enclose.

Thus I recognize clearly that I have need of a special (73) mental effort in order to imagine, which I do not require in order to ⌜conceive ⟨or⟩ understand⟩, and this ⌜special⌝ mental effort clearly shows the difference that exists between imagination and pure intellection ⌜or conception⌝. In addition, I notice that this ability to imagine which I possess, in so far as it differs from the power of conceiving, is in no way necessary to my ⌜nature or⌝ essence, that is to say, to the essence of my mind. For even if I did not possess it, there is no doubt that I would still remain the same person I now am, from which it seems to follow that it depends upon something other than my mind. And I readily conceive that if some body exists with which my mind is so joined ⌜and united⌝ that it can consider it whenever it wishes, it could be that by this means it imagines corporeal things. Thus this method of thinking only differs from pure intellection in that the mind, in conceiving, turns somehow toward itself and considers some one of the ideas which it possesses in itself, whereas in imagining it turns toward the body and considers in the latter something conformable to the idea which it has either thought of by itself or perceived through the senses. I easily conceive, I say, that the imagination can work in this fashion, if it is true that there are bodies; and because I cannot find any other way in which this can be explained ⟨equally well⟩, I therefore conjecture that bodies probably exist. But this is only a probability; and although I carefully consider all aspects of the question, I nevertheless do not see that from this distinct idea of corporeal nature which I find in my imagination, I can derive any argument which necessarily proves the existence of any body. (74)

But I have become accustomed to imagine many other things besides that corporeal nature which is the object of ⟨pure mathematics ⌈or⌉ geometry⌉, although less distinctly, such as colors, sounds, tastes, pain, and other similar qualities. And inasmuch as I perceive those qualities much better by the senses, through the medium of which, with the help of the memory, they seem to have reached my imagination, [59] I believe that in order to examine them more readily it is appropriate to consider at the same time the nature of the sensation and to see whether, from those ideas which are perceived by the method of thinking which I call "sensation," I will not be able to derive some certain proof of the existence of corporeal things.

First, I shall recall in my memory what are the things which I formerly held to be true because I had received them through the senses, and what were the bases on which my belief was founded. Afterward I shall examine the reasons which since then have obliged me to consider them doubtful, and finally, I shall consider what I ought now to believe ⟨about them⟩.

First, then, I felt that I had a head, hands, feet, and ⌈all the⌉ other members which compose this body which I thought of as a part, or possibly even as the whole, of myself. Furthermore, I felt that this body was one of a world of bodies, from

which it was capable of receiving various advantages and disadvantages; and I identified these advantages by a certain feeling of pleasure ⌈or enjoyment⌉, and the disadvantages by a
feeling of pain. Besides this pleasure and pain, I also experienced hunger, thirst, and other similar appetites, as well as
certain bodily tendencies toward gaiety, sadness, anger, and
other similar emotions. And externally, in addition to the extension, shapes, and (75) movements of bodies, I observed in
them hardness, warmth, and ⌈all the⌉ other qualities perceived
by touch. Furthermore, I noticed in them light, colors, odors,
tastes, and sounds, the variety of which enabled me to distinguish the sky, the earth, the sea, and ⌈, in general, all⌉ other
bodies, one from another.

And certainly, considering the ideas of all these qualities
which were presented to my mind [1] and which alone I directly
sensed, in the true significance of that term, it was not without reason that I believed I had sensory knowledge of things
entirely different from my thought—of bodies, namely, from
which these ideas came. For I was aware that these ideas occurred without the necessity of my consent, so that I could
not perceive any object, however much I wished, unless it was
present to one of my sense organs; nor was it in my power
not to perceive it when it was present. [60] And because the
ideas I received through the senses were much more vivid,
more detailed, and even in their own way more distinct than
any of those which I could picture to myself ⌐with conscious
purpose⌐ while meditating, or even than those which I found
impressed upon my memory, it seemed that they could not be
derived from my own mind, and therefore they must have
been produced in me by some other things. Of these things I
have no knowledge ⌐whatsoever,⌐ except that derived from the
ideas themselves, so nothing else could occur to my mind except that those things were similar to the ideas they caused.
And since I remembered that I had used my senses earlier
than my reason, and since I recognized that the ideas I formed
by myself were not as detailed as those I received through the

---

1 L. *cogitatio;* F. *pensée.*

senses and were most commonly composed of the latter as parts, I easily became persuaded that I had no idea in my mind which I had not previously acquired through my senses.

It was also not without reason that I believed that this body, which by a certain particular privilege I called mine, (76) belonged to me more ⌜properly and strictly⌝ than any other. For in fact I could never be separated from it, as I could be from other bodies; I felt in it and for it all my appetites and all my emotions; and finally I experienced ⌜the sensations of⌝ pain and ⌜the thrill of⌝ pleasure in its parts, and not in those of other bodies which are separated from it.

But when I inquired why any particular sensation of pain should be followed by unhappiness in the mind and the thrill of pleasure should give rise to happiness, or even why a particular feeling of the stomach, which I call hunger, makes us want to eat, and the dryness of the throat makes us want to drink, and so on, I could give no reason except that nature teaches me so. For there is certainly no affinity ⌜and no relationship⌝, or at least none that I ⌜can⌝ understand, between the feeling in the stomach and the desire to eat, no more than between the perception of the object which causes pain and the feeling of displeasure produced by it. And in the same way, it seemed to me that I had learned from nature all the other beliefs which I held about the objects of my senses, since I noticed that the judgments I habitually made about these objects took form in my mind before I had the opportunity to weigh ⌜and consider⌝ any reasons which could oblige me to make them. [61]

Later on, various experiences gradually destroyed all my faith in my senses. For I often observed that towers which, viewed from far away, had appeared round to me, seemed at close range to be square, and that colossal statues placed on the highest summits of these towers appeared small when viewed from below. And similarly in a multitude of other experiences, I encountered errors in judgments based on the external senses. And not only on the external senses, but even on the internal ones, (77) for is there anything more intimate

⌈or more internal⌉ than pain? Yet I have learned from certain persons whose arms or legs had been amputated that it still seemed to them sometimes that they felt pain in the parts which they no longer possessed. This gives me reason to think that I could not be ⌈entirely⌉ sure either that there was something wrong with one of my limbs, even though I felt a pain in it.

And to these reasons for doubting I have recently added two other very general ones. The first is that I have never thought I perceived anything when awake that I might not sometimes also think I perceived when I am asleep; and since I do not believe that the things I seem to perceive when asleep proceed from objects outside of myself, I did not see any better reason why I ought to believe this about what I seem to perceive when awake. The other reason was that, not yet knowing, or rather pretending not to know the author of my being, I saw nothing to make it impossible that I was so constructed by nature that I should be mistaken even in the things which seemed to me most true.

And as for the reasons which had previously persuaded me that sensible objects truly existed, I did not find it very difficult to answer them. For as nature seemed to lead me to many conclusions from which reason dissuaded me, I did not believe that I ought to have much faith in the teachings of this nature. And although my sense perceptions do not depend upon my volition, I did not think that I should therefore conclude that they proceeded from things different from myself, since there might perhaps be some faculty in myself even though it has been thus far unknown to me, which could ⌈be their cause and⌉ produce them.

But now that I am beginning to know myself better and to discover more clearly the author of my origin, I do not think in truth that I ought rashly to admit everything which the senses seem to teach us, (78) but on the other hand I do not think that I should doubt them all in general. [62]

First, since I know that all the things I conceive [2] clearly

2 L. *intelligo;* F. *concevoir.*

and distinctly can be produced by God exactly as I conceive them, it is sufficient that I can clearly and distinctly conceive one thing apart from another to be certain that the one is distinct ⌐or different⌐ from the other. For they can be made to exist separately, at least by ⌐the omnipotence of⌐ God, and we are obliged to consider them different no matter what power produces this separation. From the very fact that I know with certainty that I exist, and that I find that ⟨absolutely⟩ nothing else belongs ⌐necessarily⌐ to my nature or essence except that I am a thinking being, I readily conclude that my essence consists solely in being a body which thinks ⌐or a substance whose whole essence or nature is only to think⌐. And although perhaps, or rather certainly, as I will soon show, I have a body with which I am very closely united, nevertheless, since on the one hand I have a clear and distinct idea of myself in so far as I am only a thinking and not an extended being, and since on the other hand I have a distinct idea of body in so far as it is only an extended being which does not think, it is certain that this "I" ⌐—that is to say, my soul, by virtue of which I am what I am—⌐ is entirely ⌐and truly⌐ distinct from my body and that it can ⌐be or⌐ exist without it.

Furthermore, I find in myself various faculties of thinking which each have their own particular characteristics ⌐and are distinct from myself⌐. For example, I find in myself the faculties of imagination and of perception, without which I might no doubt conceive of myself, clearly and distinctly, as a whole being; but I could not ⟨, conversely,⟩ conceive of those faculties without me, that is to say, without an intelligent substance ⌐to which they are attached ⟨or⟩ in which they inhere⟩. For ⌐in our notion of them or, to use the scholastic vocabulary,⌐ in their formal concept, they embrace some type of intellection. From all this I reach the conception that these faculties are distinct from me as ⌐shapes, movements, and other⌐ modes ⌐or accidents of objects⌐ are distinct from ⌐the very⌐ objects ⌐that sustain them⌐.

I also recognize ⌐in myself⌐ some other faculties, such as the power of changing location, of assuming various postures, and

other similar ones; which cannot be conceived without some
substance in which they inhere, any more than the preceding
ones, (79) and which therefore cannot exist without such a
substance. But it is ⌜quite⌝ evident that these faculties, if
⌜it is true that⌝ they exist, must inhere in some corporeal or
extended substance, and not in an intelligent substance, since
their clear and distinct concept does actually involve some
sort of extension, but no sort of intelligence whatsoever. [63]
Furthermore, ⌜⌜I cannot doubt that⌝⌝ there is in me a certain
passive faculty of perceiving, that is, of receiving and recognizing the ideas of sensible objects; but ⌜it would be valueless
to me, and⌝ I could in no way use it if there were not ⌝also⌝
in me, or in something else, another active faculty capable of
forming and producing these ideas. But this active faculty
cannot be in me ⌜, in so far as I am a thinking being⌝, since it
does not at all presuppose ⌜my⌝ intelligence and also since
those ideas often occur to me without my contributing to
them in any way, and even ⌝frequently⌝ against my will. Thus
it must necessarily exist in some substance different from myself, in which all the reality that exists objectively in the
ideas produced by this faculty is formally or eminently contained, as I have said before. This substance is either a body—
that is, a corporeal nature—in which is formally ⌜and actually⌝
contained all that which is contained objectively ⌜and by rep-
resentation⌝ in these ideas; or else it is God himself, or some
other creation more noble than the body, in which all this is
eminently contained.

But since God is not a deceiver, it is very manifest that he
does not send me these ideas directly by his own agency, nor
by the mediation of some creation in which their ⌝objective⌝
reality does not exist formally but only eminently. For since
he has not given me any faculty for recognizing what that creation might be, but on the contrary a very great (80) inclination to believe that these ideas come from corporeal objects, I
do not see how we could clear God of the charge of deceit if
these ideas did in fact come from some other source ⌜or were
produced by other causes⌝ than corporeal objects. Therefore

we must conclude that corporeal objects exist. Nevertheless, they are not perhaps entirely what our senses perceive them to be, for there are many ways in which this sense perception is very obscure and confused; but ⌈we must⌉ at least ⌈admit that⌉ everything which I conceive clearly and distinctly ⌈⸜as occurring⸝ in them—that is to say, everything, generally speaking, which is discussed in pure ⸜mathematics ⌈or⸝ geometry⌉—does in truth occur in them.

⸜As for the rest,⸝ there are other beliefs, which are very doubtful and uncertain, which are either merely particular—as, for example, that the sun is of such a size and such a shape —or else are conceived less clearly ⌈and less distinctly⌉—such as light, sound, pain, and other similar things. Nevertheless, from the mere fact that God is not [64] a deceiver, and that in consequence he has not permitted any falsity in my opinions without having given me some faculty capable of correcting it, ⌈I think I can conclude with assurance that⌉ I have ⸜some hope of learning the truth even about these matters ⌈and⸝ the means of knowing them with certainty⌉.

First, there is no doubt but that all that nature teaches me contains some truth. For by nature, considered in general, I now understand nothing else but God himself, or else the ⌈order and⌉ system that God has established for created things; and by my nature in particular I understand nothing else but the arrangement ⌈or assemblage⌉ of all that God has given me.

Now there is nothing that this nature teaches me more expressly ⌈or more obviously⌉ than that I have a body which is in poor condition when I feel pain, which needs food or drink when I have the feelings of hunger or thirst, and so on. And therefore I ought to have no doubt that in this there is some truth. (81)

Nature also teaches me by these feelings of pain, hunger, thirst, and so on that I am not only residing in my body, as a pilot in his ship, but furthermore, that I am intimately connected with it, and that ⌈the mixture is⌉ so blended ⸜, as it were,⸝ that ⌈something like⌉ a single whole is produced. For if that were not the case, when my body is wounded I would not therefore feel pain, I, who am only a thinking being; but I would perceive that wound by the understanding alone, as a pilot perceives by sight if something in his vessel is broken. And when my body needs food or drink, I would simply know the fact itself, instead of ⌐receiving notice of it by⌐ having confused feelings of hunger and thirst. For actually all these feelings of hunger, thirst, pain, and so on are nothing else but certain confused modes of thinking, which have their origin in ⌐and depend upon⌐ the union and apparent fusion of the mind with the body.

Furthermore, nature teaches me that many other bodies exist in the vicinity of my own, of which I must seek some and avoid others. And certainly, from the fact that I perceive different kinds of colors, odors, tastes, sounds, heat, hardness, and so on, I very readily conclude that in the objects from which these various sense perceptions proceed there are some corresponding variations, although perhaps these variations are not really similar to the perceptions. And from the fact that some of these ⌐various sense⌐ perceptions are agreeable to me and others are disagreeable, [65] there is absolutely no doubt that my body, or rather my whole self, in so far as I am composed of body and mind, can in various ways be benefited or harmed by the other objects which surround it. (82)

But there are many other opinions that nature has apparently taught me which, however, I have not truly learned from her, but which were introduced into my mind by my habit of judging things inattentively. Thus it can easily happen that these opinions contain some falsity—as, for example, my opinion that all spaces in which there is nothing which ⌐affects and⌐ makes an impression on my senses are empty; that in an object which is hot there is some quality similar to my idea of heat; that in a white, ⌐or black,⌐ ⌐or green⌐ object there is the same whiteness, ⌐or blackness,⌐ ⌐or greenness⌐ that I perceive; that in a bitter or sweet object there is the same taste ⌐or the same flavor⌐, and so on for the other senses; and that stars, towers, and all other distant objects are the same shape and size that they appear ⌐from afar⌐ to our eyes, and so forth.

In order that there should be nothing in this matter that I do not conceive ⸂sufficiently⸃ distinctly, I should define ⸂more⸃ precisely what I properly mean when I say that nature teaches me something. For I am here using the word "nature" in a more restricted sense than when I use it to mean a combination ⌈or assemblage⌉ of everything God has given me, seeing that this ⌈assemblage or⌉ combination includes many things which pertain to the mind alone, to which I do not intend to refer here when speaking of nature—as ⌈for example⌉ my knowledge ⌈of this truth:⌉ that what has ⌈once⌉ been done can never ⌈after⌉ not have been done, and ⸂all ⌈of⸃ an infinity of⌉ other ⌈similar⌉ truths known to me by the light of nature ⌈without any aid of the body⌉. Such an assemblage also includes many other things which belong to body alone and are not here included under the name of "nature," such as its quality of being heavy and many other similar ones; for I am not concerned with these either, but only with those things which God has presented to me as a being composed of mind and body. This nature effectively teaches me to avoid things which produce in me the feeling of pain and to seek those which make me have some feeling of pleasure ⸂and so on⸃. But I do not see that beyond this it teaches me that I should ever conclude anything from these various sense perceptions concerning things outside of ourselves, unless the mind has ⌈carefully and⌉ maturely examined them. For it seems to me that it is the business of the mind alone, and not [66] of the being composed of mind and body, to decide the truth of such matters. (83)

Thus, although a star makes no more impression on my eye than the flame of a candle, and there is no real ⸂or positive inclination⸃ ⌈or natural faculty⌉ in me that leads me to believe that it is larger than this flame, nevertheless I have so judged it from infancy for no adequate reason. And although in approaching the flame I feel heat, and even though in approaching it a little too closely I feel pain, there is still no reason that can convince me that there is some quality in the flame similar to this heat, any more than to this pain. I only have reason to believe there is some quality in it, whatever it may be, which arouses in me these feelings of heat or pain.

Similarly, although there are parts of space in which I find nothing that ⌐excites and⌐ affects my senses, I ought not therefore to conclude that they contain no objects. Thus I see that both here and in many other similar cases I am accustomed to ⌐misunderstand and⌐ misconstrue the order of nature, because although these ⌐sensations or⌐ sense perceptions were given to me only to indicate to my mind which objects are useful or harmful to the composite body of which it is a part, and are for that purpose sufficiently clear and distinct, I nevertheless use them as though they were very certain rules by which I could obtain direct information about the essence ⌐and the nature⌐ of external objects, about which they can of course give me no information except very obscurely and confusedly.

In the previous discussion I have already explained sufficiently how it happens, despite the supreme goodness of God, that error occurs in my judgments. One further difficulty, though, presents itself here. This concerns objects which I am taught by nature to seek or avoid and also the internal sensations which she has given me. For it seems to me that I have noticed error here ⌐and thus that I am sometimes directly deceived by my nature⌐—as, for example, when the pleasant taste of some food in which poison has been mixed can induce me to take the poison, and so misleads me. (84) It is nevertheless true that in this case nature ⌐can be excused, for it⌐ only leads me to desire the food in which a pleasant taste is found, and not [67] to desire the poison which is unknown to it. Thus I cannot conclude anything from this except that my nature is not entirely and universally cognizant of all things. And at this there is no reason to be surprised, since man, being of a finite nature, is also restricted to a knowledge of a limited perfection.

But we also make mistakes sufficiently frequently even about matters of which we are directly informed by nature, as happens to sick people when they desire to drink or eat things which ⌐can⌐ ⟨later⟩ harm them. It might be argued here that the reason that they err is that their nature is corrupted. But this does not remove the difficulty, for a sick man is in truth no less the creation of God than is a man in full health, and therefore it is just as inconsistent with the goodness of God for him as for the other to have a ⌈misleading and⌉ faulty nature. A clock, composed of wheels and counterweights, is no less exactly obeying all the laws of nature when it is badly made and does not mark the time correctly than when it completely fulfills the intention of its maker; so also, the human body may be considered as a machine, so built and composed of bones, nerves, muscles, veins, blood, and skin that even if there were no mind in it, it would not cease to move in all the ways that it does at present when it is not moved under the direction of the will, nor consequently with the aid of the mind ⌈, but only by the condition of its organs⌉. I readily recognize that it is quite natural, for example, for this body to suffer dryness in the throat as a result of a dropsical condition, and thus to produce a feeling of thirst in the mind and a consequent disposition on the part of the mind to stimulate the nerves and other parts in the manner requisite for drinking, and so to increase the body's illness ⌈and injure itself⌉. It is just as natural, I say, as it is for it to be beneficially influenced to drink by a similar dryness of the throat, when it is not ill at all. (85)

And although in considering the purpose for which a clock has been intended by its designer, I can say that it is false to its nature when it does not correctly indicate the time, and although in considering the mechanism of the human body in the same way as having been formed ⌈by God⌉ to provide all the customary activities, I have reason to think that it is not functioning according to its nature when its throat is dry and drinking injures its chances of self-preservation, I nevertheless recognize that this last usage of the word "nature" is very different from the other. For the latter is nothing else but an arbitrary appellation [68] which depends entirely on my own idea in comparing a sick man and a poorly made clock, and contrasting them with my idea of a healthy man and a well-made clock; this appellation refers to nothing which is actually found in the objects of which we are talking. On the contrary, by the other usage of the word "nature," I mean something which is actually found in objects and which therefore is not without some truth.

But certainly, although as far as a dropsical body is concerned, it is only an arbitrary appellation to say that its nature is corrupted when, without needing to drink, it still has a dry and arid throat; nevertheless, when we consider the composite body ⌐as a whole⌐—that is to say, the mind ⌐or soul⌐ united with the body—it is not a pure appellation, but ⌐truly⌐ an actual error on the part of nature that it is thirsty when it is very harmful to it to drink. Therefore we must examine how it is that the goodness of God does not prevent man's nature, so considered, from being faulty ⌐and deceptive⌐.

⌐To begin this examination,⌐ I first take notice here that there is a great difference between the mind and the body, in that the body, from its nature, is always divisible and the mind is completely (86) indivisible. For in reality, when I consider the mind—that is, when I consider myself in so far as I am only a thinking being—I cannot distinguish any parts, but I ′recognize ⌐and∖ conceive ′very clearly∖⌐ that I am a thing which is ′absolutely∖ unitary and entire. And although the whole mind seems to be united with the whole body, nevertheless when a foot or an arm or some other part ′of the body∖ is amputated, I recognize quite well that nothing has been lost to my mind on that account. Nor can the faculties of willing, perceiving, understanding, and so forth be ⌐any more properly⌐ called parts of the mind, for it is ′one and∖ the same mind which ⌐as a complete unit⌐ wills, perceives, and understands ⌐, and so forth⌐. But just the contrary is the case with corporeal or extended objects, for I cannot imagine any ⌐, however small they might be,⌐ which my mind does not very easily divide into ⌐several⌐ parts, and I consequently recognize these objects to be divisible. This ′alone∖ would suffice to show me that the mind ⌈or soul of man⌉ is altogether different from the body, if I did not already know it sufficiently well for other reasons. [69]

I also take notice that the mind does not receive impressions from all parts of the body directly, but only from the brain, or perhaps even from one of its smallest parts—the one, namely, where the senses in common have their seat. This makes the mind feel the same thing whenever it is in the same condition, even though the other parts of the body can be differently arranged, as is proved by an infinity of experiments which it is not necessary to describe here.

I furthermore notice that the nature of the body is such that no one of its parts can be moved by another part some little distance away without its being possible for it to be moved in the same way by any one of the intermediate parts, even when the more distant part does not act. For example, in the cord A B C D ⌈which is thoroughly stretched⌉, if (87) we pull ⌈and move⌉ the last part D, the first part A will not be moved in any different manner from that in which it could also be moved if we pulled one of the middle parts B or C, while the last part D remained motionless. And in the same way, when I feel pain in my foot, physics teaches me that this sensation is communicated by means of nerves distributed through the foot. When these nerves are pulled in the foot, being stretched like cords from there to the brain, they likewise pull at the same time the ⸌internal⸍ part of the brain ⌈from which they come and⌉ where they terminate, and there produce a certain movement which nature has arranged to make my mind feel pain as though that pain were in my foot. But because these nerves must pass through the leg, the thigh, the loins, the back, and the neck, in order to extend from the foot to the brain, it can happen that even when the nerve endings in the foot are not stimulated, but only some of the ⸌intermediate⸍ parts ⌈located in the loins or the neck⌉, ⸌precisely⸍ the same movements are nevertheless produced in the brain that could be produced there by a wound received in the foot, as a result of which it necessarily follows that the mind feels the same pain ⌈in the foot as though the foot had been wounded⌉. And we must make the same judgment about all our other sense perceptions.

Finally, I notice that since each one of the movements that occurs in the part of the brain from which the mind receives impressions directly can only produce in the mind a single sensation, we cannot ⌈desire or⌉ imagine any better arrangement than that this movement should cause the mind to feel that sensation, of all the sensations the movement is [70] capable of causing, which is most effectively and frequently useful for the preservation of the human body when it is in full health. But experience shows us that all the sensations which nature has given us are such as I have just stated, and therefore there is nothing in their nature which does not show the power and the goodness of ⌈the⌉ God ⌈who has produced them⌉.

Thus, for example, (88) when the nerves of the foot are stimulated violently and more than is usual, their movement, passing through the marrow of the backbone up to the ⟨interior of the⟩ brain, produces there an impression upon the mind which makes the mind feel something—namely, pain as though in the foot—by which the mind is ⌈warned and⌉ stimulated to do whatever it can to remove the cause, taking it to be very ⌈dangerous and⌉ harmful to the foot.

It is true that God could establish the nature of man in such a way that this same brain event would make the mind feel something quite different; for example, it might cause the movement to be felt as though it were in the brain, or in the foot, or else in some other ⟨intermediate⟩ location ⌈between the foot and the brain⌉, or finally it might produce any other feeling ⌈that can exist⌉; but none of those would have contributed so well to the preservation of the body ⌈as that which it does produce⌉.

In the same way, when we need to drink, there results a certain dryness in the throat which affects its nerves and, by means of them, the interior of the brain. This brain event makes the mind feel the sensation of thirst, because under those conditions there is nothing more useful to us than to know that we need to drink for the conservation of our health. And similar reasoning applies to other sensations.

From this it is entirely manifest that, despite the supreme goodness of God, the nature of man, in so far as he is composed of mind and body, cannot escape being sometimes ⌈faulty and⌉ deceptive. For if there is some cause which produces, not in the foot, but in some other part of the nerve which is stretched from the foot to the brain, or even in the brain ⌈itself⌉, the same effect which ordinarily occurs when the foot is injured, we will feel pain as though it were in the foot, and we will naturally be deceived by the sensation. The reason for this is that the same brain event can cause only a single sensation in the mind; and this [71] sensation being much more frequently produced by a cause which wounds the foot than by another acting in a different location, it is much more reasonable (89) that it should always convey to the mind a pain in the foot rather than one in any other part ⌈of the body⌉. And if it happens that sometimes the dryness of the throat does not come in the usual manner from the fact that drinking is necessary for the health of the body, but from some quite contrary cause, as in the case of those afflicted with dropsy, nevertheless it is much better that we should be deceived in that instance than if, on the contrary, we were always deceived when the body was in health; and similarly for the other sensations.

And certainly this consideration is very useful to me, not only so that I can recognize all the errors to which my nature is subject, but also so that I may avoid them or correct them more easily. For knowing that each of my senses conveys truth to me more often than falsehood concerning whatever is useful or harmful to the body, and being almost always able to use several of them to examine the same object, and being in addition able to use my memory to bind and join together present information with what is past, and being able to use my understanding, which has already discovered all the causes of my errors, I should no longer fear to encounter falsity in the objects which are most commonly represented to me by my senses.

And I should reject all the doubts of these last few days as exaggerated and ridiculous, particularly that very general uncertainty about sleep, which I could not distinguish from waking life. For now I find in them a very notable difference, in that our memory can never bind and join our dreams together ⌈one with another and all⌉ with the course of our lives, as it habitually joins together what happens to us when we are awake. And so, in effect, if someone suddenly appeared to me when I was awake and ⟨afterward⟩ disappeared in the same way, as ⌈do images that I see⌉ in my sleep, so that I could not determine where he came from or where he went, it would not be without reason that I would consider it a ghost (90) or a phantom produced in my brain ⌈and similar to those produced there when I sleep⌉, rather than truly a man.

But when I perceive objects in such a way that I distinctly recognize both the place from which they come and the place where they are, as well as the time when they appear to me; and when, without any hiatus, I can relate my perception of them with all the rest of my life, I am entirely certain that I perceive them wakefully and not in sleep. And I should not in any way doubt the truth of these things [72] if, having made use of all my senses, my memory, and my understanding, to examine them, nothing is reported to me by any of them which is inconsistent with what is reported by the others. For, from the fact that God is not a deceiver, it necessarily follows that in this matter I am not deceived.

But because the exigencies of action frequently ⌈oblige us to make decisions and⌉ do not ⌈always⌉ allow us the leisure to examine these things with sufficient care, we must admit that human life is very often subject to error in particular matters; and we must in the end recognize the infirmity ⌈and weakness⌉ of our nature.

RULES FOR THE
DIRECTION OF THE MIND

BOOK ONE

RULE I

The purpose of our studies should be the direction of the mind toward the production of firm and true judgments concerning all things which come to its attention.

As soon as men recognize some similarity between two things, it is their custom to ascribe to each of them, even in those respects in which they are different, what they know to be true of the other. Thus they erroneously compare the sciences, which consist exclusively of intellectual knowledge, with the arts, which require some bodily use and skill; and they see that not all the arts can be learned by the same man, but that a man can perform an art best and most easily who performs that one only, (360) since the same hands are not so suitable for both agriculture and playing the lute, or for various other tasks of diverse sorts, as they would be for only one of these. Consequently, they believe the same to be true of the sciences, and, distinguishing them one from another by the diversity of their objects, believe that each should be pursued by itself to the exclusion of all others. In this they are certainly mistaken, for all the sciences are nothing else but human wisdom, which always remains one and the same, however many different subjects it is applied to. And since wisdom is no more altered by the topics with which it is concerned than is the light of the sun by the variety of the objects it illuminates, it is not necessary for the mind to be confined within any limits. For the learning of one truth does not hinder us from discovering another, as does the practice of an art, but rather assists us to discover more truths. It seems especially remarkable to me that so many people should most diligently investigate the customs of men, the properties of plants, the motions of the heavens, the transmutations of metals, and the objects of similar disciplines, and at the same time give hardly a thought to proper thinking or to universal wisdom, although all other subjects should be esteemed, not so much for themselves, as because they contribute something to this wisdom.

And so it is not without justice that we propose this rule first of all, because nothing will sooner lead us away from the correct path in the search for truth than if we direct our studies, not toward this comprehensive purpose, but toward several particular ones. I am not speaking of perverse and harmful pursuits, such as empty glory or base gain, for it is clear that false reasons and absurdities suited to the vulgar mind (361) open up a much more advantageous route to these than can the firm knowledge of the true. Rather, I am concerned with honest and even praiseworthy pursuits, because we are often more insidiously deceived by these, as, for example, if we are seeking knowledge useful to achieve a more pleasant life or to achieve that happiness which is found in the contemplation of the true, and which is almost the only joy in this life which is complete and free from sorrow. For we are indeed entitled to expect these legitimate fruits of the sciences; but if we are concerned with them while we are carrying on our researches, the result is often that we overlook many things which are necessary to the knowledge of other matters, because at first glance they seem either of little value or devoid of interest. And it must be believed that all things are so interconnected that it is much easier to learn them all together than to study each in isolation.

Therefore, if someone wishes to make a serious investigation of the truths of nature, he should not choose some particular science, for they are all interconnected and interdependent; but he should seriously study to improve the natural light of his reason, not in order to solve this or that difficulty of scholastic thought, but so that his intellect may guide his will toward what should be sought in the various contingencies of life. And if he does this, he will soon be surprised at how much greater strides he has made than have those who study particular subjects, and find that he has achieved not only all those things which others searched for, but greater things than they could even imagine. (362)

RULE II

We should be concerned only with those objects regarding which our minds seem capable of obtaining certain and indubitable knowledge.

All science is certain, evident knowledge, and he who doubts many things is not more learned than he who has never thought about these things; on the contrary, he seems even less learned if he has conceived some false opinion about them. And therefore it is better never to study than to turn our attention to such difficult topics that, being unable to distinguish the true from the false, we are forced to accept doubtful conclusions as certain, since in such cases there is not as much hope of increasing our knowledge as there is danger of diminishing it. And so, in accordance with this rule, we reject all knowledge which is merely probable,[1] and judge that only those things should be believed which are perfectly known, and about which we can have no doubts. Learned men may perhaps persuade themselves, nevertheless, that hardly any such knowledge exists, because, due to a common fault of human nature, they have failed to consider such knowledge for the very reason that it is so simple and obvious to everyone. Nevertheless, I advise them that there is much more such knowledge than they think, and knowledge such

[1] The word *probabile* may be rendered "plausible," which perhaps is closer to the emotional flavor of the original, although "probable" correctly gives the intellectual content. It is translated here in either way, depending upon the context.

as will suffice to provide certain demonstrations of innumerable propositions which they have hitherto been unable to discuss except as merely probable. And because they have believed it unworthy (363) of a learned man to confess there is something he does not know, they have been accustomed so to elaborate their pretended reasons that they then have gradually persuaded themselves, and so offered these reasons to others as genuine.

And truly, if we make good use of this rule, there will be very few things left to the investigation of which it will be permissible to direct our efforts. For there is hardly any question in the sciences concerning which talented men do not often differ among themselves. But whenever the judgments of two persons concerning the same thing are opposed, it is certain that at least one of them is wrong, and there is not even one of them who seems to have knowledge. For if one person's argument were certain and evident, he could propose it in such a way to the other one that even the latter's mind would eventually be convinced. Therefore, we do not seem able to acquire perfect knowledge of anything about which there are merely plausible opinions of this sort, because we have no right, without vanity, to hope to achieve more ourselves than others have accomplished. And thus, if we argue correctly, only arithmetic and geometry remain of the sciences already discovered, to which we are reduced by the observation of this rule.

But we should not for this reason condemn that method of philosophizing which others have thus far used, and these very convenient weapons of debate, the probable syllogisms [2] of the Scholastics; for they train the minds of the young and stimulate them by means of a certain rivalry. And it is far better for young persons to be educated by opinions of this sort, (364) even though they appear to be uncertain since there are controversies among the learned, than to be left free

[2] Reference is to the "dialectic syllogism" of Aristotle, i.e., to reasoning based on premises that are only probably true, or which appear to be such to the learned.

to their own devices. For perhaps they would push into danger without a leader; but as long as they follow in the foot-
steps of their teachers, though they may sometimes stray from
the truth, they will nevertheless engage in a method that is
at least more secure in the respect that it has already been
approved by the more prudent. We ourselves may rejoice that
we were once thus taught in the schools; but we were eventually freed from the bond which tied us to the words of our
teacher when we were withdrawn from the hand of authority
on reaching a sufficiently mature age. So if we really wish to
propose rules for ourselves, by the aid of which we may scale
the heights of human knowledge, the following must certainly
be accepted among the first: that we should be on guard not
to abuse our leisure, as many do, neglecting whatever is simple and being concerned only with difficult matters. For
though these persons ingeniously prepare some most subtle
conjectures and very plausible reasons concerning these matters, they finally discover, after a great deal of effort and when
it is too late, that they have only increased the multitude of
their doubts, and have reached no true knowledge.

A little while before, we said that of the disciplines known
to others, only arithmetic and geometry are free from the
taint of any falsity or uncertainty. In order to inquire more
carefully why this should be so, we should note that there are
two paths available to us leading to the knowledge (365) of
reality, namely, experience and deduction. It should also be
noted that our experiences with things often lead to error,
but "deduction," or the pure logical inference from one thing
to another, can never be performed improperly by an intellect
which is in the least degree rational, although it may escape
our attention if we do not happen to notice it. And it seems
to me that there is very little benefit in those chains of reasoning by which logicians believe they can regulate human reasoning, though I do not deny that they are very suitable for other
purposes. For no error which can happen to human beings—
I say to human beings, not to animals—arises from incorrect
inference, but only from the fact that certain poorly under-

stood experiences are falsified, or certain opinions are accepted rashly and without justification.

From this we can easily understand why arithmetic and geometry are much more certain than the other disciplines, because only these are concerned with an object so pure and simple that nothing need be assumed which experience has rendered uncertain, and because they consist wholly of rationally deduced consequences. These disciplines are therefore the easiest and most obvious of all, and they have the kind of characteristic we require, since, except by oversight, it hardly seems that in this case it is human to err. Nevertheless it ought not to be surprising that many people prefer to turn their attention to other arts or to philosophy: this happens because each person takes the liberty of prophesying with greater confidence in an obscure matter than in one that is evident, and (366) it is much easier to make some conjecture concerning any subject that happens to arise rather than to reach the real truth about one question, however trivial it may be.

Now from all of this it is to be concluded, not that arithmetic and geometry are the only subjects to be studied, but only that in seeking the correct path to truth we should be concerned with nothing about which we cannot have a certainty equal to that of the demonstrations of arithmetic and geometry.

RULE III

Concerning the subjects proposed for investigation, we should seek to determine, not what others have thought, nor what we ourselves conjecture, but what we can clearly and evidently intuit, or deduce with certainty; for in no other way is knowledge obtained.

The books of the ancients should be read, because it is an enormous advantage to us to be able to make use of the works of so many men, both in order to know those things which have already been discovered before our time, and also in order to be advised which things still remain to be discovered in all fields. But at the same time there is a real danger that we may be infected with the faults and errors which we pick up by reading them with insufficient care, however much we try to avoid it. For authors, when they render an unconsidered decision about some controversial matter, are accustomed to use their ingenuity in trying to carry us along with them by very subtle arguments; and, on the other hand, whenever they fortunately discover something certain and evident, (367) they never communicate this to us except in an ambiguous manner, for fear, perchance, that the merit of the invention will be diminished by the simplicity of the evidence, or because they begrudge us the full truth.

Moreover, even if everyone were frank and open, and never thrust any doubtful opinions upon us as true, and set forth everything in good faith; nevertheless, because there is hardly anything that has been said by one person, the contrary of which has not been asserted by someone else, we would always be uncertain which of them should be believed. And it will do no good to count votes in order to follow the opinion held by the greater number of authors, for if we are concerned with a difficult question, it is more likely that the truth about it would have been discovered by few than by many. And even if everyone were in agreement, nevertheless their beliefs would not be enough, for we never, for example, become mathematicians by remembering all the demonstrations of others unless we are also capable of solving any kind of problem that may be proposed, nor do we become philosophers by reading all the arguments of Plato and Aristotle, for if we cannot ourselves reach a firm judgment concerning whatever is at issue, it would appear that we are not devoting ourselves to science, but to history.

Let us also take heed never to confuse any conjectures with our judgments about the true state of things. Attention to this matter is of no little importance, for there is no stronger reason why contemporary philosophy has found nothing so evident and certain that it cannot be controverted, than because those eager for knowledge, not content to learn obvious and certain things, (368) venture to affirm even obscure and unknown ones, about which we can make only plausible conjectures, and then give their whole credence to these, confusing them indiscriminately with the true and evident. Thus they can finally reach no conclusion which does not seem to depend upon some proposition of this sort, and all their conclusions are therefore doubtful.

But lest we should fall into the same error, let us reconsider all the acts of our mind by which we may arrive at a knowledge of things without any fear of error. I accept only two, namely, intuition and deduction.[1]

By "intuition" I understand, not the fluctuating faith in the senses, nor the false judgment of badly constructed imaginings, but the conception of the pure and attentive mind which is so simple and distinct that we can have no further doubt as to what we understand; or, what amounts to the same thing, an indubitable conception of the unclouded and attentive mind which arises from the light of reason alone, and is more certain than deduction itself, even though we have noted above that human beings cannot make errors in deduction. Thus everyone can intuit in his mind that he exists, that he thinks, that a triangle is bounded by three lines, that a sphere has only one surface, and other similar things, of which there are many more than most people notice because they disdain to consider such simple matters. (369)

For the rest, lest anyone should be disturbed by this new usage of the word "intuition" and of other words which I am similarly forced to use in an uncommon sense in the following pages, I give notice that in general I pay no attention to the manner in which words are made use of in these recent times in the schools, because it would be very difficult to use the same meanings when the inner conception is so different.

---

[1] The manuscripts here read "induction," and this reading is perfectly acceptable if this paragraph is read in isolation. But the author's further elucidation makes it clear that "deduction" is meant.

Rather, I will pay attention to what each word means in Latin, so that, in so far as appropriate ones are lacking, I will convert to my meaning whichever seem to me to be most suitable.

But in truth this evidence and certainty of intuition is not only necessary for the enunciation of individual propositions; it is also necessary for any implications. Thus, for example, if we consider the conclusion that 2 and 2 are the same as 3 and 1, we must not only intuit that 2 and 2 make 4 and that 3 and 1 also make 4, but, in addition, that the third proposition necessarily follows from these two.

At this point it may be questioned why we have another method of knowing beyond intuition, that is, "deduction," by which we understand everything which is necessarily concluded from other premises which are known with certainty. We had to assert this because many things are known with certainty although they are not evident in themselves for the sole reason that they are deduced from true and known principles by a continuous and uninterrupted process of thought, in which each part of the process is clearly intuited. In the same way we recognize that the last link of some long chain is connected with the first link, even though we do not notice at one and the same glance (370) all the intermediate links upon which this connection depends, but have only examined them in sequence and remember that each of them is connected with its neighbors from the first to the last. We can therefore distinguish an intuition of the mind from certain deduction by the fact that in the latter we perceive a movement or a certain succession of thought, while we do not in the former; and furthermore, because present evidence is not necessary to the latter, as it is to intuition, but rather, in a certain measure, it derives its certainty from memory. From this it follows that certain propositions which are immediately derived from first principles can be said to be known in different ways, now by intuition, now by deduction. But the first principles themselves are known only by intuition, while, on the other hand, ultimate conclusions are known only by deduction.

And these two methods are the most certain paths to knowledge, and no others should be admitted by the intellect. All other ways ought to be rejected as suspect and as liable to error; but this nevertheless does not prevent us from believing that those things which are divinely revealed are more certain than any other knowledge, since faith in them, to whatever extent they are obscure, is not an act of the intellect, but of the will. If this faith has some basis in the intellect, it can be, and, more than anything else, ought to be, found by one or the other of the methods already described, as we may perhaps explain sometime at greater length. (371)

RULE IV

Method is necessary for discovering the truths of nature.

Mortals are endowed with so blind a curiosity that they often let their minds wander through unknown paths without any ground for hope, just being willing to suffer danger wherever that which they are seeking may be hidden. It is as though someone were so inflamed with the senseless desire of finding a treasure that he constantly wanders through the streets, seeking whether he may, perchance, find something that a passerby has lost. This is the way in which almost all chemists, many geometricians, and not a few philosophers pursue their studies; and while I do not deny that they may sometimes wander so felicitously that they discover some truth, nevertheless I do not concede that they are, on that account, any more diligent, but only more fortunate. It is much more satisfactory never to think of searching for the truth about anything than to make the search without method, for it is absolutely certain that by disorderly studies of this sort, and by obscure meditations, the natural light is confused and our minds are blinded; and whoever thus becomes accustomed to

wander in the dark so weakens the power of his eyes that later
he cannot bear the full light of day. This is confirmed by experience, for we very often see that those who have never
pursued their studies seriously make much firmer and clearer
judgments of things at hand than do those who have been
continuously trained in the schools.

By "method," I mean rules so clear and simple that anyone (372) who uses them carefully will never mistake the
false for the true, and will waste no mental effort; but by
gradually and regularly increasing his knowledge, will arrive
at the true knowledge of all those things which he is capable
of knowing.

Two more things should also be noted here: that nothing
actually false should be taken as true, and that we should
arrive at the knowledge of everything. Because, if we are ignorant of some one of the things we are able to know, this
ignorance can only be attributed to our failure to notice a
path which would have led us to such knowledge, or to our
falling into a contrary error. But if our method correctly explains how intuition is to be used so that we do not fall into
the latter error, and how deductions are to be discovered so
that we reach the knowledge of everything, it seems that nothing is lacking for it to be complete, since no knowledge can
be attained except by intuition or deduction, as has been said
before. For method cannot be extended to teach how these
operations themselves are to be performed, because they are
the simplest and most elemental of all and, unless our intellect
is already able to make use of them, it will not comprehend any
instructions on how to use them, however simple. Moreover, the
other rules, by the aid of which logic tries to direct the operations of the mind, are useless here, or rather are to be considered hindrances, (373) because nothing can be added to the
pure light of reason which does not in some manner obscure it.

Therefore, since the usefulness of this method is so great
that in its absence to take pains with studies seems to be
harmful rather than profitable, I am forced to conclude that
the greater minds have already in some fashion discovered

it, or have been led to it by nature alone. For the human mind has a certain touch of divinity in which the first seeds of useful thought already lie, so that often, no matter how much they are neglected and suffocated by interfering studies, they spontaneously produce fruit. We experience this in the easiest branches of knowledge, arithmetic and geometry, for it is sufficiently evident that the ancient geometricians made use of some kind of analysis which they extended to the solution of all problems, even though they begrudged it to posterity. And there now flourishes a certain kind of arithmetic called "algebra," for demonstrating in the area of numbers that which the ancients were wont to do in the area of figures. And these two are nothing else but the fruit sprung spontaneously from the principles engendered by our method; and I am not surprised that among all the arts, these two, concerned with the simplest objects, have thus far grown more satisfactorily than have the others, which are frequently suffocated by their greater difficulties. We can hardly doubt, nevertheless, that even these, if they are cultivated with the greatest care, will attain a more perfect development.

This is what I had especially in mind to accomplish in writing this treatise; for I would not think much of these rules if they were not sufficient to do anything but solve those useless problems with which logicians or geometricians play when they have nothing better to occupy their time. For in that case I would believe that I excelled in no other way than that I could perhaps trifle more subtly than others do. And although (374) I speak a good deal here of figures and numbers, since in no other disciplines can we find so evident and so certain examples, nevertheless anyone who pays close attention to my meaning will easily observe that I am not thinking at all of common mathematics, but am setting forth a certain new discipline of which these illustrations are the outer husk rather than the kernel. For this discipline ought to contain the first rudiments of human reason, and be broad enough to bring out the truths of any subject whatsoever. And to speak freely, I am persuaded that it is a more powerful tool for the acquisition of knowledge than any other handed down to us in the human tradition, since it is the source of all others. And when I spoke of the husks, it was not that I wished to cover this doctrine with one, and to hide it from the public; I would rather clothe and adorn it, so that it could be more acceptable to the human mind.

When I first turned my attention to the mathematical disciplines, I thoroughly and continuously examined much of what the authors who treat of them usually discuss, and I particularly cultivated arithmetic and geometry because they were said to be the simplest of them, and, (375) as it were, the pathway to the others. But in neither discipline did I happen to come upon writers who were altogether satisfactory. I did, indeed, read in them many things about numbers which I found by computation to be true; and in a way they showed many things about figures which struck the eye, and from which they deduced appropriate consequences; but they did not seem to show with sufficient intellectual clarity why these things were so and how they were discovered. And I was therefore not surprised that many people, even some of the most intelligent and studious, either neglected these arts, disparaging them as vain and childish, or, on the contrary, were discouraged from commencing their study by hearing that they are very difficult and intricate. For in reality nothing is more futile than to be so learned about abstract numbers and imaginary figures that we seem willing to be satisfied with the knowledge of such abstractions; and so to devote ourselves to these superficial demonstrations, which are more often discovered by accident than by skill and are more concerned with the eyes and the imagination than with the intellect, that we become to some extent unaccustomed to making use of reason itself. At the same time there is nothing more perplexing than the attempt to clarify the new difficulties which arise from the confusion of numbers in such a method of proof. But later, when I wondered why it happened that the first discoverers of philosophy in earlier times wished to admit no one to the study of wisdom who was unskilled in mathematics, since this discipline (376) seemed the easiest approach of all and very necessary to educating and preparing the mind for understanding the other major branches of knowledge, I strongly suspected that what they recognized as mathematics was very different from that which people accept in our times. I did not think that they knew this perfectly, for their foolish and excessive festivals and rejoicings over the slightest discoveries clearly show how ignorant they were. Nor am I turned from this opinion by certain of their devices which were celebrated in history; for if there were, perhaps, some very simple ones, they could easily be exalted by the ignorant and astonished throng into reputed miracles. But I am persuaded that there are certain basic roots of truth implanted in the human mind by nature, which we extinguish in ourselves daily by reading and hearing many and varied errors; and that these were so powerful in that unpolished and simple age of antiquity that the ancients saw by this light of the mind how virtue was to be preferred to pleasure and honesty to utility, even though they were ignorant why this was so; and they also recognized true ideas in philosophy and mathematics, although they could never achieve true mastery of these sciences. And, indeed, some traces of this true mathematics seem to me to be found in Pappus [1] and Diophantus,[2] who lived, if not in the earliest ages, at least many centuries before these present times. Indeed, I could readily believe that this mathematics was suppressed by these writers with a certain pernicious craftiness, just as we know many inventors have suppressed their discoveries, being very much afraid that to publish the method, since it was quite easy and simple, would make it seem worthless. And I believe they preferred to show us in its place, as the product of their art, certain barren truths which they cleverly demonstrate deductively so that we should admire them, (377) rather than teach us the method itself, which would indeed detract from the admiration. Finally, there were certain very ingenious men who tried to revive the same practice in this century, for that

---

[1] Greek algebraist of Alexandria, circa third century.
[2] Greek geometrician of Alexandria, circa third century.

art appears to be nothing else but what they call by the barbarous name of algebra, which, if it could be freed from the vast array of numbers and inexplicable figures with which it is overrun, would no longer lack that clarity and great simplicity of application which we presume should characterize the true mathematics.

When these thoughts had led me from the study of arithmetic and geometry in particular to an investigation of mathematics in general, I sought first to learn what, precisely, everyone understands by that name, and why not only the subjects already mentioned, but also astronomy, music, optics, mechanics, and many others are said to be parts of mathematics. And here it was not enough to consider the origin of the word, for since the name "mathematics" means the same thing as learning, the other disciplines [3] are called mathematical with no less propriety than geometry itself. But we observe that there is hardly anyone, even among those who have barely commenced their studies, who does not easily distinguish which of the subjects he considers to belong to mathematics, and which to other disciplines. But as I considered this more attentively, it finally became clear that only those subjects (378) in which order or measure are considered are regarded as mathematical, and it makes no difference whether such measure is sought in numbers, or figures, or stars, or sounds, or any other object whatever. It then follows that there must be a certain general science which explains everything which can be asked about order and measure, and which is concerned with no particular subject matter, and that this very thing is called "pure [4] mathematics," not by an arbitrary appellation, but by a usage which is already accepted and of long standing, because in it is contained everything on account of which other sciences are called "parts of mathematics." How much this science surpasses both in usefulness and in facility the others which are subordinate to it is apparent from the fact that it

[3] "The other disciplines" is a phrase missing in the original, but supplied by many commentators.

[4] Lit., "universal."

is concerned with everything with which the latter are concerned, and many other things in addition; and if it contains any difficulties, the same exist in the others; in addition to this the latter have their own difficulties derived from their particular subject matters, which pure mathematics does not. Now everyone knows the name of mathematics, and understands what it is about, even if he is not a student of it: so how does it happen that many people laboriously pursue the other disciplines which depend upon it, but no one cares to pursue mathematics itself? I would indeed be surprised, if I did not know that it is considered very simple by everyone, and if I had not noticed long ago that the human mind, putting aside those things in which it believes that it can easily excel, constantly hastens on to new and more impressive matters.

But, conscious of my limitations, I decided pertinaciously to follow an order in seeking knowledge of the world (379) in which I always begin with the simplest and easiest things, and never proceed to the rest until it seems to me that nothing further remains to be sought concerning the simple ones. Because of this I have hitherto cultivated this pure mathematics as much as my abilities permitted, so that I think I can deal with more profound sciences a little later and not do so prematurely. But before I make this advance, I will try to bring together whatever I have noticed to be more worthy of attention in my previous studies, and put them in order, so that at some future time, when my memory is weakened by increasing age, I can, if need be, readily be reminded of them by referring to this book, and also so that at the present time my memory can be relieved of these things and I can more freely pay attention to what remains to be studied.

RULE V

Method consists entirely in the order and arrangement of those things upon which the power of the mind is to be concentrated in order to discover some truth. And we will follow this method exactly if we reduce complex and obscure propositions step by step to simpler ones and then try to advance by the same gradual process from the intuitive understanding of the very simplest to the knowledge of all the rest.

In this one rule is contained the sum of all human endeavor, and it is to be followed no less in (380) acquiring the knowledge of nature than is the thread of Theseus in entering the labyrinth. But many persons do not reflect upon the principle which is here laid down, or they do not know it at all, or they presume that they have no need of it. Thus they often examine difficult questions out of order, which seems to me to be the same as though they strove to jump from the bottom to the top of some edifice in one leap, either neglecting the staircase which is provided for this purpose or not noticing it. This is the way all astrologers act who hope to be able to predict the results of heavenly motions without any knowledge of the heavens, and without even observing their motions accurately. This is the way many do who study mechanics apart from physics, and rashly invent new instruments for initiating motion. So also do those philosophers who neglect experience and believe that truth will arise from their own heads as Minerva did from that of Jove.

And, indeed, all these persons obviously violate this rule. But because the order which is here sought is often so obscure and intricate that not everyone can recognize it, it is hardly possible to be sufficiently careful not to go wrong, unless we carefully follow what is set forth in the following proposition.

RULE VI

In order to distinguish the simplest things from complex ones and to put them in order, we should observe in every series of propositions in which we have directly deduced some truths from others, which one is the simplest of all, and how far from this one each of the others is removed, either more, or less, or equally.

Even though this proposition appears to teach nothing new, it nevertheless contains the principal secret of the art, and there is nothing more useful in the whole of this treatise. For it shows that all propositions can be arranged in such a series, not indeed insofar as they are referred to particular classes of entities, as philosophers divide them into categories, but for purposes of investigation. Some of them can be distinguished from others in such a way that, whenever some difficulty arises, we can immediately notice whether it will be worth while to examine some other propositions first, and which ones, and in what order.

Moreover, so that this can be done correctly, we must first notice that all things in the sense in which they are pertinent to our purposes, that is, where we do not consider their natures in isolation, but where we compare them to each other in order to deduce some from others, may be said to be either absolute or relative.

I call "absolute" whatever contains in itself the pure and simple essence with which we are concerned; such as all which is considered as independent, causal, simple, universal, unitary, equal, similar, straight, or as having other qualities of this sort; and I call "the absolute" itself that which is the simplest (382) and clearest of all, and which we can therefore use in solving further problems.

And the "relative" is that which, while having the same nature or at least participating in it to some degree, is secondary in that it can be traced back to the absolute, and deduced from it by some chain of reasoning. But, in addition, it involves in its conception certain other things which I call "relations," such as whatever is said to be dependent, resultant, compound, particular, multiple, unequal, dissimilar, oblique, and the like. And these relative things are the further removed from the absolute, the more such relational qualities they contain in subordination to one another. We are warned in this rule that all these things should be distinguished, and that their connections with one another and the natural order among them should be observed, so that we can pass from the last to the most absolute by traversing all the other steps.

In this respect, the secret of the entire method consists in the fact that in all things we diligently note that which is most absolute. For from some points of view certain things are more absolute than others, while from another point of view they are more relative; just as the universal is more absolute than the particular, because it has a simpler essence, but at the same time it can be said to be more relative, because it depends upon individuals for its existence, and so on. In the same way, certain things are actually more absolute than others, but nevertheless are not the most absolute of all. Thus, if we consider individuals, the species is something absolute, but if we consider the genus, the species is something relative; and thus, among measurable objects, extension is something absolute, but among dimensions, length is, (383) and so forth. In the same way, finally, in order to understand more fully that we are considering the series of hypotheses and not the nature of each of them individually, we have intentionally listed cause and equality among the absolutes, although their nature is really relational; for although among philosophers cause and effect are correlative, if we inquire how a particular thing is really an effect, we must first recognize the cause, and not the other way around. Equals, moreover, are correlative with each other, but we recognize that things are unequal only by comparing them with equals, and not the other way around.

We should note, second, that there are very few pure and simple essences which can be recognized at first and in themselves, independently of all others, either by means of our experience of them or by some intuitive light in ourselves; and we say that these should be carefully noted, for they are the essences which we term the simplest of all in any series whatsoever. Moreover, all other things can only be perceived as being deduced from these, whether immediately and directly, or only through two or three or more intermediate conclusions; and the number of these intermediate conclusions should be noted, in order to recognize whether these things are separated by many or by few steps from the first and most simple proposition. And everywhere we look, this deductive relationship from which arises that chain of hypotheses to which every question should be reduced, is such that it can be investigated with certainty by our method. But because it is not (384) easy to recollect everything, and, in addition, because these things are not so much retained in the memory as discerned by a sort of sharpness of insight, we should seek whatever will so train our intelligence that it will immediately notice as many of these things as necessary. For this purpose, I have found nothing more appropriate than for us to accustom ourselves to reflect, with a certain sagacity, upon every least item of those things which we have previously discovered.

Then we should note, third, that we should not begin our studies with the investigation of difficult matters; but, before we prepare ourselves for certain problems we have decided to tackle, we should first freely and unselectively collect obvious truths and later see whether we can deduce some other truths step by step from these, then some more from those newly deduced, and so on. Then, when this has been done, we should reflect attentively upon the truths discovered, and carefully consider why we were able to discover some earlier and more easily than others, and which ones they were. We can then judge, when we attack some question that we have selected for study, what other things it would be useful to consider first. For example, if it should occur to me that the number six is twice three, I might then inquire what is twice six, namely twelve; and inquire again, if I please, as to its double, namely twenty-four, and the latter's, namely forty-eight, and so on. And from this I might quite easily deduce that the same proportion exists between three and six as between six and twelve, and the same between twelve and twenty-four, and thus that the numbers 3, 6, 12, 24, 48, and so on form a geometrical series. And although all these things are so obvious that they seem almost childish, I understand by carefully considering them, (385) how all questions which can be asked about the proportions or the characteristics of things are related, and in what order they should be asked; and this one thing sums up the whole science of pure mathematics.

For I notice, first of all, that it was not more difficult to discover the double of six than the double of three; and similarly in all cases: as soon as we have discovered a ratio between any two numbers, innumerable others can be found which have the same ratio between them. Nor is the degree of difficulty changed if three or four or more numbers of this kind are sought, because each one of them must be found by itself and with no regard for those remaining. And then I notice that, although when the numbers three and six have been given, you easily discover a third in the same proportion, namely twelve, nevertheless it is not so easy to discover the mean, namely six, when the two extremes, three and twelve, are given; and the reason for this lies open to the discerning mind, in that this is another kind of difficulty, clearly different from the preceding one. This is because, in order to discover the mean proportional, we must simultaneously pay attention to the two extremes and to the ratio between them, in order to obtain something new from the division of the latter; and this is clearly different from what is required when two magnitudes are given, in order to discover a third member of the geometrical series. I will even pursue this further and examine whether, when the two numbers three and twenty-four are given, we can find equally easily one of the two mean proportionals, namely six and (386) twelve. A new kind of difficulty occurs here, more involved than the earlier ones, for here we do not have to pay attention to only one or to two, but to three different things simultaneously in order to find a fourth. Let us continue even further to see whether, when only three and forty-eight are given, it would be still more difficult to find one of the three mean proportionals, namely six, twelve, and twenty-four, as it would seem at first glance. But we can soon notice that this difficulty can be divided and diminished, for we can seek at first only the single mean proportional between three and forty-eight, namely twelve, and later seek another mean proportional between three and twelve, namely six, and another between twelve and forty-eight, namely twenty-four, and thus reduce the difficulty to the second kind already described.

In all the above I notice how the knowledge of the same thing may be sought in different ways, one of which is much more difficult and more obscure than the other. In finding the progressive ratio of the four numbers, three, six, twelve, and twenty-four, in order to discover the remaining members of the series from these, the task will be most easily accomplished if we separate from them a pair of adjacent numbers, such as three and six, or six and twelve, or twelve and twenty-four, and in this case we say that the proportion to be discovered is examined directly. But if we should take two alternate numbers, such as three and twelve or six and twenty-four, then we say that the difficulty is examined indirectly by the first method. If in the same way the two extremes are taken, namely three and twenty-four, so that the intermediates six and twelve are sought from these, then it will be examined (387) indirectly by the second method. And I might continue further in this way and deduce many other things from this one example, but these suffice for the reader to understand what I mean when I say that a proposition is deduced directly or indirectly, and for him to know how, from the knowledge of the simplest and most basic things, many things, even in other disciplines, can be discovered by careful reflection and wise investigation.

RULE VII

For the consummation of knowledge it is necessary to examine each and every item which pertains to our design in a continuous and uninterrupted process of thought and to include all of these in an adequate and orderly enumeration.

The observation of the points here proposed is necessary before we can admit as known those truths which we have previously said were not immediate consequences of first and self-evident principles. For this may sometimes be accomplished through such a long chain of inferences that when we have arrived at the conclusions we do not easily remember the whole procedure which led us to them; and thus we say that we must come to the assistance of our weak memory by means of a certain continuous process of thought. If, therefore, for example, by means of various procedures I should first recognize what the relation between the magnitudes A and B is, then between B and C, then between C and D, and finally between D and E, I do not on that account see the relation between (388) A and E, nor can I deduce it precisely from the relationships I already know, unless I remember all of them. Because of this, I have learned to consider each of these steps by a certain continuous process of the imagination, thinking of one step and at the same time passing on to others. Thus I go from first to last so quickly that by entrusting almost no parts of the process to the memory, I seem to grasp the whole series at once. The memory is assisted by this device, and at the same time the sluggishness of the intellect is lessened, and its ability is in some measure increased.

We must add, however, that this process should be nowhere interrupted, for frequently those who strive to deduce something too quickly and from distantly related principles do not cover the whole chain of intermediate conclusions with sufficient accuracy to avoid passing over many points without adequate consideration. But clearly, when the least part that you choose is omitted, the whole chain is immediately broken, and all the certainty of the conclusion falls to the ground.

We say, furthermore, that enumeration is required in order to complete our knowledge, since other precepts aid somewhat in resolving many problems, but only with the aid of enumeration is it possible always to reach a true and certain judgment about whatsoever engages our attention, and in the same way it is clear that nothing escapes us, but that we seem to have some knowledge of the whole matter.

This enumeration or induction ought therefore to be so careful and accurate a search for all things which bear upon any suggested inquiry that we can certainly and clearly conclude from it that we have omitted nothing by oversight. In consequence, whenever we have (389) used this method, if the desired knowledge escapes us, we are at least wiser in that we clearly perceive that there is no known way in which it can be discovered by us. And if perchance—as often happens— we are able to examine all the paths to this goal which lie open to human beings, we could boldly affirm that the knowledge of this thing lies beyond the power of the human mind.

We should take note, furthermore, that by a sufficient enumeration or induction we only mean one from which a truth can be reached with greater certainty than by any other kind of proof except simple intuition. Whenever a certain problem cannot be solved by intuition, and we have eliminated the possibility of dealing with it by syllogisms, only one path is open to us, and in this we should place our complete confidence. For whenever one proposition is deduced directly from others, it has been known by a true intuition if the inference was evident. But if what we infer is based on many and various items, it often happens that the capacity of our intellect is not great enough to comprehend all of it in a single act of intuition; and for this reason the evidence of the process of enumeration must be sufficient. This is how we proceed in the case of some long chain, all the separate links of which we cannot distinguish at one glance; but nevertheless if we notice the connection of each one of them with its neighbors we are able to say that we have seen how the first and the last links are connected.

I have said that this process must be sufficient because it can often be defective and, consequently, is subject to error. For occasionally, even if we carefully enumerate a large number of items which are quite evident, nevertheless if (390) we have omitted the least one, the chain is broken, and all the certainty of the conclusion is destroyed. At times, also, everything is indeed included in the enumeration, but we do not distinguish each item from all the rest, so that we know the whole only confusedly.

Furthermore, this enumeration must sometimes be complete, sometimes distinct, and sometimes there is no need of either quality; and that is why we have said only that it ought to be sufficient. For if I wish to establish by enumeration how many kinds of entities are corporeal, or are in some manner perceptible, I will not assert that they are just this many and no more unless I can first know with certainty that I have included everything in the enumeration and have distinguished each from the rest. But if I wish to show in the same way that the rational mind is not corporeal, it is not necessary for the enumeration to be complete, but it is sufficient if all bodies are divided together in several categories so that I show that the rational mind can belong to none of them. Finally, if I wish to show by enumeration that the area of a circle is greater than the areas of any other figures of equal periphery, it is not necessary to consider every possible figure, but it is enough to demonstrate this about some figures in particular, and conclude by induction that the same is true of all others.

I have also added that the enumeration should be methodical; not only because there is no more effective remedy for the defects already discussed than if we scrutinize everything in an orderly fashion, but also because it often happens that if (391) we had to examine individually each separate item which bears on the problem, no man's life would be long enough, either because there are too many items or more frequently because the same items occur over and over again.

But if we arrange all of these in the best possible way in order to reduce them to certain classes, it may be sufficient to examine carefully perhaps one of these, or perhaps something about each one, or some rather than all the rest; at any rate, we shall never unnecessarily examine the same one more than once. And this method is so helpful that often, when the order has been properly arranged, many things can be quickly and easily examined which at first glance appeared to be overwhelming.

Moreover, the order in which things are to be investigated frequently admits of variation, and depends upon the decision of each person, so that to arrange matters most profitably we should recollect what has been said in the fifth rule. There are also among men many trivial games which depend entirely for their solution upon the method used to attack them; thus if you wish to make the best anagram from the letters of someone's name, it is not necessary to go from the evident to the most difficult, nor to distinguish the absolute from the relative, for these are not involved here; but it will suffice to arrange such an order for examining the transpositions of the letters that we never try the same ones twice, and so that they are grouped in such classes that it is immediately apparent in which there is the greater chance of finding what we are seeking, for thus the task will often be not long, but childishly simple. (392)

For the rest, these last three rules should not be separated, because most commonly they must all be considered simultaneously, and all contribute equally to the perfection of the method. Nor does it make much difference which is explained first. We have discussed them here only briefly, because there is little else left to consider in the rest of this treatise, which will present in detail what we have explained here in general.

RULE VIII

If, in a series of things being investigated, we come upon one which our intellect cannot adequately comprehend, we must immediately call a halt. We should not examine what follows, but refrain from a useless task.

The three preceding rules prescribe and explain order; this one shows, in addition, when it is absolutely necessary and when it is only convenient. For whatever constitutes an entire rank in this series, by which we must travel from the relative to the absolute or in the other direction, must necessarily be examined before any which follow. But if, as often happens, many things belong to the same rank, it is still always useful to examine them all in order. Nevertheless, we are not strictly and rigidly required to adhere to this, and most of the time (393) we can progress further even if we do not understand clearly all of these, but only a few or even one.

This rule follows necessarily from the reasons given for the second. Nevertheless we should not assume that this one contains nothing new which can be used for the advancement of knowledge, even though it seems only to warn us away from the investigation of certain things and not to set forth any new truth. As far as tyros are concerned, it teaches them only how not to lose their labor, in almost the same way as the second rule; but those who fully understand the preceding seven rules learn from this one how they can so satisfy themselves, in any science whatsoever, that they will desire nothing more. For whoever follows the previous rules exactly in the solution of some difficulty, and nevertheless is directed to cease by this last one, knows with certainty that he could not have discovered the desired knowledge by any effort whatsoever. He has been kept from this discovery, not by a fault of his mind, but by the nature of the difficulty itself, or by his nature as a human being. And this recognition is no less knowledge than that which reveals the nature of the object itself; and the person who carried his curiosity further would betray a lack of judgment.

All these things should be illustrated by an example or two. If, for instance, someone who was a student of mathematics alone sought that line which in optics is called "anaclastic," (394) in which parallel rays are so refracted that they all intersect each other in a single point after the refraction, he will readily notice, following rules five and six, that the determination of this line depends upon the relation which the angles of refraction bear to the angles of incidence. But, because he will not be competent to investigate this, since it pertains not to mathematics but to physics, he will be forced to stop here at the threshold, nor would it be of any help if he desired to obtain this information from philosophers or to find it by experiment, for he would violate the third rule. Furthermore, this proposition is composite and relative; and it is only concerning genuinely simple and absolute matters that we can have certain knowledge, as we will explain in the proper place. It would also be useless to conjecture a certain relationship between angles of this kind which is presumed to be the most probably true, for then he would no longer be seeking the anaclastic, but only the line which fits the nature of his beliefs.

But if a person who is not a student of mathematics alone, but who, obedient to the first rule, desires to seek the truth about everything he encounters, comes upon the same difficulty, he will discover further that this relationship between the angles of incidence and of refraction itself varies according to the kind of media involved [1] and that this variation depends in turn on how the ray of light penetrates through the whole transparent body. The knowledge of this penetration suggests that the nature of illumination (395) must also be known; then, in order to understand illumination, he must

[1] Lit., "This relationship between the angles of incidence and of refraction depends upon their variation on account of the variety of media."

know what a natural power is in general—the final term which
is the most absolute in this whole series. Therefore, after
he has clearly understood this by an intuition of the mind, he
will go through the same steps, up to rule five; and as soon as
he finds that he cannot understand the nature of illumination
in the second step, he should enumerate, in conformity with
rule seven, all other natural powers, so that from the recognition of some others he may understand this one also, at least
by analogy, which I shall discuss later. Having done this, he
will inquire how the ray penetrates through the whole transparent body, and so will follow through the whole sequence
until he arrives at last at the anaclastic itself. Even though
this line has been sought by many, so far in vain, nevertheless
I see nothing which could prevent someone who makes perfect use of our method from achieving a clear knowledge of it.

But let us give the noblest example of all. If someone takes
for his problem the examination of all truths which human
reason is capable of knowing—which it seems to me should be
done once in his life by everyone who seriously strives to develop wisdom—he will surely discover through the rules given
that nothing can be known prior to the intellect itself, since
the knowledge of all other things depends upon this, and not
conversely. Then, when he has examined all those things
which follow directly from the knowledge of the pure intellect, he will, among other things, enumerate whatever other
means of knowing we possess in addition to the intellect; and
there are only two of these, namely, (396) imagination and
sensation. He will therefore employ all his efforts in distinguishing and examining these three methods of knowing and,
seeing that truth or falsity, properly speaking, cannot exist
except in the intellect alone, but often derive their origin from
the other two, he will pay great attention to all the ways in
which he can be deceived, in order to be on guard against
them. And he will enumerate carefully all the paths to truth
which lie open to men, so that he may follow the certain one:
for there are not so many of them but that he can easily, by

means of a sufficient enumeration, find all of them. And it will seem marvelous and incredible to the uninitiated that he will have immediately distinguished the items of information concerning each object which only burden or adorn the memory from items which, if possessed, will entitle one to be termed generally more erudite. And this can be readily understood.[2]

This man will recognize fully that there is nothing further of which he is ignorant because of a lack of intelligence or of skill, and that there is absolutely nothing that can be known by another man of which he is not also capable, provided only that he applies his mind to the same thing in the proper way. And although many things can often be proposed to him, the investigation of which is forbidden by the present rule, he will nevertheless not consider himself more ignorant, because he clearly perceives that those same things exceed the capabilities of the human mind. The very fact that he knows that the matter under inquiry can be known by no one, will, if he is sensible, abundantly satisfy his curiosity.

And lest we should remain forever uncertain as to what our mind can compass, and lest it should make ill-advised and foolish efforts, we must, for once in our lives, before setting ourselves to discover particular truths, make careful inquiry into what knowledge (397) the human reason is capable of discovering. And in order to accomplish this better, we should always investigate first, as between things of equal difficulty, those which are more useful.

This method somewhat resembles those of the mechanical arts which do not require the assistance of others, but themselves show how their tools are to be made. For if anyone wished to ply one of these trades, that of the blacksmith, for example, and lacked all instruments, he would be forced at first to use a hard stone or some unshaped mass of unwrought iron as an anvil, to take a rock instead of a hammer, to pre-

---

[2] In the margin of the manuscripts is written: "Hic deficit aliquid" (something is missing here).

pare wood as tongs, and to arrange other things as they may
be necessary. Then when these things have been done, he will
not immediately attempt to forge swords or helmets or any
of those things which are made of iron for others to use, but
before anything else will make hammers, an anvil, tongs, and
other tools useful to himself. We are taught by this example
that when in these first attempts we have been able to discover
nothing but rather confused precepts which seem innate in
our minds rather than skillfully derived, we should not immediately try by the aid of these to settle the disputes of
philosophers or to solve the difficulties of mathematicians, but
they should first be used in searching diligently for whatever
other things are most necessary for the examination of truth.
This is particularly true since there is no reason why it would
seem more difficult to discover these things than it would be to
solve any of the other problems usually propounded in geometry or physics or in other disciplines.

In fact, there is nothing more useful to inquire about than
the nature and limits of human knowledge. And therefore all
our search now reduces to the single question which (398) we
evaluate as the one which should be examined before all
others according to the rules previously laid down. This inquiry should be undertaken once in his life by any person
who has the slightest regard for the truth, because in this investigation is contained the true means and the whole method
of acquiring knowledge. Moreover, nothing seems more ab-
surd to me than rashly to dispute about the secrets of nature,
the influence of the stars on the world below, the prediction
of future events, and similar things, as many do, and yet never
to have made any investigation as to whether human reason
is capable of discovering these things. Nor should it appear
to be a tedious or difficult task to define the limits of the mind
in dealing with what we feel within ourselves, as we often
have no hesitation in making this judgment about what is
outside of ourselves and completely alien. Nor is it an enormous task to try to grasp in thought everything which is con-

tained in this universe, in order to recognize how each one of them is subject to examination by our mind, for nothing can be so complex or varied that we cannot, by means of that enumeration with which we are concerned, delimit them within certain bounds and place them in a certain number of categories. In order to do this in the matter under discussion, we first divide all the pertinent facts into two classes, for each one should be related, either to us who are capable of thinking, or to the matters which can be known; and we will discuss these two categories separately.

We notice in ourselves that the intellect alone is capable of knowledge; but it can be aided or impeded by three other faculties, namely, imagination, sensation, and memory.[3] We must therefore consider, in order, what each of these faculties can do to impede us, so that (399) we may be on guard against these possibilities, and what they can do to aid us, so that we may employ their full assistance. And thus this part of our inquiry will be discussed by the use of an adequate enumeration, as will be shown in the following rule.[4]

Then we must come to reality itself, which must be considered only in so far as it can be dealt with by the intellect. From this point of view we divide real things into those which have very simple essences and those which are complex or composite. No essences can belong to the simple class unless they are either spiritual or corporeal or both. Then, in the composite class, the intellect must experience what some of them are before it can make any judgments about them; others of this class are invented by the intellect itself. All of these things will be explained more fully in the twelfth rule, where it will be demonstrated that there can be no falsity except in the last type, which is invented by the intellect. This composite class we therefore further divide into those which are deduced from

---

[3] It has been suggested that the passage which begins here, naming three associated faculties, may have been intended to be substituted for the previous passage which names only two. (See p. 31 [396]; see also p. 44 [411].)

[4] This enumeration actually appears in Rules XII and XIV.

the simplest essences and which are self-evident, about which we will be concerned in the whole following book; and those which presuppose others which we discover empirically to be composite, to the explanation of which we plan to devote the whole third book.[5]

And in the entire treatise we shall strive to follow so accurately and explain so simply all paths which lie open to men for the knowledge of truth that anyone who has learned this whole method perfectly, however humble his abilities may be, will nevertheless perceive that none of these ways is less open to him (400) than to anyone else, and that there is nothing further of which he is ignorant because of any failure of ability or method. But whenever he applies his mind to any problem, he will either solve it completely or he will observe that it depends upon some experiment which it is not within his power to perform, and he can therefore not be blamed for being compelled to stop at that point; or, finally, he will show that the desired information is altogether beyond the capacity of the human mind [6] and therefore he will not be thought more ignorant, because the knowledge of limitation is no less truly knowledge than is any other sort.

RULE IX

We should bring the whole force of our minds to bear upon the most minute and simple details and to dwell upon them for a long time so that we become accustomed to perceive the truth clearly and distinctly.

Having set forth the two operations of our intellect, intuition and deduction, upon which alone we have said we can depend for the acquisition of knowledge, we continue to ex-

---

[5] Each book was to consist of twelve rules, but only Book One was completed. Book Two is represented by the completed rules XIII through XVII; Rule XVIII is incomplete; Rules XIX, XX, and XXI are represented by their titles only; and Rules XXII, XXIII, and XXIV are missing. Book Three does not exist.

[6] Lit., "exceeds the whole capacity of the human mind."

plain, in this and the following rule, how we can render ourselves more able to accomplish this, and at the same time to improve the two principal faculties of the mind, that is, perspicacity in intuiting every object distinctly and sagacity in deducing one thing from another skillfully.

How the intuition of the mind should be used can be learned by a comparison with the perception of the eyes. For whoever tries to observe many objects at the same time with a single glance (401) sees none of them distinctly; and likewise, whoever is accustomed to consider many things at the same time by a single act of the understanding is confused in his mind. But those artisans who work on minute tasks, and are accustomed to direct their glance attentively to a single point, acquire by experience the ability to distinguish any number of minute and tiny objects perfectly. And in the same way those who never divide their attention among many objects at the same time, but always direct it wholly upon the simplest and easiest matters, are the ones who become perspicacious.

It is, moreover, a common failing among mortals to consider difficult matters most attractive; and many consider that they know nothing when they discover a very obvious and simple cause of something, and at the same time admire the sublime and profound reasoning of philosophers, even though this reasoning depends upon principles which have never been sufficiently examined by anyone. How foolish they are who prefer darkness to light! And we should notice that those who truly know recognize each truth with equal ease whether they have derived it from a simple source or from a difficult one, for they comprehend each truth by a similar but unique and distinct act, as soon as they have reached it. The difference lies wholly in the chain of reasoning, which certainly ought to be longer if it leads to a truth further removed from the first and most absolute principles.

Everybody should therefore become accustomed to consider such simple things and so few at a time that they think they never know anything which they do not grasp as distinctly (402) as that which they know most distinctly of all. Some persons, no doubt, are much better equipped at birth to do this than others, but anyone can make himself much more skillful by study and practice. And there is one thing, it seems to me, which should be pointed out above all, namely, that each person should become firmly persuaded that even the most obscure sciences should be deduced, not from impressive and difficult matters, but only from the easy and more obvious ones.

Thus, for example, if I should wish to inquire whether any natural force can travel instantaneously to a distant point and pass through all intermediate points, I will not immediately consider magnetism, nor the influence of the stars, nor even the velocity of light, in order to find out whether these forces are instantaneous, for this would be more difficult to investigate than the original question; but I will rather think about the motion of bodies in space, because nothing in this category can be more apparent. And I will notice that a stone cannot travel instantaneously from one place to another, because it is a body; but that a power, such as that which moves the stone, cannot be communicated otherwise than instantaneously if it goes by itself from one object to another. For example, if I move one end of a very long rod, I easily conceive that the power which moves that end of the rod also necessarily moves all the other parts at the same instant, because then it is communicated by itself, and does not exist in some body, such as the stone, by which it is carried.

In the same way, if I wish to learn how contrary effects can be produced simultaneously by one and the same simple cause, (403) I will not borrow examples from the doctors, whose drugs expel certain humors and retain others; nor will I talk nonsense about the moon, saying that it heats by its light and cools by an occult quality; but rather I will consider a balance, in which the same weight causes one pan to rise at one and the same instant that it depresses the other, and other similar cases.

RULE X

For the mind to become wise, it must have practice in seeking those things which have been previously discovered by others, and in studying methodically even the most trivial human skills, but, above all, those which explain or presuppose order.

I confess that I was born with such a disposition that I always took the greatest delight in studies, not in hearing the arguments of others, but in discovering them by my own devices; and this alone attracted me, as a youth, to the study of the sciences. Whenever some book gave promise, in its title, of a new discovery, I tried, before reading further, whether perchance I could deduce something similar by some inborn sagacity, and I was very careful not to deprive myself of this innocent pleasure by precipitate reading. And I succeeded in this so often that I finally noticed that I no longer achieved knowledge of things, as others usually do, by vague and blind investigations, aided by luck rather than by skill, but that by long experience I had discovered certain rules which aided not a little, and by the use of which I later (404) succeeded in making many discoveries. And so I diligently pursued the whole method, and I was persuaded that from the beginning I had followed the most useful method of studying.

But because not everyone's mind is so disposed by nature to search for truth by his own exertions, this rule teaches us that we ought not to concern ourselves immediately with the more difficult and arduous problems, but that the easiest and simplest should be investigated first. We should especially investigate those arts in which there is more order, such as those of the artisans who weave fabrics and tapestries or those of women who embroider or weave threads in an infinite variety of patterns, and likewise all those numerical games, and everything which pertains to arithmetic and other things of the sort. All of these train the mind admirably, provided we do not owe the solutions of them to others, but to ourselves. For since there is nothing in all these things which remains obscure, and they are entirely within the capacity of the human mind, they offer us very distinct examples of innumerable orders, all different from each other and nevertheless quite regular; and the scrupulous observation of these orders constitutes almost all of human sagacity.

We have therefore pointed out that these things should be pursued with method, which, in these simpler matters, is usually nothing more than careful observation of the order which either exists in the object itself, or is cleverly devised by the intellect. Thus, if we wished to read a writing veiled in unknown characters, we would certainly perceive no order, but nevertheless we can imagine one, both for the purpose of examining all hypotheses we can think of concerning individual letters or words or sentences, and (405) also for that of arranging them so that we can determine by enumeration what can be deduced from them. And we should be very careful not to waste time by trying to guess such matters by chance and without method, for even if such things can often be discovered without skill, and sometimes possibly more rapidly by chance than by method if we are lucky, nevertheless it blunts the acuteness of the mind, and so accustoms it to vain and childish procedures that afterward it always clings to superficialities and cannot penetrate into the heart of things. But neither should we fall into the error of those who occupy their minds only with deep and serious matters, of which, after much effort, they acquire only a confused knowledge, while they hoped for a profound one. It is therefore in these easier matters that we should first exercise our minds, but methodically, so that we become accustomed to penetrate each time, by open and recognized paths and almost as in a game, to the inner truth of things. In this way, soon afterward, and in less time than one could hope, we will find ourselves

able to deduce with equal ease and from self-evident principles, many propositions which appear very difficult and intricate.

But perhaps some will be astonished that in this study,
where we are inquiring how we can be made more competent
to deduce some truths from others, we omit all the rules by
which the logicians think they regulate human reason. These
prescribe certain forms of argument which involve such necessary implications that the mind which relies upon this method,
even though it neglects (406) to give clear and attentive consideration to the reasoning, can nevertheless reach certain conclusions on the strength of the form of the argument alone.
The reason for our omission is that we have noticed that truth
often escapes from these fetters, while at the same time the
persons who use them remain entrapped. This does not happen so frequently to those who are not logicians, and we observe that the cleverest sophistries usually deceive no one who
uses pure reason, but only deceive the sophists themselves.

For this reason, and being particularly careful lest our reason might be deceived when we examine the truth of something, we reject this formal logic as opposed to our teaching,
and seek rather all the aids by which our mind may remain
alert, as will be shown in the sequel. And so that it will be
more evident that the syllogistic art is of practically no assistance in the search for truth, we should notice that logicians
can form no syllogism which reaches a true conclusion unless
the heart of the matter is given, that is, unless they previously
recognized the very truth which is thus deduced. From this it
is clear that the logicians themselves learn nothing new from
such formal procedures, and that ordinary logic is completely
useless to those who seek to investigate the truth of things.
It is only useful for more readily explaining to others principles which are already known. It follows, therefore, that formal
logic should be transferred from philosophy to rhetoric. (407)

RULE XI

After we have recognized several simple propositions by intuition, if we deduce something else from them, it is useful to run through them all by a continuous and uninterrupted process of thought, to consider their connections with one another, and to conceive distinctly as many of them as possible at the same time, for in this way our knowledge is made much more certain and the capacity of our minds is increased as much as possible.

This is the time to explain more clearly what has previously been said about intuition in the third and seventh rules; because in one place we have contrasted it with deduction, and in another only with "enumeration," which we have defined as the inference drawn from many and distinct things, while we have said in the same place that the simple deduction of one thing from another is accomplished by intuition.

We had to proceed in this way, because two things are requisite for intuition; namely, that the proposition be understood clearly and distinctly, and also that it be perceived at one glance and not successively. But deduction, if we consider it as a process as we do in the third rule, does not seem to be accomplished all at once, but rather involves a certain movement of our mind in inferring one thing from another, and therefore we rightly distinguished it from intuition there. But if we consider deduction as already accomplished, (408) as in what was said in rule seven, then it no longer designates a process, but the product of the process, and therefore we suppose that it is perceived by intuition when it is simple and clear, but not when it is complex and involved. To the latter we have given the name of "enumeration" or "induction," because it cannot be understood all at once by the intellect, its certainty depending to some extent upon the memory in which the judgments about each of the parts of the enumeration

must be retained in order that from all of them a single conclusion can be reached.

And all these distinctions had to be made in order to interpret this rule, for, while [1] the ninth rule treats of intuition
alone and the tenth of enumeration alone, the present one explains how these two operations mutually assist and comple-
ment one another. Thus they seem to coalesce into one, in a
certain process of thought which attentively observes each
thing and at the same time passes on to others.

In this we observe a double utility, namely, to know more
certainly the conclusion about which we are concerned, and
to make our minds more capable of discovering other truths.
For because the certainty of any conclusion which contains
more than we can comprehend by a single intuition depends
upon memory, as we have said, and because memory is fleeting
and infirm, it ought to be reconsidered and confirmed by this
continuous and repeated process of thought. Thus, if by many
operations I have first recognized what the relationship is between the first and second quantities, then between the second
and third, then between the third and fourth, (409) and then
between the fourth and fifth, I can not therefore see what is
the relation between the first and the fifth, nor can I deduce
it from what is already known, unless I remember everything
at once. For this reason it is necessary for me to go over them
in thought again and again, until I pass from the first to the
last so quickly that I seem to perceive the whole series simultaneously while entrusting hardly any parts of it to the memory.

Everyone sees that in this way the sluggishness of the mind
is corrected and its grasp enlarged. But, in addition, it should
be noticed that the greatest usefulness of this rule consists in
this fact: that by reflecting upon the mutual dependence of
simple propositions, we acquire the habit of distinguishing immediately which is more or less relative, and by what path it
is reduced to the absolute. For example, if I consider some
numbers in geometrical proportion, I think of all the following:
that it is by the same concept, and neither more nor less easily,

[1] Lit., "after."

that I recognize the relationship between the first and the second, the second and the third, the third and the fourth, and so on, while I cannot as readily conceive what is the dependence of the second upon the first and third together, and it is still much more difficult to conceive that of the second upon the first and the fourth, and so on. From these things, I then recognize why, if the first and the second only are given, I can easily find the third and fourth, and so on, because this is done by individual and distinct conceptions. But if the first and the third only are given, I cannot recognize the mean as readily, (410) because this can only be done by a conception which involves both given numbers at once. If the first and the fourth alone are given, I will recognize the two mean proportionals with still more difficulty, because this involves three concepts at once. In consequence, it would seem even more difficult to find three mean proportionals between the first and the fifth; but there is a reason why it turns out otherwise. Even though there are really four concepts joined together here, they can nevertheless be separated, because four is divisible by another number. For this reason I can seek the third alone as the mean between the first and the fifth, then the second as the mean between the first and the third, and so on. Whoever becomes accustomed to reflect upon these and similar matters will immediately recognize, whenever he examines a new question, what produces the difficulty in it, and what is the very simplest method of solving it and this is of the greatest assistance in learning the truth.

RULE XII

Lastly, we must make use of every assistance of the intellect, the imagination, the senses, and the memory; not only for understanding simple propositions distinctly, but also for correctly comparing what is being sought with what is known, in

*order that they may be recognized; and for finding those things
which ought to be compared with each other, so that no aspect
of human effort is omitted.*

This rule comprehends everything which has been said before, (411) and teaches in general what had to be explained
previously in detail.

For the knowledge of objects, only two things need to be
considered: we who know, and the objects themselves which
are to be known. In us there are only four faculties which we
can use for this purpose, namely, intellect, imagination, sensation, and memory. Only the intellect, of course, is capable
of perceiving truth, but it must make use, nevertheless, of the
imagination, sensation, and memory, if we are not to miss
something which is within our grasp.

In respect to objects, it is sufficient to examine these three
things: first, what is immediately evident; then, how one
thing is learned from another; and finally, what may be further deduced from these. And this enumeration seems complete to me, nor does it omit any things to which the human
mind can attain.

Turning to the first point, then, I would have liked to explain in this place what the human mind is, and what the
body is; how the latter is molded by the former; what the
faculties are which serve in this composite whole for recognizing objects, and what each of these does. But space seems to me
to be too restricted to do all the things which would be pre-
requisite before the truth about these matters could be demonstrated to all. For I always hope to write in such a way that I
assert nothing about controversial matters unless I first set
forth (412) the reasons which have led me to my conclusion,
and by which I believe that others can also be convinced.

But because this is not now possible, it will be enough for
me to explain as briefly as possible which manner of conceiving our powers of recognizing objects will be most useful
for my plan. You need not believe that the facts are thus, unless you choose; but what is to keep you from following these

suppositions, nevertheless, if it appears that they are in no way opposed to the truth about these matters, but only make everything much clearer? It is no different than when in geometry you make certain assumptions about quantity,[1] by which the force of the demonstration is in no way diminished, although you often have a different opinion of its nature in physics.

We must therefore conceive first that all the external senses, in so far as they are parts of the body, perceive only passively, in the same way that wax receives an impression from a seal, even though we apply them to objects by a positive action, that is to say, by motion in space. Nor must it be thought that this is said as an analogy; it must be understood that the external shape of the perceiving body is really changed by the object, just as the shape of the surface of the wax is changed by the seal. This must be accepted not only when we perceive through touch that a body has shape, or is hard, or rough, and so forth; but also when by touch we perceive heat or cold or similar qualities. It is the same with the other senses. For example, the first opaque part of the eye receives a shape impressed upon it by illumination of various colors; and the outer (413) skin of the ears, the nose, and the tongue, impervious to the object, is thus changed into some new shape by sound, odor, and taste.

And it helps a great deal to conceive all these things in this manner, since nothing is more susceptible to examination than shape, for it is both felt and seen. Moreover, that no falsity follows from making this assumption rather than any other is demonstrated by the fact that the concept of shape is so common and simple that it is involved in every perception. For example, suppose that color is whatever you choose, nevertheless you will not deny that it is also extended, and consequently that it has shape. What objection would therefore be entailed, if, guarding against the unnecessary assumption and rash hypothesis of some new entity, we should deny nothing of what others have been pleased to say about color, but only abstract from everything else whatever is of the nature of

[1] The assumption, for example, that quantities are infinitely divisible.

shape, and conceive the differences between white, blue, red, and so forth, as similar to those which exist between the following shapes, or similar ones?

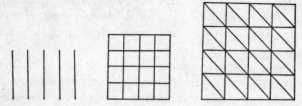

The same can be said about all the senses, since it is certain that the infinite multitude of shapes is sufficient to explain all the differences of perceptible objects.

Second, it must be conceived that when the external senses (414) are affected by an object, the shape which they receive is passed on to some other part of the body, which is called the seat of the senses in common,[2] instantaneously and without the passing of any real entity from one place to another. In exactly the same way I now know, as I write, not only that the lower part of the pen is moved at the same moment in which each character is written on the paper, but also that no slightest motion of this pen can be made without at the same time moving the whole pen. I know that all these various motions are also described in the air by the upper part, even though I understand that no real object has passed from one end to the other. For who would believe that there is less connection between the parts of the human body than between those of a pen, and what could be a more simple way of explaining this?

Third, it must be conceived that the seat of the senses in common also performs a function like that of the seal in impressing upon the imagination, as upon wax, the same shapes or ideas which they receive in pure and immaterial form from the external senses. And this imagination is a real part of the body, and of such a size that various portions of it can be impressed with many figures, distinct from one another, and

[2] Latin, "sensus communis"; French, "sens commun."

ordinarily retain them for a long time; and this, then, is what is called "memory."

Fourth, it must be conceived that the motive force, or the nerves themselves, originate in the brain, in which the imagination is found, and is affected by the latter in various ways, just as the senses in common are affected by the external senses, or as the whole pen is moved by its lower part. This example also shows (415) how the imagination can be the cause of many motions in the nerves, although it does not possess the specific images of these motions, but certain other images from which these motions can follow. For the whole pen is not moved in the same way as its lower part, but, on the contrary, its largest part is seen to move with a very different and contrary motion. And from these considerations we can understand how all the motions of the lower animals can come about even though they have absolutely no awareness of objects, but only a purely corporeal imagination. In the same way we also understand how all those of our own actions are performed which we accomplish without any assistance from reason.

Fifth and last, it must be conceived that that force by which we know a thing, in the true sense of the word "know," is purely spiritual, and that it is no less distinct from everything corporeal than blood is from bone, or the hand from the eye. It is of a simple nature, which either receives shapes from the senses in common as does the imagination, or applies itself to those which are preserved in the memory, or forms new ones by which the imagination is so occupied that it is often unable, at the same time, to receive ideas from the senses in common, or passes them on to the motive force almost in the same way as by the control of the body alone. In all these cases this cognitive faculty is sometimes passive, sometimes active; sometimes acting like the seal, sometimes like the wax. But the last must be understood only as an analogy, for in corporeal matters nothing is ever found exactly like this. And it is one and the same force which, when it applies itself with imagination to the senses in common, (416) is said "to see, to feel," and so forth; when it applies itself to the imagination alone as it contains various shapes, is said "to recollect"; when it applies itself to the imagination in order to create new ideas, is said "to imagine" or "conceive"; and finally, when it acts alone, is said "to understand." I will explain later, in its proper place, how this last is accomplished. For this reason this force is called, according to its various functions, either "pure intellect" or "imagination" or "memory" or "sensation"; but it is properly called "mind," whether it is forming new ideas in the imagination or is considering ideas already produced. We consider it therefore to be capable of these various operations, and the difference between these names will be considered later. Moreover, when all these things are thus conceived, the attentive reader will easily comprehend what is to be sought by the aid of each faculty, and to what extent human efforts can serve to repair the deficiencies of the mind.

For since the intellect can affect or be affected by the imagination, and in the same way the imagination can affect the senses by using the motive force to apply them to objects, and the senses can affect the imagination in which they depict the images of objects; and since the memory, at least that part which is corporeal and similar to retention in animals, is in no way distinct from the imagination, it can be concluded with certainty that if the intellect is concerned with those things in which there is nothing corporeal or similar to the corporeal, it cannot be assisted by these faculties. On the contrary, it must, to avoid being hindered by them, maintain its independence of the senses, and, as far as possible, divest the imagination of every distinct impression. But if the intellect proposes to examine something which can be related to body, it should produce in the imagination the most distinct idea of it (417) possible; and in order to do this more readily, the object which this idea represents should be exhibited to the external senses. Nor can the intellect be aided by the number of objects in understanding each one distinctly; but in order to deduce one thing from many objects, which often has to be done, we must reject whatever is irrelevant in the conception of them so that we can more readily retain the rest in our memory. In the same way, the objects themselves should not be presented to our external senses, but rather some simple sketches of them; and provided that these are sufficient to guard against a lapse of memory, the simpler they are, the better. Whoever observes all these rules, it seems to me, will overlook nothing which pertains to this part.

Now we approach the second part of our exposition wherein we wish to distinguish accurately between the notions of simple things and those which are compound, and also to see what falsity can exist in either in order to guard against it, and what things can be known with certainty, so that we may pay attention to these alone. Here, as earlier, certain ideas must be assumed which are not accepted by everyone; but it makes little difference if they are regarded as no more true than those imaginary circles by which astronomers describe phenomena, provided that with their assistance we may distinguish the true opinion on any subject from the false. (418)

We therefore say, first, that each thing must be regarded in a different manner when we are concerned with its relationship to our knowledge of it, than when we speak of it in reference to its actual existence. For if, for example, we consider some body with extension and shape, we acknowledge that it is, in reality, a certain unique and simple entity; for in this sense we cannot say that it is composed of the nature of body, of extension, and of shape, since these constituents never exist apart from one another. But in relation to our mind, we say that it is composed of these three natures, because we have first understood each of them separately before we were able to judge that those three were found together in one and the same object. For this reason, since we are not here considering objects except in so far as they are perceived by the mind, we call simple only those of which the perception is so clear and distinct that they cannot be divided by the mind into many and more distinct perceptions. Examples of this are figure, extension, motion, and so on; and we conceive that everything else is somehow composed of these. This is to be understood in so general a manner that we do not even except those things which we sometimes derive by abstraction from the simple things themselves, as is done if we say that shape is the boundary of an extended thing, conceiving by "boundary" something more general than by "figure," because obviously it could also be said that there is a boundary of duration, a boundary of motion, and so on. For then, even if the meaning of "boundary" is abstracted from "figure," it nevertheless should not seem to be more simple than "figure"; but rather, since (419) it is also applied to other things, such as the limits of duration or motion and so on, which are altogether different from "figure" in kind, that it should be abstracted from these also, and therefore that it is composed of various natures which are clearly different, and to which it does not apply except in different senses.

Second, we say that those things which we call "simple" in relation to our intellect are either purely intellectual, or purely material, or a mixture of both. Those things are purely intellectual which are recognized by the intellect by means of a certain inborn light, and without the assistance of any corporeal image, for it is certain that some such exist. No corporeal idea can be imagined which would represent to us what thinking is, what doubt is, what ignorance is, and, likewise, what the action of the will that may be called "volition" is, and so forth. Nevertheless we obviously recognize all these things, and so easily that for this it is sufficient that we are endowed with reason. Those things are purely material which are known to exist only in the body, as are figure, extension, motion, and so on. Finally, those things should be said to be a mixture of both which apply indiscriminately to corporeal things and to spirits, such as existence, unity, duration, and so on. Here also are to be classified those mixed notions which are like certain chains joining other simple natures together, and on the basis of which rests whatever we conclude by reasoning, as, for example: that those things which are equal to a third thing are equal to each other; or that things which cannot be related to the same third thing have some difference between them, and so forth. These mixed entities can be known either by the intellect alone, (420) or by the intellect making use of images of material things.

For the rest, it is also desirable to count among these simple natures their privations and negations, in so far as they are understood by us; because that is no less true knowledge by which we intuit what is nonexistent, or instantaneous, or motionless, than that by which we understand what is existence, or duration, or motion. And this method of conceiving things will enable us, subsequently, to say that everything else that we know is composed of these simple natures. Then, when I judge that some figure is not moving, I will say that my thought is somehow composed of shape and rest, and similarly in other instances.

We say, third, that these simple natures are all self-evident, and never contain any falsity. This is easily demonstrated if we distinguish that faculty of the intellect by means of which it intuits and recognizes objects from that by which it judges by affirming or denying, for it could happen that we think we are ignorant of those things which we really know, as when we suspect that they contain something unknown to us beyond that which we intuit, or which we learn by thought, and when this suspicion of ours is false. For this reason it is evident that we err if we think that the whole of one of these simple natures is not known to us, for if we can conceive it in the very slightest degree, which is certainly necessary since we are supposed to have made some judgment about it, it must, for this very reason, be concluded that we know it all, for otherwise it could not be said to be simple, but (421) composed of that which we perceive in it and of that which we judge we do not know.

We say, fourth, that the connection between these simple things is either necessary or contingent. It is necessary whenever one thing is so involved in the rather confused concept of the other that we cannot conceive either distinctly if we consider them to be separated from one another. In this way figure is conjoined with extension, motion with duration or time, and so forth, because it is not possible to conceive figures devoid of all extension, nor motion devoid of all duration. So even if I say that four and three are seven, this connection is necessary, for we cannot clearly conceive of seven unless we include three and four in it somewhat confusedly. And in the same way whatever is demonstrated about figures or numbers is necessarily connected with that of which it is affirmed. Nor is the necessity found only in sensible objects, but in others as well, for example: if Socrates says that he doubts everything, it necessarily follows that he at least knows this, that he doubts, and in the same way he knows that something can be true or false, and so on; for this is necessarily connected with the nature of doubt. But the union of those things which are joined by no inseparable relationship is contingent, as when we say that a body is alive, that a man is clothed, and so on. And often, also, there are many things necessarily joined together, which are considered to be contingently joined by many who do not notice the relationship, as in this proposition: "I exist, therefore God exists"; or similarly: (422) "I understand, therefore I have a mind distinct from the body," and so on. Finally, it is to be noted that the converses of many necessary propositions are contingent, for example: although from the fact that I exist I conclude with certainty that God exists, it is nevertheless not permissible to affirm that from the fact that God exists, I also exist.

We say, fifth, that we can never understand anything beyond these simple natures and a certain mixture or composition of them; and it is often easier to notice several of them joined together all at once, than to separate one of them from the others. Thus, for example, I can recognize a triangle, even though I have never thought that in that concept there is also contained the concept of angles, lines, the number three, figure, extension, and so on. Nevertheless this does not prevent our saying that the nature of the triangle is composed of all these natures, and that these are better known than the triangle, since they are the same ones as are recognized in it. Furthermore, there are perhaps many other ideas in that of the triangle which escape us, such as the size of the angles, which are equal to two right angles, and innumerable relationships between the sides and the angles, or the size of the area, and so forth.

We say, sixth, that those natures which we call composite are known by us, either because we have experienced what they are, or because we have composed them ourselves. We experience whatever we perceive by the senses, whatever we hear from others, and generally whatever reaches our understanding either from outside ourselves, or by introspection about ourselves. (423) Here it should be noted that the intellect can never be deceived by any experience, provided that the intellect intuits precisely the thing which is presented to it as occurring only within itself or in an image, and provided, further, that it does not judge that the imagination faithfully reflects physical objects, nor that the senses represent the true shapes of things, nor, finally, that external objects are always what they appear to be. For in all these matters we are liable to error, as, for example, if someone tells us a story and we believe that it has actually occurred; or if a man suffering from jaundice believes that everything is yellow because his eyes are shot with yellow; or if, finally, when the imagination is disordered, as happens in melancholia, we think that its disturbed visions represent real things. But these same things do not deceive the mind of a wise man, because even though he judges that whatever image he has received from the imagination is really depicted there, he nevertheless never asserts that this same image has been acquired intact and without alteration by the senses from external objects, and by the imagination from the senses, unless he has previously concluded this on some other grounds. We ourselves, on the other hand, compose those things which we understand, in so far as we believe that something is contained in them which is immediately perceived by our mind without being found in experience. Thus if the jaundiced person persuades himself that the things he sees are yellow, this idea of his will be composed of that which his imagination represents to him and that which he assumes for himself, namely, that the yellow color does not come from the defect of his eyes, but because the things he sees are really yellow. From this we conclude that we can only err when the things which we believe to be real are in some manner composed by ourselves. (424)

We say, seventh, that this composition may be produced in three ways, namely: by impulse, by conjecture, or by deduction. Those persons produce their judgments of things by impulse who are not led to a belief by any consideration of reason, but are caused to reach it either by some superior force, or by their own free choice, or by the state of their imagination. The first type of impulse, where we are persuaded by superior force, never deceives; the second rarely; the third almost always; but we are not concerned with the first type in this place, since our method is not concerned with it. Persons compose their judgments by conjecture if, for example, considering the fact that water, which is further from the center of the globe than earth, is also more tenuous, and that air, higher than water, is still more tenuous, they conjecture that above the air there is nothing but a certain very pure ether, and that it is much more tenuous than the air itself, and so on. The judgments we compose in this manner do not deceive us either, if we consider them to be only probable and never affirm that they are true, but they do not make us any more learned.[3]

Deduction alone therefore remains, by which we can so compose judgments that we are certain of their truth. Nevertheless there can also be many defects in this, as when, for example, from the fact that we perceive nothing in this space which is full of air, neither by sight nor by touch nor by any other sense, we conclude that it is empty, incorrectly connecting the nature of vacuum with that of this space. And

[3] There has been a dispute about the text at this point, the Hanover manuscript using an abbreviation that could be taken as either *nos* (us) or *non* (not). The Amsterdam text uses *non*, which makes the sentence meaningless; A-T conjecture *nos*, which provides meaning, but it does not seem likely that Descartes intended to praise the method of unconfirmed hypothesis. It is translated here—not for the first time—as *nos non*.

this also occurs whenever we think we can deduce something universal and necessary from a particular or contingent fact. But it is in our power to avoid this error (425) if we never connect any things together unless we intuit that the connection of one with the other is absolutely necessary, as when we deduce that nothing can have figure which is not extended, from the fact that figure is necessarily joined with extension, and so forth.

From all these things we conclude, first, that we have now demonstrated distinctly, and, I believe, by a sufficient enumeration, what we could show at first only confusedly and crudely, namely, that there are no paths to the certain knowledge of truth open to man except evident intuition and necessary deduction; and, likewise, why these natures are simple, about which we will write in the eighth point. And it is clear that the intuition of the mind is sometimes extended to all of these objects, and sometimes to recognizing their necessary connections with one another, and sometimes, finally, to all the other things which the intellect clearly perceives to exist, either in itself or in imagination. Concerning deduction, more will be said below.

We conclude, second, that no effort need be made to learn these simple natures, because they are sufficiently self-evident, but only to distinguish them from one another and to intuit each one separately by a firm mental glance. For no one is so weak in mind that he does not perceive that while he is seated he is in some way different from what he is when he is standing on his feet; but not everyone perceives with equal clarity (426) the difference between the nature of position and the rest of what is contained in this thought, nor can they affirm that nothing is then changed except position. We are not pointing this out without a purpose, because often educated people are accustomed to be so ingenious that they find a way of obfuscating even that which is self-evident and which is never unknown even to the ignorant. This happens to them whenever they try to explain self-evident things by something still more evident, for then they explain something else or nothing at all. For who does not perceive the whole entity, whatever it is, which remains unchanged when we change location; and who is there who will then conceive the same thing when he is told that "location is the surface of a moving body," since this surface can be changed while I am unmoved and do not change position; or, on the other hand, since I can be so moved that although the same things surround me, I am nevertheless no longer in the same place? And in truth will they not seem to prefer magic words which have an occult power beyond the grasp of the human mind, if they say that "motion," a thing most perfectly known to everyone, "is the act of an entity in potentiality, in so far as it is in potentiality"? For who understands these words? Who does not know what "motion" is? And who does not admit that those who talk thus are busily engaged in a search for the nonexistent? [4] It must therefore be said that matters should never be explained by any definitions of this kind, lest we should conceive them as composite instead of simple, but that they should only be intuited attentively by everyone, apart from all other things (427) and by the light of his mind.

We conclude, third, that all human knowledge consists of this one thing, that we perceive distinctly how these simple natures combine to produce other things. It is very important to note this, for whenever some difficulty is proposed for examination, almost everyone hesitates at the beginning, uncertain what ideas they should offer the mind, and supposing that they must seek some new kind of entity, previously unknown to them. For example, if they should seek to learn the nature of a magnet, they foresee that the problem will be knotty and difficult and therefore constantly turn their attention from everything obvious and consider the most difficult points, hoping that while wandering at random through the fruitless field of imaginable [5] causes, they may happen to hit upon something new. But he who believes that whatever can be known about a magnet must be known in terms of certain simple

[4] The proverbial Latin expression is literally translated: "have sought for a knot in a bulrush."

[5] Lit., "many."

and self-evident natures, will not be uncertain about what should be done, and will first diligently collect all the information he can obtain about this stone, from which he will then try to deduce what combination of simple natures is necessary to produce all those effects which are discovered in the magnet. Once he has discovered this, he can boldly assert that he has found the true nature of the magnet, in so far as it can be discovered by man on the basis of the available information.

Fourth, and finally, we conclude from what has been said that no knowledge of objects should be thought to be more obscure than any other such knowledge, since (428) they are all of the same nature and consist solely in the combination of self-evident things. Hardly anyone notices this, but the more confident, prejudiced in favor of the contrary opinion, permit themselves to assert some of their conjectures as though they were true demonstrations, and in matters of which they are completely ignorant they often have a feeling that they glimpse truths darkly, as in a fog. These they do not fear to propose, enveloping their conceptions with certain phrases by means of which they are accustomed to carry on discussions at great length and with logical arguments, all of which, however, neither they nor their hearers understand. The more modest often abstain, on the other hand, from examining many things which are simple and very necessary to life, just because they think they are unequal to the task, and since they think that these same things can be perceived by others endowed with greater ability, they embrace the opinions of those whom they believe have greater authority.

We say, eighth,[6] that we can only deduce things from words, or the cause from the effect, or the effect from the cause, or like from like, or parts or the whole itself from parts . . . . [7]

For the rest, lest the chain of our argument should perhaps escape anyone, let us divide whatever can be known into sim-

[6] Incorrectly given as "fifth" in the Hanover manuscript, but it does not follow the "fourth and last" just preceding, but the "seventh" on page 54.

[7] This thought remains uncompleted in the manuscripts. It is repeated later in Rule XIII, and amplified.

ple propositions and problems. For simple propositions, we do not propose other precepts than those which prepare the cognitive faculty more distinctly to intuit and more wisely to scrutinize whatever objects it encounters, because these ought to occur spontaneously and cannot be sought. (429) All this we have discussed in the twelve previous rules, in which we believe we have exhibited everything which we thought could make the use of the reason in any way easier. Among the problems, some are perfectly understood, even if their solution is unknown, and we are concerned with these alone in the twelve rules next following. Finally, there are others which are not perfectly understood, which we reserve for the twelve last rules. We did not reach this division without design, intending both to avoid being forced to discuss anything which presupposes the knowledge of what follows, and also to show those things first to which we think we should first apply ourselves for the cultivation of ingenuity. It is to be noted that among the problems which are perfectly understood, we place only those in which we perceive three things distinctly, namely, by what signs we can recognize what is sought when we encounter it, what it is precisely from which we ought to deduce it, and how it is to be proved that these things so depend upon one another that it is in no way possible to change one without changing the other. Thus we possess all our premises and nothing remains to be done except to show the way to find the conclusion—not, indeed, by deducing one item from one other simple thing (because that can be done without rules, as we have said)—but in disengaging a determinate object which is dependent on a complex of many involved things from them so skillfully that no step requires a greater capacity of the mind than is needed for making the most simple inference. Problems of this kind, since they are for the most part abstract and occur almost exclusively in arithmetic or geometry, (430) seem of little use to the uninitiated. But I warn them that they ought to apply themselves to this art for a long time, and practice it, if they wish later to acquire a perfect knowledge of the last part of this method, in which we treat of all other problems.

BOOK TWO

CONCERNING PROBLEMS WHICH CAN BE PERFECTLY UNDERSTOOD

RULE XIII

If we understand a problem perfectly, it should be considered apart from all superfluous concepts, reduced to its simplest form, and divided by enumeration into the smallest possible parts.

In only one thing do we follow the logicians, in that we assume, as they do, that the terms or subject matter must be known before we can proceed with inference: we even go further and presuppose in this section of our work that the problem is perfectly understood. But we do not, as they do, distinguish two extreme terms and a middle one. We treat the whole matter in this way: first, in any problem it is necessary that something is unknown, for otherwise it would be pointless to search for it; second, this unknown must be designated in some manner, for otherwise we would not be led to the discovery [1] of that thing rather than any other; and third, it cannot be so designated except in terms of something else which is already known. All this is also true about imperfectly known problems. Thus if we are investigating the nature of a magnet, (431) we know what is meant by these two words, "magnet" and "nature," because of which we have decided to investigate this problem rather than something else, and so on. But in order that the problem be perfectly understood, we wish it

[1] Lachelier proposed to read "investigation."

to be completely determinate, so that nothing need be discovered other than what can be deduced from the given. An example of this would be if we ask what I can infer about the nature of the magnet just from those observations which Gilbert says he made, whether they are true or false; or, similarly, if we ask what conclusion can be made about the nature of sound, just from the fact that three strings, A, B, and C, give the same tone, supposing that B is twice as thick as A but no longer, and that it is stretched by twice as heavy a weight, and that C is no thicker than A, but just twice as long, and is stretched by a weight four times as great, and so on. From these examples it is easily perceived how all imperfect problems can be reduced to perfect ones, as will be explained at greater length in the proper place. It is also apparent how this rule can be observed, by abstracting the well-understood difficulty from every superfluous concept, and by reducing it to such a point that we no longer feel that we are considering this or that object, but only that we are concerned in a general way with certain magnitudes that are to be compared with each other. For example, after we have decided to consider only this or that set of observations about the magnet, there is no longer any difficulty in ignoring all other observations. (432)

We add, furthermore, that the difficulty should be simplified as far as possible according to the fifth and sixth rules, and divided according to the seventh. For example, if I consider a magnet on the basis of a number of experiments, I will consider them separately one after another; and in the same way if I consider sound, as suggested before, I will compare strings A and B together without C, then A and C, and so forth, so that I will finally include them all together in a sufficient enumeration. And these are the only three procedures that the pure intellect can use when concerned with the terms of any problem before we approach its final solution, although that final solution will require the use of the eleven following rules. How these things are to be accomplished will be more fully clarified in the third book of this treatise.

By "problems," moreover, we refer to every situation in which we seek to distinguish the true from the false. The various types of these problems are to be enumerated, in order to determine what we are able to accomplish in each of them.

We have already said that there can be no falsity in the pure intuition of objects, whether they are simple or composite; and in this sense they cannot be called "problems," although they acquire this name as soon as we decide to make a determinate judgment about them. And we do not consider as problems only those questions which are raised by others, but considering the very ignorance, or rather doubting, of Socrates —a problem was created as soon as Socrates, turning his attention to this point, set himself to inquire whether it were true that he doubted everything and affirmed that he did. (433)

Moreover we seek either objects, given words; or causes, given effects; or effects, given causes; or the whole or other parts, given parts; or finally, several of these at once, given others.

We say that we seek objects, given words, whenever the difficulty consists in the obscurity of speech. We are here concerned not only with riddles, such as the one proposed by the Sphinx concerning that animal which at first walks on four legs, then on two, and finally on three; or similarly that of the fishermen who, standing on the shore and furnished with lines and nets for catching fish, asserted that they no longer had those which they had caught, but on the contrary did have those that they had not yet been able to catch, and so on. These riddles are not the only instances of this form of problem—the greater part of the problems discussed by the erudite are almost always questions of words. Nor should we have so poor an opinion of the better minds as to think that they have a poor conception of things in themselves whenever they are unable to express them satisfactorily in words. For example, when they call a "place" the "surface of the surrounding body," they do not really have a false idea of the object, but only misuse the word "place," which in common usage signifies that simple and self-evident nature by virtue of which something is said to be here or there, and which consists wholly in a certain relationship of the object, which is said to be in a place, to regions of extended space.[2] Some persons, seeing that the name "place" is given to the external surface, have improperly called it the intrinsic location. So it is (434) in other cases: for these questions about names occur so frequently that if philosophers were always in agreement about the meaning of words, almost all their disputes would evaporate.[3]

[Problems concerning objects can be reduced to four principal types. The first is when we seek causes, given their effects. We know, for example, the various effects of the magnet, and we seek their cause. We know the various effects which are usually attributed to nature's abhorrence of a vacuum: we seek to discover whether this is the true cause (*and we have found that it is not* [4]). We know the ebb and flow of the sea, and ask what can be the cause of so great and so regular a movement.

The second is when we seek effects, given their causes. We have always known, for example, that wind and water were

---

[2] Georges LeRoy conjectures "external" instead of "extended."

[3] At this point, the manuscripts start a new paragraph, as follows: "Given the effects, we seek the causes, whenever we are concerned with whether something exists, or what it is," and then breaks off. But the original manuscript, which is now missing, continued, and we may reproduce the missing part, to some extent, from the second edition of the *Port Royal Logic*. For Clerselier possessed this manuscript and gave it to Arnauld to translate into French, and while Arnauld may have condensed, elaborated, or paraphrased Descartes, and while one of the illustrations—that concerning nature's abhorrence of a vacuum—could not have been from the pen of Descartes, the passage clearly bridges the gap in the existing manuscripts. In this *Port Royal Logic,* the two paragraphs preceding are condensed to approximately one-fifth of their original length, and the part succeeding the gap is only slightly condensed. It is entirely possible, therefore, that the part of the *Port Royal Logic* we here insert may be condensed also, but it is not necessarily so. [471]

[4] This refers, presumably, to Pascal's posthumous work, *Treatise on the Equilibrium of Liquids and of the Weight of a Mass of Air.* As this was published in 1663, it could not have been seen by Descartes, but it was available to Arnauld, writing in 1664.

very powerful in moving objects; but the ancients, not having sufficiently considered what could be the effects of these causes, did not apply them as has been done since, by means of mills, to a great number of purposes which have been very useful to human society and have notably lightened the burden of human labor, which should be the goal of true physics. Thus we can say that the first kind of problem, where causes are sought, effects being given, constitutes the theory of physics; and the second, where effects are sought, causes being given, is its practice.

The third kind of problem is that in which, parts being given, we seek the whole. An example is when we have several numbers and we seek their sum by adding them one to another, or when we have two numbers and we seek their product by multiplying them.

The fourth is that in which, having the whole and some part, we seek another part. An example is when we have a number and the part that should be taken away, and seek what will be left, or when we have a number and seek what will be such and such a part of it.

But it should be noticed that in order to extend further these last two types of problems, and to include in them whatever does not properly belong in the first two, we must take the word "part" in a very general sense as including everything which makes up an object, such as its modes, its limits, its accidents, its properties, and in general all its attributes. Thus we would be searching for the whole, given its parts, if, for example, we were seeking the area of a triangle, given its altitude and its base; and it would be seeking a part, given the whole and another part, if, on the contrary, we were seeking the side of a rectangle, given the area and one of its sides.[5]]

For the rest, since when some problem is propounded to us for solution we frequently do not immediately notice to what class it belongs, nor whether we should seek objects, given words; or causes, given effects; and so forth, it seems to me

[5] Here ends our insertion from the *Port Royal Logic.* We now continue with the presently available manuscripts. (434)

completely useless to give more details about these things. For it will be more concise and convenient if we make orderly inquiry about everything that should be done upon encountering any difficulty whatsoever. Therefore, whenever any problem occurs, we should first make it clear what is sought, so that we understand it distinctly.

It frequently happens that individuals are so eager to investigate problems that they apply their capricious intelligence to finding a solution before they have determined by what signs they will recognize the object of their search, if they should stumble upon it by accident; these persons are no less foolish than would be a boy, sent somewhere by his master, who was so eager to obey that he started to run without waiting for instructions, and without knowing where he was ordered to go.

Actually, although something must be unknown in every problem—for otherwise it would be vain to seek — nevertheless this unknown ought to be designated by conditions so certain (435) that we are directed to the investigation of this one thing rather than any other. And these are the conditions which we have said should be examined at the very start; and this can be done if we direct our intelligence to understanding each item distinctly, inquiring diligently how far this unknown we are seeking is limited by each condition. For in this matter human intelligence usually errs in two ways, either by assuming something more than is given for the solution of the problem, or, on the contrary, by overlooking something.

We must beware of supposing that we know more things than we actually do, or that we know them more accurately than we really do, especially in riddles and other problems purposely contrived to perplex the mind. We must occasionally beware of this error in other problems, when for their solution it almost seems permissible to take something as certain, of which one is in fact persuaded not by any good reason, but by long-standing opinion. For example, in the riddle of the Sphinx, it is not to be thought that the word "feet" applies only to the true feet of animals, but it must also be considered whether its meaning can be extended to certain other things, as it happens in this case, such as the hands of babies and the canes of old men, since both of these are used somewhat as feet as aids in walking. In the same way, in the riddle of the fishermen we must beware lest the thought of fish so occupies our mind that it forgets to think of those creatures which are often carried unwillingly by the poor, who throw them away when they catch them. In the same way, let us suppose we are seeking to discover how a vase was constructed, which we saw (436) once upon a time, in the middle of which rose a column depicting Tantalus trying to drink, the water being contained perfectly in this vase as long as it does not rise as high as the mouth of Tantalus, but all the water flows out instantly as soon as it reaches the lips of the unfortunate one. It seems at first glance that the whole art consisted in the construction of this figure of Tantalus; but in reality, this does not solve the problem in the slightest. For the difficulty lies in this one point: how can a vase be so constructed that water flows out of it completely as soon as it reaches a certain height, although previously it did not flow out at all? In the same way, finally, if from everything we know about the stars we seek to affirm whatever we can about their motions, we must not gratuitously assume that the earth is motionless and in the center of things, as the ancients did, just because it has seemed this way to us since infancy. Even this should be considered doubtful, so that we may examine later what we may judge to be certain on this subject; and, so, for all other problems.

But we err by omission whenever there is some other condition necessary for the solution of the problem, either expressed in the problem or to be discovered in some other way, to which we pay no attention. This occurs, for example, when we seek perpetual motion, not in nature, as in the motion of stars or springs, but in the products of human effort. Someone (437) may think that he will have perpetual motion if he places a magnet so that it moves in a circle, or so that it may communicate its motion to the iron along with its other properties. For some believe that this is possible, knowing that the earth moves perpetually in a circle around its axis, and believing that a magnet has all the properties of the earth. Even if this succeeded, such a person would not make perpetual motion artificially, but would only utilize that which occurs in nature, just as when a water wheel is placed in a stream so that it moves forever—his trouble is that he has omitted a condition necessary for the solution of the problem.

When the problem is sufficiently understood, we must observe precisely in what the difficulty consists, so that, by considering the difficulty apart from everything else, it may be more easily solved.

It is not always sufficient to understand the problem to recognize in what point its difficulty lies; but we must, in addition, consider each of the points about which our information is deficient so that we may omit any which appear easy to solve, and, setting these aside, leave for examination only that which we do not know. For example, in that problem of the vase described a little while before, we easily discern how the vase should be made, how the column should be placed in its center, how it should depict a bird,[6] and so forth, and having dismissed all this as not bearing on the question, there remains the basic difficulty, which is that the water previously contained in the vase flows (438) out completely when it has reached a certain height: what we are to discover is how this happens.

We say, therefore, that the whole secret of the task is this: to examine in order all those things which are given in the proposition, and, after rejecting those which we see clearly do not bear on the issue, to retain those that are necessary and to reserve the doubtful points for more careful examination.

---

[6] Tantalus, Aeolus, and birds were favorite designs for this type of vase.

RULE XIV

The same problem should be understood as relating to the actual extension of bodies and at the same time should be completely represented by diagrams to the imagination, for thus it will be much more distinctly perceived by the intellect.

In order to use the assistance of our imagination, it should be noted that whenever something unknown is deduced from something else previously known, we have not necessarily found some new kind of entity, but have only extended our previous knowledge so that we perceive that the investigated object participates in some manner or other in the nature of other things which are presupposed in this problem.

For example, if someone has been blind from birth, it is not to be hoped that by any of our arguments we can ever bring him to perceive the true ideas of colors such as we receive from the senses. But if someone has once seen the primary colors, although never the intermediate and mixed ones, it is possible for him to (439) imagine the appearance of those which he has not seen by a certain deduction from their similarity to the others. In the same way, if there is a certain type of entity in a magnet, nothing similar to which has ever been perceived by our minds, it is not to be hoped that we can ever recognize it by reasoning: we would rather have to receive information from some new sense or from the divine mind. We believe that we have done whatever the human mind can do in this situation if we recognize as distinctly as possible that mixture of previously known natures or entities which would produce the same effects that appear in the magnet.

And actually all these things already spoken of, such as extension, figure, motion, and other things which are not appropriately enumerated here, are known by the same concept in various cases; for we do not imagine the figure of a crown differently if it is silver than if it is golden. This common idea [1] is transferred from one subject to another by simple comparison, by which we affirm that the sought-for entity is in one way or another similar or identical or equal to the given entity. In all reasoning, therefore, we obtain a precise knowledge of the truth only by comparison. For example, in the argument—all A is B, all B is C, therefore all A is C—we compare to each other the given terms of the sought-for conclusion, that is, A and C, in the light of whether either is B, and so forth. But because the forms of the syllogisms, as we have already pointed out, give no assistance in (440) perceiving the truth about objects, it will assist the reader, after he has completely rejected the syllogism, if he will recognize that absolutely every item of knowledge which he does not acquire through the simple and pure intuition of a single object in isolation, is obtained through the comparison of two or more with each other. And therefore practically the whole aim of the human mind consists in the accomplishment of that task, for, when it is obvious and simple, there is no need of method—nothing but the light of nature alone is needed for intuiting the truth which is obtained by it.

It is to be observed that I refer only to simple and obvious comparisons, whenever the sought-for conclusion and the given participate equally in a certain nature; but all other cases require preparation only because this common nature is not equally present in both, but varies according to certain other conditions or proportions in which it is involved. The principal function of human investigation consists only in reducing these proportions to such a form that we can clearly perceive an equality between the entity sought for and something else which is known.

It is then to be observed that nothing can be reduced to this equality unless it can exist as more or less, and all this is included in the term "magnitude." In consequence, we recognize that when, according to the preceding rule, the terms of the difficulty have been abstracted from any subject, we

---

[1] "Idea" in the Platonic sense: form.

are, in the last analysis, concerned only with magnitude in general.

In order to have something to imagine, let us, instead of using the intellect alone, make use of the intellect aided by figures represented in the imagination; (441) it ought to be noted, finally, that nothing can be said about magnitudes in general which cannot be said about some magnitude in particular.

From this it is readily concluded that it will be of no little advantage if we translate what we understand to be affirmed about magnitudes in general into that particular magnitude that we can most easily and distinctly picture in our imagination. That this is in fact the real extension of a body, abstracted from everything else which has shape, follows from what has been said in rule twelve, where we perceived that the imagination itself, together with the ideas existing in it, is nothing else but a genuine body having real extension and shape. This is also evident by itself, since in no other subject are all the differences in proportions more distinctly exhibited; for although a thing can be said to be more or less white than another, or a sound higher or lower, and so on, we nevertheless cannot define exactly whether such an excess amounts to a double or triple quantity, and so forth, unless by a certain analogy with the extension of a figured body. Let it then be taken as established and certain that perfectly determined problems contain hardly any difficulty beyond that which consists in reducing proportions to equalities or equations.[2] The whole area in which such a difficulty is found can easily be separated from every other subject, and should be so separated, and then translated into extension and figures. We will now treat of these matters, neglecting all other considerations, until we reach the twenty-fifth rule. (442)

It is to be hoped at this point that the reader possesses a propensity for the studies of arithmetic and geometry, even though I would prefer him never to have studied them, rather

2 "To equalities" is the proposal of Hamelin, as opposed to "of inequality" in the Amsterdam manuscript, and "in inequalities" in the Hanover manuscript.

than to have studied them in the customary manner, for the use of the rules which I will give here in expounding these subjects, for which they are entirely sufficient, is much easier than is their use in any other kind of question. And the utility of this method in attaining deeper understanding is so great that I am not afraid to say that this part of our method has not been devised for the sake of solving mathematical problems, but rather that mathematics is principally to be studied for the sake of perfecting our skill in this method. In my treatment, I will therefore presuppose no previous knowledge of these disciplines, except perhaps of some things which are self-evident and obvious to everyone. For even though the knowledge of these things, as commonly held by our contemporaries, may not be corrupted by obvious errors, it is obscured by many imperfect and badly conceived principles; and these we will try to correct from time to time in the remainder of this book.

By "extension" we understand everything which has length, breadth, and depth, without inquiring whether it is really a body or only space; nor does it seem to need more explanation, since there is nothing more easily perceived by our imagination. Nevertheless, since learned men often make use of such fine distinctions that they dissipate the light of nature and find obscurities even in those things which are never unknown even by rustics, they should be warned that by "extension," at this time, we do not mean something distinct and separate from the object itself, nor in general do we recognize philosophical entities of this sort, which in fact do not occur to the imagination. For even if someone can persuade himself, for example, that if everything extended in nature were annihilated, (443) it would still not prevent extension from existing in itself; nevertheless a corporeal idea is not used for this concept, but only an intellectual idea involving a mistaken judgment. And he will himself confess this, if he will attentively reflect on the very image of extension itself, forcing himself to picture it in his imagination, for he will notice that he does not perceive it devoid of all content, but imagines it quite otherwise than he judges it. These abstract entities, therefore, such as extension, are never formed in the imagination apart from something which is extended, whatever the intellect believes about the truth of the matter.

And because we are to do nothing from this point on without the aid of the imagination, it is useful to distinguish carefully the ideas by which the meaning of the several words are represented to our intellect. For this reason we propose for consideration these three ways of speaking: "extension occupies space," "body has extension," and "extension is not body."

The first of these shows how extension is taken for that which is extended; for clearly I have the same conception if I say, "extension occupies space," as if I say, "that which is extended occupies space." Nevertheless, this is not to say that it is better to say, "that which is extended," in order to avoid ambiguity, for it does not express so clearly what I conceive, namely, that some object occupies space because it is extended. And someone might only understand, "that which is extended is an object occupying space," just as when we say, "that which is alive occupies space." This explains why we have said that we will be concerned here with extension, rather than with that which is extended, even though we believe that we cannot conceive of it in any other way than that which is extended. (444)

Now let us pass on to these words, "body has extension," wherein we understand "extension" to signify something other than "body." Nevertheless we do not form two distinct ideas in our imagination, one of body and the other of extension, but only the one idea of extended body in respect to the matter at issue; and it is just as though I should say, "body is extended," or rather, "that which is extended is extended." This is a peculiarity found in those entities which only inhere in something else, and can never be conceived alone; and the situation is quite different in the case of those qualities which are really distinct from objects in which they inhere. If I said, for example, "Peter has wealth," the idea of Peter is clearly distinct from that of wealth; so that if I say, "Paul is wealthy,"

I am contemplating something altogether different from what I would mean if I said, "the wealthy are wealthy." Not making this distinction, many people falsely believe that extension contains something distinct from that which is extended, in the sense that Paul's wealth is different from Paul.

Finally, if it is said that "extension is not body," the meaning of extension is understood in a very different way than before, and in this sense no particular idea in the imagination corresponds to it. This whole pronouncement is made by the pure intellect, which alone has the ability to distinguish abstract entities of this type. And this is a source of error to many, who, not noticing that extension so considered cannot be comprehended by the imagination, represent it to themselves by an actual image. As such an image necessarily involves the concept of body, if they say that extension so conceived is not body, they unfortunately contradict themselves in that the same thing (445) is at once body and not body. And it is of great importance to distinguish those ways of speaking in which words of this type: "extension," "figure," "number," "surface," "line," "point," "unity," and so on, have such a restricted meaning that they exclude something from which they are not in reality distinct, as, for example, when it is said that "extension or figure is not body"; or "number is not things numbered"; "surface is the boundary of a body, and a line of a surface, and a point of a line"; "unity is not quantity"; and so on. All these propositions and others like them have nothing at all to do with the imagination, even if they should be true, and for this reason we will not be concerned with them in what follows.

We should diligently note that there are other propositions in which these names, although they retain the same meaning and are used in the same way as abstracted from their objects, nevertheless exclude nothing and deny nothing from which they are not really distinct. In all such cases, we should carefully observe that we can and should use the assistance of our imagination; because then, even if the mind pays close attention only to what is designated by the word, nevertheless the imagination ought to depict a true idea of the object. In this way, whenever the situation requires it, the intellect can be directed to other aspects of the situation not expressed literally by the words, and will never incautiously judge that these aspects were excluded. Thus, if it is a question of number, let us imagine some object measuring a great many units; while the intellect perhaps reflects at present only on the multitude of these units, we will take care lest it will therefore later reach some conclusion in which it is supposed that the object so numbered was excluded from our concept as do those who (446) attribute mysterious magic, vain and pretentious, to numbers. They would not have so much faith, certainly, in this belief, if they did not conceive the number to be distinct from the thing numbered.

In the same way, if we are concerned with a figure, let us consider that we are concerned with an extended object, considered only in so far as it is figured; if we are concerned with a body, let us consider that we are concerned with it in so far as it is long, wide, and deep; if with a surface, let us think of it in the same way as being long and wide, depth being omitted but not denied; if with a line, as being long only; if with a point, the same, but omitting from consideration everything else but the fact that it is an entity.

At whatever great length I examine all these things, nevertheless the minds of men are so preoccupied that I still fear that there are very few who are sufficiently safe from all risk of error in this matter and who will not find the explanation of my meaning too brief, for all its length. For the very arts of arithmetic and geometry, although most certain of all, nevertheless deceive us here, for what arithmetician does not think his numbers are really independent of any object, abstract, not only intellectually, but even in the imagination? And what geometrician does not confuse the clarity of his subject with contradictory principles, when he judges a line to be without width, and a surface without depth, and nevertheless goes on to construct some of these from others, not noticing that the line, from the movement of which he conceives a surface to be constructed, is really a body; and moreover that that which lacks width is nothing unless it is a mode of body, and so forth? But lest we should dally too much longer in enumerating these things, it will be more expeditious to explain how we suppose our subject should be conceived, (447) so that we can use it to demonstrate most easily whatever truth there is in arithmetic and geometry.

We are therefore concerned here with an extended object, considering in it nothing else at all except extension itself, and deliberately avoiding the word "quantity" because certain philosophers are so subtle that they also distinguish quantity from extension. We will suppose that all problems have been reduced to the point where nothing else is sought but to recognize a certain extension from the fact that it is compared with a certain other known extension. For we do not here expect to learn of any new entity, but wish to consider everything only as proportion, however involved, until we discover that what is unknown is equal to a certain known value. It is certain, consequently, that whatever differences in proportion exist in other characteristics may also be found in two or more extensions; and therefore it is sufficient for our purpose if we consider in extension itself all those things which can help explain differences in proportion. Only three things of this type are to be found, namely, dimension, unity, and figure.

By "dimension," we understand nothing else than the method and law according to which some object is considered to be measurable, so that not only are length, width, and depth dimensions of body, but also gravity is the dimension according to which an object is weighed, speed is the dimension of motion, and we have an infinite number of other dimensions of this kind. For the very division into (448) many equal parts, whether they are real or only conceptual, is actually the dimension according to which we number objects; and that method which produces number is, properly speaking, a kind of dimension, although there may be some variation in the meaning of the word. For if we consider parts as constituting a whole, then we are said to "number"; if, on the contrary, we regard the whole as divided into parts, we "measure" it. For example, we measure centuries by years, days, hours, and minutes, but if we count minutes, hours, days, and years, at length we complete the centuries.

From this it is clear that there can be an infinity of different dimensions in the same object, and that they add absolutely nothing to the object measured, but are understood in the same manner whether they have a real basis in the objects themselves, or whether they are arbitrarily conceived by our mind.

For the weight of an object is something real, or the speed of motion, or the division of the century into years and days, but not the division of days into hours and minutes, and so on.[3] Nevertheless all these are used in the same way, if they are considered only as dimensions, as is done here and in the disciplines of mathematics; it is more properly the function of the physicist to examine whether their basis is real.

The consideration of this matter sheds a great light upon geometry, because in geometry almost everyone erroneously thinks that there are three species of quantity: the line, the surface, and the solid, or body. For it has already been said that the line and the surface do not fall into the concept of being distinct from body, (449) or from each other in reality; but if they are considered simply as abstractions of the intellect, then they are no more distinct species of quantity than "animal" and "living" are different species of substance in man. And in passing, it should be noticed that the three dimensions of body—length, breadth, and depth—are differentiated from one another by name only, for nothing prevents us from selecting any extension we please in a given solid as length, and another as width, and so on. And although these three dimensions have a real basis in every object, in so far as it is extended and considered simply as extended, nevertheless we are not concerned with them here any more than with an

---

[3] Descartes does not distinguish clearly here, as a "century" is as arbitrary a unit as an "hour" or a "minute."

infinite number of other ones which are imagined by the intellect or which have other bases in objects. Thus, in the triangle, if we wish to measure it precisely, three items must be known about it, that is, either three sides, or two sides and one angle, or two angles and the area, and so forth. In the same way, we need five items for a trapezoid, six in a tetrahedron, and so on; and all these can be called "dimensions." Moreover, in order to choose those here which will give most assistance to our imagination, we should never pay attention to more than one or two simultaneously in our imagination, even though we understand that in the proposition with which we are concerned there are any number of others. For it is the point of the method to make as many distinctions as possible, so as to pay attention to only as few as possible at once, but to all of them in due order.

By "unity" I understand that common measure or unit which we have previously said should be equally participated in by all things which are compared to each other. And unless some such is already (450) given in the problem, we can assume it to be any one of the given magnitudes, or any other whatsoever, and it will be the common measure of all the others. We will understand [4] in this matter, that there are as many dimensions in our unit as there are common dimensions in the most diverse items which are to be compared with each other and we will conceive the object either simply as something extended, abstracting it from everything else, and then it will be the same as the point of geometricians when they construct a line by its movement; or as a finite line; or as a square.

As far as "figures" are concerned, it has already been shown how the ideas of all things can be represented by them alone. It remains for us to give warning at this point that out of the innumerably different varieties of figures, we should use only those by which all the differences of relationship or propositions are most easily expressed. But there are only two kinds of things which are compared among themselves, and they are

---

4 The manuscripts read: "We understand."

quantities and magnitudes; and we also have two kinds of figures to represent them to our conception. Thus, for example,

(450)

the points by which the number of triangles [5] is designated, or the family tree which explains someone's ancestry,

FATHER

SON   DAUGHTER

(450)

(451) and so on, are figures for exhibiting quantity; while those which are continuous and undivided, as a triangle, a square, and so on,

(451)

illustrate magnitudes.

And now, in order to explain which of all these figures we are to use here, we should know that all the relationships which can exist among entities of this type can be reduced to two classes, namely, to order and to measure.

We should know, in addition, that it is no slight task to devise some order, as can be seen everywhere in this method, which teaches hardly anything else. However, to recognize order, once it has been discovered, involves no further difficulty; and we can easily consider each of its parts serially, according to the seventh rule. This is because in the relationship of order each item is related to the others directly, and not through the mediation of a unit, as is the case in measuring; and in consequence we will concern ourselves here with the elucidation of the latter only. For I know what is the order between A and B, without considering anything else but the

[5] Adam and Tannery propose "triangular numbers," i.e., 1, 3, 6, 10, 15 . . . .

two extremes, but I do not know what is the ratio of magnitude between two and three unless I consider a third term which is the unit serving as the common measure of both.

We must also recognize that continuous magnitudes (452) can occasionally be completely reduced to quantity by the aid of an assumed unit, and this can always be done at least partially; and the quantity of units can subsequently be put in such an order that the difficulty involved [6] in recognizing measure finally depends upon the observation of order only— and the assistance of our method is of the greatest importance to this progress.

We must recognize, finally, that among dimensions of continuous magnitudes, none can be more distinctly conceived than length and width and that we should not pay attention simultaneously in the same figure to more than two, in order to compare them with each other, because it is part of the method that if we have to compare more than two different things together, we should take them in succession, and attend only to two at the same time.

Having recognized these things, it is easily concluded that propositions must be abstracted from the figures with which geometricians are concerned, if the problem concerns them, no less than from any other matter; and that we should retain for this purpose nothing but rectilinear and rectangular surfaces, or straight lines, which we also call "figures" because by their means we can imagine a genuinely extended object no less than by surfaces, as has been said before; and finally, that by these same figures we must represent, now continuous magnitudes, now also a quantity or a number; and that nothing more simple can be discovered by human efforts for the explanation of all differences of relationships. (453)

[6] Manuscripts have: "which might be involved."

RULE XV

It is usually helpful, also, to draw these diagrams and ob-
serve them through the external senses, so that by this means
our thought can more easily remain attentive.

The way these figures are to be drawn so that their images
will be formed more clearly in our imagination when they are
presented to our eyes is self-evident. For, first, we depict unity

in three ways, namely, by a square, ☐ , if we consider

only length and width, or by a line, ————, if we consider only length, or, finally, by a point, . , if we consider
nothing else but that it is to form part of a quantity. But in
whatever way it is depicted and conceived, we always understand that it is an object extended in every way and capable of
an infinity of dimensions. In the same way, also, we exhibit
the terms of a problem to our eyes, if we are to pay attention
to two of their different magnitudes simultaneously, by the rectangle, two sides of which are the two magnitudes under consideration: in this way should they be incommensurable [1] with

unity, ▭ , or this way, ⊡ ;

or this way, **: : :**, if they should be commensurable; and
nothing more is needed unless it is a question of a multitude
of units. (454) Finally, if we consider only one of those magnitudes, we depict it [2] either by a rectangle, one side of which

1 Manuscripts read: "commensurable."
2 Manuscripts read: "depict the line."

is the magnitude in question and the other is unity, in this

way,   [box]   , as we shall do whenever it is to be

compared with some other surface; or by a length alone in this
manner, ————————, if it should be regarded only as an incommensurable length; or in this manner, ..., if it
should be a quantity.

RULE XVI

Whatever does not require immediate attention, even
though it may be necessary to the conclusion, is better repre-
sented by very brief notes than by complete diagrams, for
thus the memory cannot fail, yet the mind will not be dis-
tracted in the meantime in trying to remember these details
while it is concerned with deducing other things.

We have said that we should consider at one and the same
time not more than two different dimensions out of the innumerable ones that can be depicted in our imagination,
whether we observe them with the eyes or in the mind. It is
therefore necessary to keep track of all the others, so that
they may easily be brought to mind whenever there is need
of them; and it is for this purpose that memory seems to have
been developed by nature. But because this memory is often
fleeting, and in order that we should not be forced to keep
some part of our attention concerned in recalling one thought
while we devote ourselves to others, the art of writing has
been most appropriately invented. (455) Relying on the aid
of this art, we will commit practically nothing to memory, but,
leaving our imagination free to be wholly concerned with its
present thoughts, we will confide to paper whatever is to be
retained. This we will do by very brief notes, so that after
we have examined each item carefully, according to the ninth
rule, we can run through all of them in a very rapid move-

ment of thought and grasp as many as possible at the same time.

Whatever is to be considered, therefore, as a unit in the solution of the problem, we will designate by a unique symbol, which can be imagined in any way we please. But because of its simplicity, we will use the characters a, b, c, and so on for magnitudes already known, and A, B, C, and so on to express unknown ones, before which we will often place the figures 1, 2, 3, 4, and so on to express their number, and in the same way we will append to them a figure to represent the number of relations which are to be understood in them. Thus if I write "$2a^3$," it will mean the same as if I had said "twice the magnitude represented by the letter a, containing three relations." And by this means we not only save the space of many words, but what is more important, express the terms of the difficulty so clearly and simply, that, even while nothing useful is omitted, still nothing superfluous will ever be found in it which might uselessly occupy the capacity of the mind by offering it many things to be considered simultaneously.

To understand all this more clearly, we should first notice that arithmeticians are accustomed to designate each magnitude by several units or by some number, but that we are abstracting in this place from numbers themselves no less than we did a little while ago from geometrical figures (456) or from anything else. We do this, not only to avoid the tedium of long and superfluous computation, but especially so that the parts of the problem which pertain to the nature of the difficulty will always remain distinct, and not be surrounded by useless numbers. For example, if we are seeking the hypotenuse of a right triangle whose sides are given as 9 and 12, the arithmetician would say that it is $\sqrt{225}$ or 15; but we will put a or b in place of 9 and 12, and find the hypotenuse to be $\sqrt{a^2 + b^2}$, and these two parts, a^2 and b^2, which are confused in the numerical expression, remain distinct.

It should also be noticed that by the number of relations we are to understand the ratios following each other in con-

tinuous order, such as others try to express in the usual algebra
by various dimensions and figures, the first of which they call
the "root," the second the "square," the third the "cube," the
fourth the "biquadratic," and so on. I confess that for a long
time I was myself deceived by these names, for nothing, it
seemed, could be more clearly apparent to my imagination,
after the line and the square, than the cube and other figures
built on this plan, and I resolved quite a few problems with
their aid. But after many experiences, I discerned that I had
never discovered anything by this method of conceiving that
I could not have learned much more easily and distinctly
without it; and that such names should be wholly rejected, lest
they disturb our understanding, since, according to a previous
rule, a magnitude should never be regarded in the imagination otherwise than as a line or a surface, even though it may
be called a "cube" or a "biquadratic." (457) It is therefore
especially to be observed that the root, the square, the cube,
and so forth, are nothing other than magnitudes in geometrical progression which we always assume are preceded by that
arbitrary unit which we have previously discussed. To this
unit the first proportional refers immediately and by a simple
relationship; but the second by the mediation of the first and
therefore through two relationships; the third by the mediation of the first and second, and by three relationships, and so
on. We shall therefore in the future use the term "first proportional" for that magnitude which in algebra is called the
"root," the "second proportional," that which is called
"square," and so on for the others.

It is to be observed, finally, that even though we are here
abstracting the elements of the problem from certain numbers
in order to discover the nature of the difficulty, nevertheless it
often happens that it can be solved in a simpler manner with
the given numbers than if it were abstracted from them. This
happens because of the two-fold use of numbers, which we
have already touched upon, because the same numbers sometimes express order, sometimes measure; and in consequence,
after we have sought it in general terms, we should refer back

to the given numbers in order to see whether they will furnish us some simpler solution. For example, after we have seen the hypotenuse of a right triangle with sides a and b to be $\sqrt{a^2 + b^2}$, we are to substitute 81 for a^2 and 144 for b^2, these added give 225, whose root, or the mean proportional between unity and 225, is 15. Thus (458) we recognize that the hypotenuse, 15, is commensurable with the sides 9 and 12, but not as a general principle from the fact that it is the hypotenuse of a right triangle, one side of which is to the other as 3 is to 4. All this we have distinguished, we who are seeking evident and distinct knowledge of things; but not the arithmeticians, who are satisified if they have discovered the number sought even though they have not noticed how it depends upon the given facts, although this latter is the only point in which science truly lies.

And furthermore, it is to be observed in general that nothing should ever be confided to the memory about those things which do not require continuous attention, if we can commit them to paper, lest perhaps the unnecessary effort of memory may withdraw some part of our mind from the study of the object present. And some record should be made in which we inscribe the conditions of the problem as it was first proposed, and then how these were abstracted and by what symbols they are designated; so that when the solution has been found in terms of these symbols, we can easily interpret it, without any effort of memory, as referring to the particular object which is in question, for nothing is ever abstracted except from something less general. I shall write, therefore, in this manner: to find the hypotenuse AC in the right triangle ABC; and I abstract the problem: how in general to find the length of the hypotenuse from the lengths of its sides. Then let a represent AB, which is given as 9; let b represent BC, which is given as 12; and so on for the rest. (459)

It is to be noted that we will use these four rules again in the third part of this treatise, and in a somewhat broader sense than has been described here, as will be stated in the proper place.

RULE XVII

The difficulty under consideration should be surveyed directly, noting that certain of its terms are known, others unknown, and intuiting by true methods the mutual dependence of each of its terms upon the others.

The four preceding rules have taught how determinate and perfectly understood problems are to be abstracted from each subject, and so simplified that nothing further is sought but the knowledge of certain magnitudes, to be determined from the fact that they bear this or that relation to certain given magnitudes. Now in these five following rules we will explain how these difficulties are to be broken down so that no matter how many unknown magnitudes there are in a problem, they may all be subordinated to one another in order, and just as the first will be related to unity, so the second is to the first, the third to the second, the fourth to the third; and so in consequence, no matter how many there are, they make a sum equal to a certain known magnitude; and this by a method so certain that we can safely assert that by no effort can this be reduced to simpler terms.

As far as the present is concerned, it is to be noted that in every problem which is to be solved by deduction, there is a certain (460) clear and direct way by which we can most easily pass from some terms to others, while all other ways are more difficult and indirect. And to understand this, we should remember what has been said in rule eleven, where we discussed chains of propositions—how when each of these is compared to its neighbors, we easily perceive how even the first and the last are related to each other, even though it is not so easy to deduce the intermediate ones from the extremes. Now, therefore, if we understand the dependence of each of them upon each other in a continuous series, so that we infer from all this how the last depends upon the first, we run through the problem directly; but if, on the contrary, we know that the first and the last are connected together in a certain manner, and we wish to deduce from this what the intermediates are which connect them, we follow an indirect and inverted order. And because we are concerned here only with complex problems, in which certain intermediates in an incomplete series are to be learned from known extremes, the whole method in this case consists in supposing the unknown to be known so we can provide ourselves with an easy and direct path for our search, however complex the difficulties may be. Nothing can prevent this from always being done, since we have supposed from the beginning of this book that we know that the dependence of the unknown terms upon the known terms in the problem is such (461) that the former are completely determined by the latter. And so, if we reflect on those terms which occur first, while we know this dependence, and if we consider the unknown as known, so that from these terms we deduce step by step and by correct procedures all the other items, even the known, just as though they were unknown, we will do exactly what this rule prescribes. We will postpone examples of this procedure, and also of many others which we will speak of shortly, for the twenty-fourth rule, because they can be more fully explained there.

RULE XVIII

For this purpose, only four operations are required: addition, subtraction, multiplication, and division; the last two of which are often not to be completed here, both to avoid unnecessary complication and because they can be completed more readily later on.

A multitude of rules is often the product of the inexperience of the teacher, and what can be reduced to a single general precept is much less clear if it is divided into many particulars. For this reason, we here reduce all our operations which are to be used in investigating problems, that is, those in which some magnitudes are to be deduced from others, into only four types. How these are sufficient will be seen from their explanation. (462)

For if we reach the knowledge of one magnitude from the fact that we know the parts of which it is composed, this is done by addition; if we learn a part from the fact that we know the whole and the excess of the whole over the part, this is done by subtraction; there are no other ways to deduce one magnitude from other absolutely given magnitudes in which it is contained in some fashion. But if some magnitude is to be discovered from others from which it is completely different, and in which it is in no way contained, it is necessary to relate it to them in some manner. If this relationship or ratio is sought for directly, then we are to make use of multiplication; if indirectly, of division.

In order to explain these two processes clearly, we must understand that unity, of which we have already spoken, is here the basis and foundation of all relationships, and in a geometric series of magnitudes it occupies the first place. The given magnitude is in the second place, and the values sought for in the third, fourth, and remaining places, if the proportion [1] is direct; but if it is indirect, the value sought is found in the second and in other intermediate positions, and the given in the last. (463)

For if it is said that unity is to a, given as 5, as b, given as 7, is to the value sought, which is ab, or 35; then a and b are in the second position, and ab, which is their product, is in the third. Then if we add that unity is to c, or 9, as ab or 35 is to the sought-for value abc, or 315, then abc is in the fourth position, and is generated by two multiplications from ab and c, which are in the second position, and so on for the rest. In

[1] Manuscripts read: "proposition."

the same way, as unity is to a or 5, so a or 5 is to a^2 or 25; and once more, as unity is to a or 5, so a^2 or 25 is to a^3 or 125; and finally, as unity is to a or 5, so a^3 or 125 is to a^4, which is 625, and so forth. The way in which multiplication is performed is no different if a magnitude is multiplied by itself, than if it is multiplied by another and completely different magnitude.

Now if it is said, on the other hand, that unity is to a given as 5, the divisor, as B or 7, the desired answer, is to ab, given as 35, the dividend; then the order is reversed and indirect. That is why the sought-for value B cannot be found except by dividing the given ab by the similarly given a. It is the same if it is said that unity is to the sought-for value A or 5 as the sought-for value A or 5 is to a^2, given as 25; or that unity is to the sought-for A or 5 as the sought-for A^2 or 25 is to a^3, given as 125; and so for the rest. All this we include in the term "division," although it is to be noted that the last two kinds of it contain more difficulty than the earlier ones, because the magnitude sought for is found in them more frequently, and they therefore involve more relationships. For the sense of these examples is the same as if we were told to extract the square root (464) of a^2 or 25, or the cube root of a^3 or 125, and so on for the rest—which mode of speaking is in use among arithmeticians. Or to explain these again with the vocabulary of the geometricians, it is the same as though we were told to find the mean proportional between that assumed magnitude which we call unity, and that designated as a^2; or two mean proportionals between unity and a^3, and so for the others.

From this it can easily be seen how these two operations suffice for discovering any magnitudes whatsoever which are to be deduced from some relationship with others. And when we have understood this, we still have to explain how these operations are to be scrutinized by the imagination, and also how they are to be exhibited to the eyes, so that we can explain their use or practice.

If addition [2] or subtraction are to be performed, we con-

[2] Manuscripts read: "division."

ceive the object in the form of a line, or as an extended magnitude in which length alone is considered: for if the line *a*
is to be added to the line *b*,

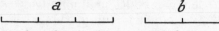

we join one to the other in this manner, *ab*,

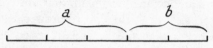

and *c* is produced:

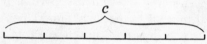

(465) If, however, the smaller is to be taken from the larger,
that is, *b* from *a*,

we place one above the other in this manner,

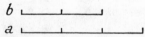

so that the answer is that part of the larger which cannot be
covered by the smaller, namely:

In multiplication we also conceive of the given magnitudes
in the form of lines, but imagine that a rectangle is formed by
them. For if we multiply *a* by *b*,

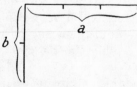

we place one on the other at right angles, in this way,

and make the rectangle:

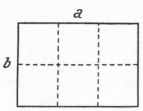

a

b

(466) In the same way, if we wish to multiply *ab* by *c,*

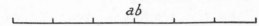

c

we should conceive *ab* as a line, namely, *ab,*

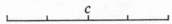

ab

so that we have for *abc:*

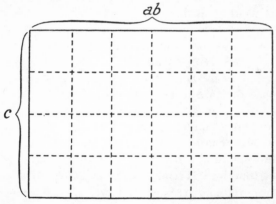

ab

c

Finally, in division in which the divisor is given, we imagine the magnitude to be divided to be a rectangle, one side of which is the divisor and the other, the quotient. If the rectangle *ab* is to be divided by *a,*

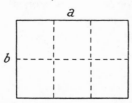

a

b

the width a is taken away from it, and b remains as the quotient,

(467) or on the contrary, if the same is divided by b, the altitude[3] b is taken away, and the quotient will be a:

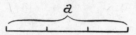

But in those divisions in which the divisor is not given, but only designated by some relationship, as when we are told to extract the square or cube root and so on, it is then to be noted that the term to be divided and all others are always to be conceived as lines existing in a geometrical series, the first term of which is the unit, and the last, the magnitude to be divided. But how we are to discover any number of mean proportionals will be explained at the proper place; here it is sufficient to have given notice that we are supposing that such operations are not yet brought to a conclusion at this point, since they are to be performed by an indirect and reversed act of the imagination, and we are now concerned only with questions examined directly.

As for what concerns other operations, they can be very easily resolved in the manner in which we have said they should be conceived. It remains to be explained, however, how their terms are to be prepared, for even though when we are first concerned with some difficulty we are free to conceive its terms as lines or rectangles, without ever making use of other figures, as was said in rule fourteen, nevertheless, after (468) a rectangle has been formed by the multiplication of two lines, it frequently must be conceived soon afterwards in the discussion as a line, for the purpose of performing another operation; or this rectangle or a line produced by some addition or subtraction must soon be conceived as some other rectangle on a base representing the magnitude by which it is to be divided.

3 Manuscripts read: "width."

It is therefore important to explain here how any rectangle can be transformed into a line, and on the other hand how a line or even a rectangle can be transformed into another rectangle whose side is given. This is very easy for geometricians, provided that they recognize that whenever we compare a line with a rectangle, as in this case, we always conceive the line as a rectangle, one side of which is that length which we have assumed as unity. Thus, in effect, all this work is reduced to the following proposition: given a rectangle, construct another rectangle equal to it on a given side of it.

Even though this is simple to novices in geometry, I nevertheless want to explain it, for fear of omitting anything. . . .[4]

RULE XIX [1]

By this method of reasoning, we should seek as many magnitudes, each expressed in two different ways, as we suppose we know there are unknowns directly pertaining to the difficulty, for in this way we will have the same number of equations between two expressions [as there are unknowns].[2] (469)

RULE XX

When we have found our equations, we must complete the operations which we have omitted, never using multiplication when there is opportunity for division.

---

[4] The discussion of this rule was not completed.

[1] This rule and the two following ones exist only as titles.

[2] Bracketed part supplied by translator.

RULE XXI

If there are many equations of this type, they must all be reduced to one, namely, to that one whose terms occupy the lowest rank in the geometrical progression of powers of the unknown, in which order they should be arranged.

RULES XXII, XXIII, XXIV [1]

BOOK III

CONCERNING PROBLEMS WHICH ARE NOT PERFECTLY UNDERSTOOD [2]

---

[1] The titles of these three rules are missing.

[2] This book, like the first two, was to have twelve rules, XXV through XXXVI, none of which is known.

The Library of Liberal Arts

The American Heritage Series